IMAGES
of America

AROUND TITUSVILLE

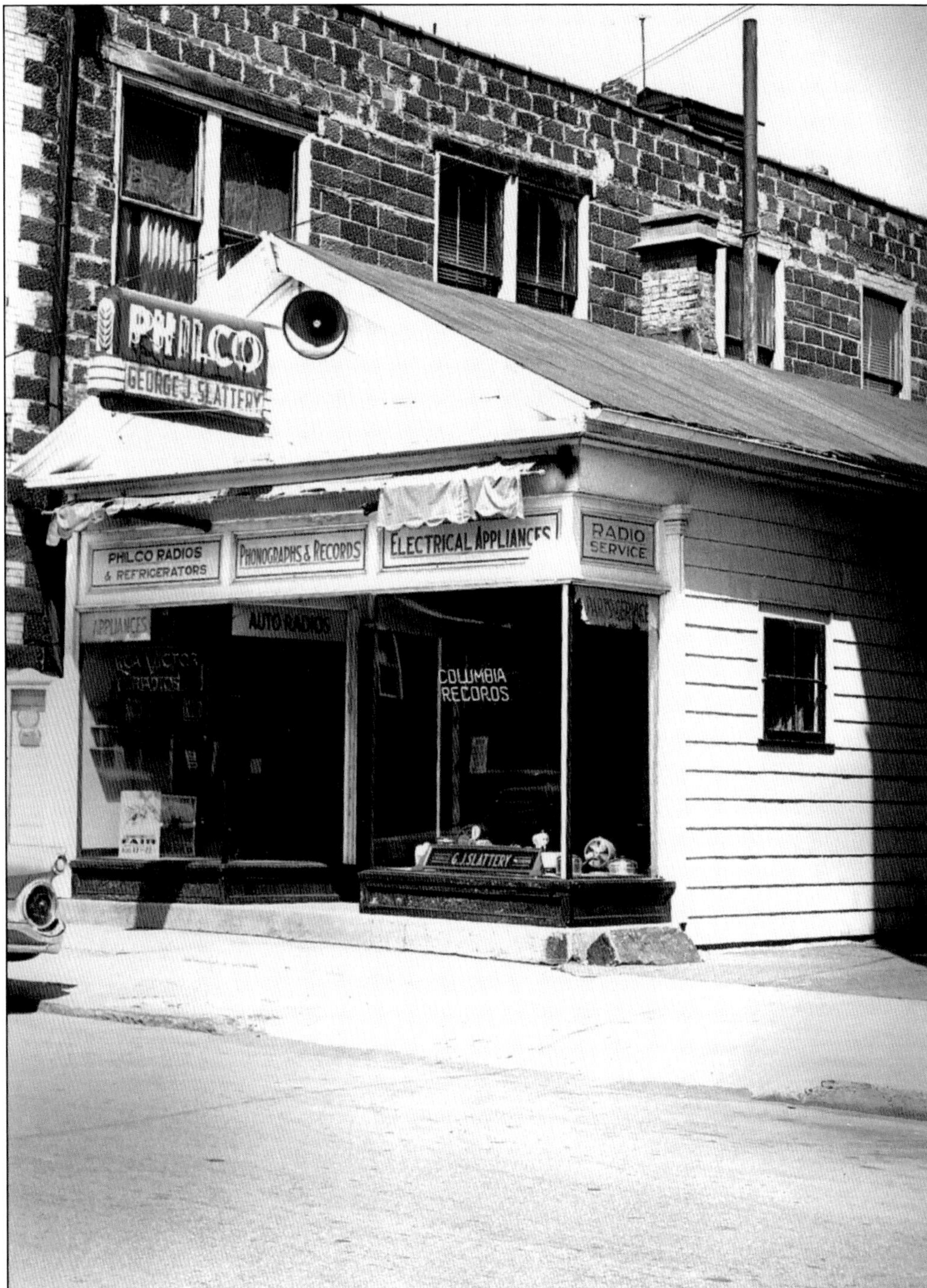

Old structures have continually been adapted to new uses. Titusville has had many of these. The former Maxwell Chick insurance and real-estate agency building later housed George J. Slattery's radio and appliance store. Slattery's North Franklin Street business featured refrigerators, small appliances, radios, phonographs, and records. This 1961 photograph was taken shortly before the building was torn down. (Courtesy of the Titusville Herald.)

IMAGES
of America

AROUND TITUSVILLE

David L. Weber

ARCADIA
PUBLISHING

ISBN 978-0-7385-3630-9

Published by Arcadia Publishing
Charleston, South Carolina

Printed in the United States of America

Library of Congress Catalog Card Number: 2004105908

For all general information contact Arcadia Publishing at:
Telephone 843-853-2070
Fax 843-853-0044
E-mail sales@arcadiapublishing.com
For customer service and orders:
Toll-Free 1-888-313-2665

Visit us on the Internet at www.arcadiapublishing.com

In memory of the Titusville-area residents who instilled in me a knowledge of local history and events. The names of these individuals are too numerous to mention on one page.

Contents

ACKNOWLEDGMENTS

Many individuals have provided assistance in making my pictorial Titusville history a reality. I first of all wish to thank Myrna Wescoat and Kathryn Newson of the Titusville Historical Society for searching through the organization's historic photographs. Others who have provided vintage photographs and just plain help include Tom and Jean Beason, Melvin and Kathy Wescoat, Frank Newson, Colleen Weekley of the Pleasantville Historical Committee, Karl Engleka and Margaret Fiely of the Titusville High School Alumni Association, Terry and Charlene Poux Ruot at Charter Plastics Inc., Brian DiFonzo, Jon Sherman and Holly Matthews of the Titusville Herald, Kim Ciccarelli at the Titusville YMCA, and Millia Armatas Sullivan.

The Drake Well Museum has also been generous with photographs, layout space, and technical assistance. Museum site administrator Barbara Zolli has let me use certain images from the collection of over 10,000 photographs housed there. Helen Boemmel and Holly Walker helped type and edit the manuscript. Museum archival curator Susan Beates helped select photographs and guided me through the project. Nate Lytle and Camille Kline, Titusville High School students, have also assisted with typing and editing.

Arcadia Publishing editor Erin Loftus has guided me through several months of frustration that have also been filled with satisfaction. I also wish to thank my parents, Elmer and Mildred Weber, for providing support and guidance through this sometimes aggravating but interesting project. Their work is greatly appreciated.

INTRODUCTION

Jonathan Titus and Samuel Kerr, two surveyors and land agents from Hollidaysburg, Pennsylvania, were sent by the Holland Land Company to survey a Northwest Pennsylvania tract in 1795–1796. The two men settled near the junction of Pine and Oil Creeks, in present-day Crawford County, and built log cabins. Within two years, the Holland Land Company erected a saw- and gristmill on Pine Creek. Titusville had begun.

Titus and Kerr opened their cabins to lumbermen and Seneca (Iroquois) hunting parties. Settlers of Irish, Ulster Scottish, and Pennsylvania German background moved into Titus's hamlet. "Yankees" from New York, Connecticut, and Vermont also settled in the vicinity.

Titusville was incorporated as a borough in 1847. Located near the junction of Crawford, Venango, and Warren Counties, the settlement became a lumbering and agricultural center. Locally cut pine lumber was rafted down Oil Creek to the Allegheny River and on to markets in Pittsburgh, Cincinnati, and elsewhere.

Other settlements were growing near Titusville, including Hydetown, Pleasantville, Cherrytree, Townville, Centerville, and Enterprise, and all had economies centering around lumbering, agriculture, and stoneware and crockery manufacturing.

A mysterious greasy substance was long known to flow from springs near Pine and Oil Creeks. Local sawmills—especially those owned by Brewer, Watson & Company—used the grease for lubrication and lighting. Experiments with this fluid led to formation of the world's first oil lease in 1853.

For the purpose of increasing petroleum production, New York and Connecticut capitalists leased Brewer, Watson & Company's upper sawmill. A former railroad conductor, Edwin L. Drake, was sent to Titusville to manage the operation.

Drake and his driller, William A. "Uncle Billy" Smith, struck a freak oil sand at 69.5 feet on August 27, 1859. Lumbermill owners, who had been skeptical of the venture, now invested capital in the new industry.

More producing wells were drilled near Titusville. The town's population increased after 1860. Machine and boiler shops, foundries, barrel factories, nitroglycerin companies, and oil refineries sprang up to serve the new industry. Lumbermills and related establishments supplied rig lumber and building materials to the oil fields. Railroads and pipelines extended through the oil region. Direct access to New York, Philadelphia, Cleveland, and Chicago was now possible.

Titusville's population swelled to 6,000 permanent and 2,000 floating residents in 1865. The town became an incorporated city in 1866. The people who settled in the area included

Civil War veterans; adventurers; and immigrants from Ireland, Britain, Germany, France, Switzerland, Sweden, and other nations.

Titusville survived the collapse of the oil market, unfair business practices, outbreaks of lawlessness, disease, floods, fires, and explosions.

Oil production eventually moved on to other western Pennsylvania fields (including some in nearby communities). Titusville remained the oil region's Queen City. It was also the region's "breadbasket" and "lumber pile."

Established lumber production (now centering around hardwoods), agriculture, and community institutions (schools, churches, and fraternal organizations) assured the city's future. Local business and civic leaders put aside their differences and began attracting and starting new industries and institutions.

Titusville's location in the Pittsburgh-Buffalo-Cleveland industrial triangle and equidistance between New York City and Chicago helped in this diversification. New industries—a specialty steel mill, a heavy forge shop, radiator factories, a silk ribbon mill, cutlery shops, furniture factories, wholesale and mail-order businesses, and dairies and creameries—came to town.

Older established concerns began the manufacture of new products, such as heating boilers and oil field gas engines. Many of these plants played important roles in the winning of World War I. They helped create the Titusville region as it exists today, attracted new immigrants (mainly from Poland, Croatia, the Ukraine, and Finland), and made the community representative of Pennsylvania.

Titusville's industrial plants have been renowned for many firsts in their respective fields. They helped win both world wars, played significant roles in later conflicts, and also made key items for the U.S. space program. Following World War II, a new material, plastic, made its impact on the local economy. Its production of the original Hula-Hoops brought the Titusville plastic-tubing industry recognition and growth lasting to the present day.

Titusville gradually lost its oil-town connections. The last oil refinery ceased operations in November 1950. Other major employers and retail businesses shut their doors in the 1960s and later decades. However, the local industrial base remains intact, largely due to newer, small manufacturing and service employers (some of which are outgrowths of the older firms), and lumber and agriculture remain significant facets of the local economy today.

Old mansions (built with lumber, oil, and industrial wealth) and the Drake Well Museum and park remain as reminders of the town's past. Other reminders are the achievements of area natives in business, historical writing, journalism, sports, and music (opera, country, and rock), all of which help define the Titusville region and its people.

One

Lumber, Leather, and Woodworking

The Holland Land Company, the original owner of much of present-day Titusville, constructed a water-powered saw- and gristmill on Pine Creek in 1798. Within a generation, approximately 20 sawmills operated on nearby Oil Creek and its tributaries. Demand for pine lumber in Pittsburgh and Cincinnati stimulated the local logging operations, and lumber was rafted downstream to market.

The presence of petroleum springs on the Brewer, Watson & Company upper mill site led to even greater economic growth. Following the Drake Well's completion, on August 27, 1859, Titusville's sawmills supplied timber for derricks, tanks, barrels, sucker rods, barges, gauge poles, homes, churches, and hotels.

After the first oil boom's collapse, hardwood- and softwood-related industries were there for Titusville to fall back on. Sawmills, with logging railroads, planing mills, millwork plants, and furniture factories, and a tannery, with facilities for extracting tannic acid from hemlock bark and chestnut wood, were part of the industrial base. Hardwood lumbermills, planing mills, concentration yards, and dimension mills remain active in Titusville today.

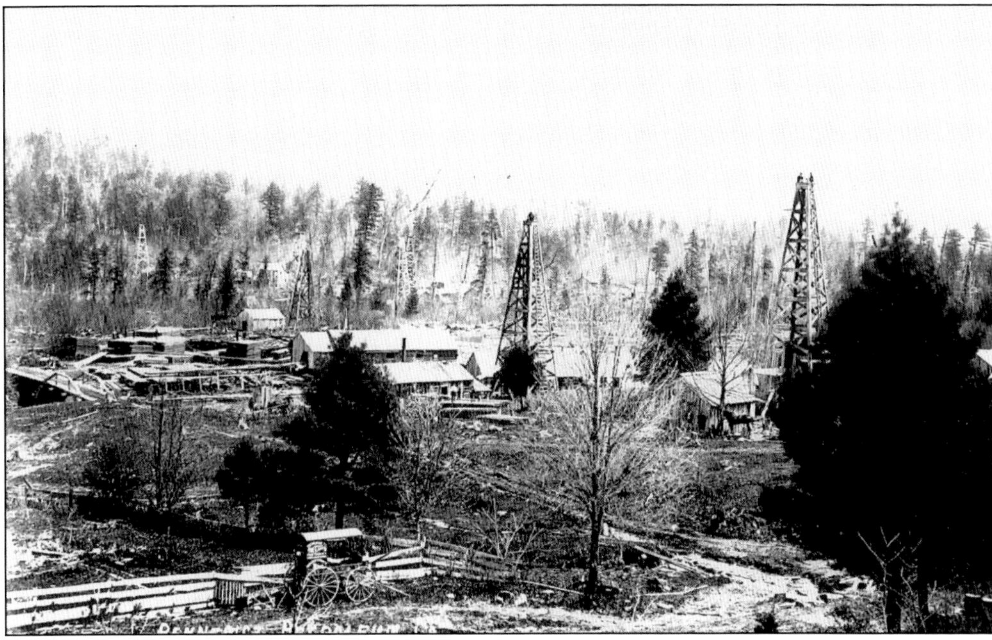

The Benedict Petroleum Company operated a lumbermill on its property near Enterprise, east of Titusville, *c.* 1870. Both water and steam were used for operating the mill. An oil well was also pumped by the steam engine. Note photographer John Mather's wagon in the foreground.

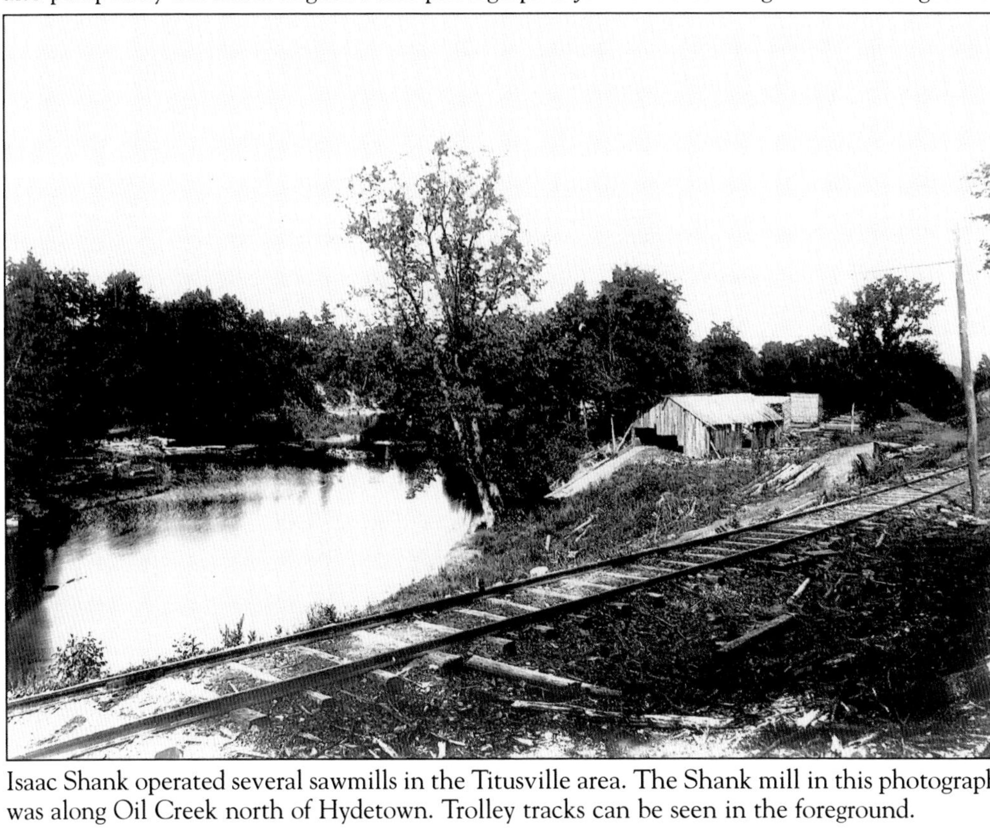

Isaac Shank operated several sawmills in the Titusville area. The Shank mill in this photograph was along Oil Creek north of Hydetown. Trolley tracks can be seen in the foreground.

Isaac Shank also operated a planing mill and custom-millwork plant on Diamond Street in Titusville from 1897 to 1930. Central Towers stands on this site today.

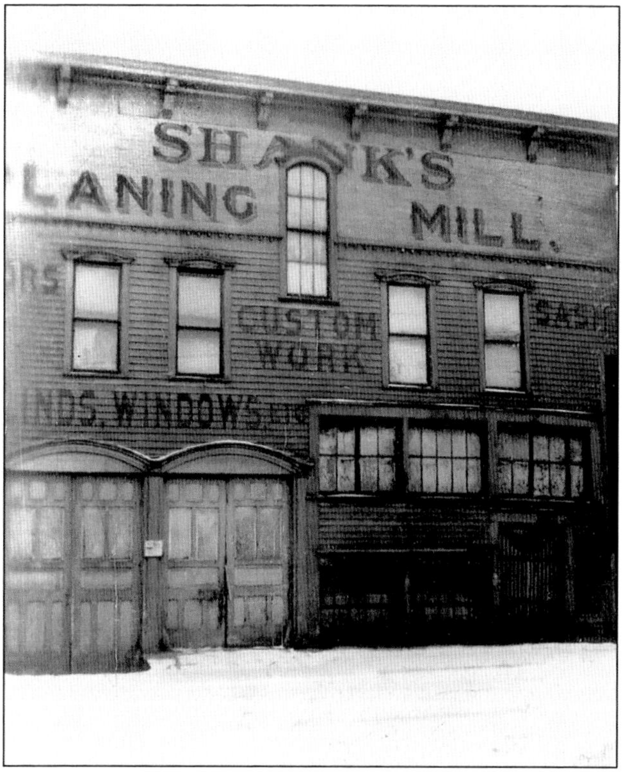

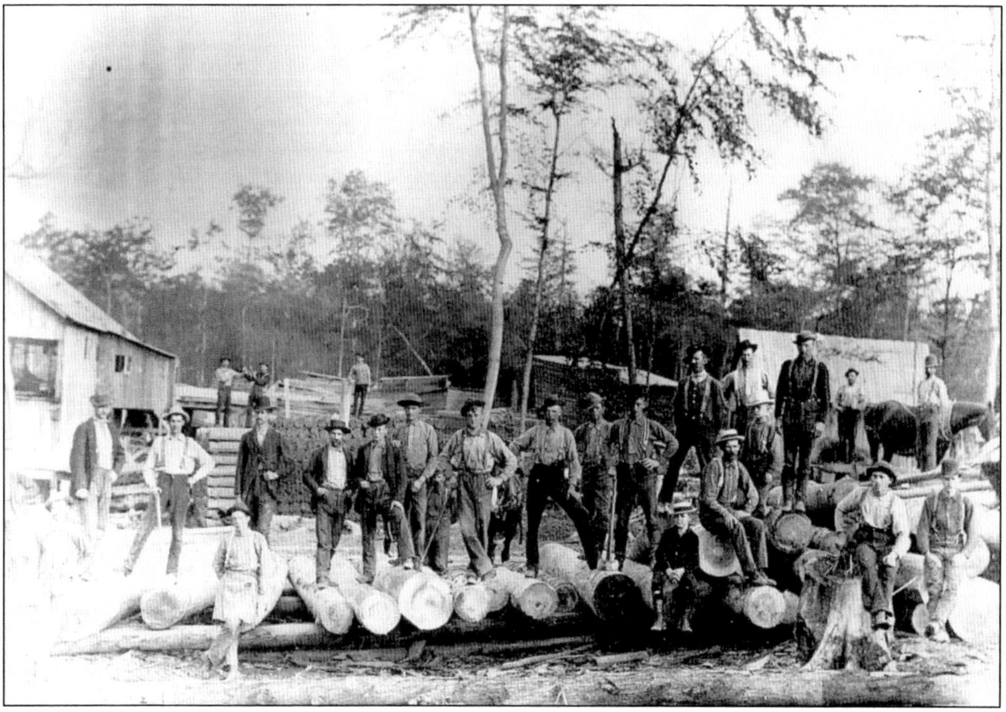

Wheelock's sawmill was located near Enterprise in Southwest Township, Warren County, east of Titusville, *c.* 1885.

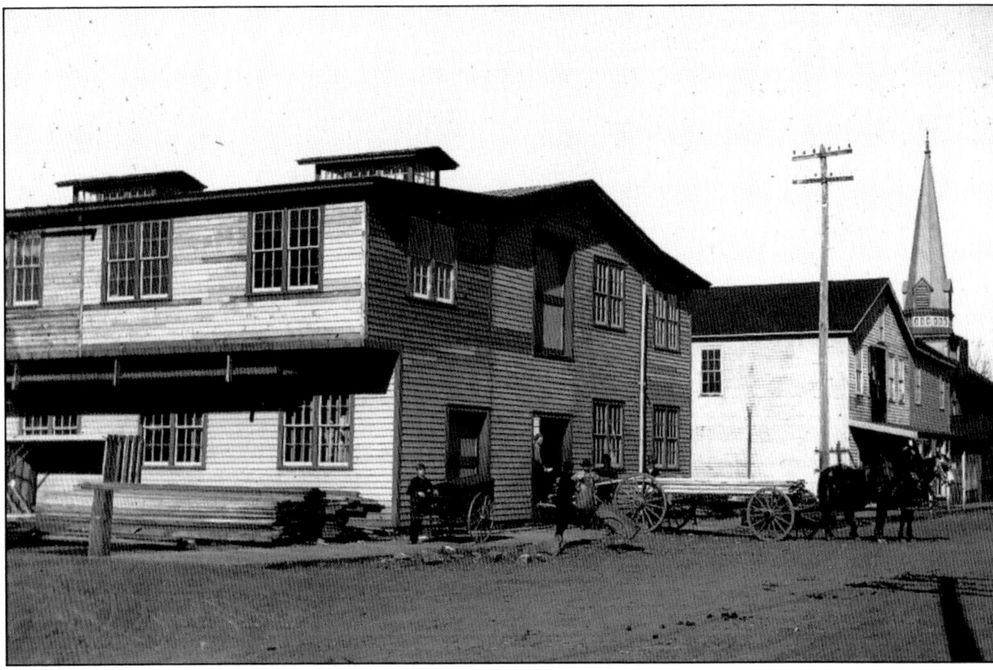

The Reuting planing mill and the Titusville Elastic Chair Company operated side by side on West Central Avenue in Titusville during the last decade of the 19th century. On the far right is the Methodist church, which was razed in 1903.

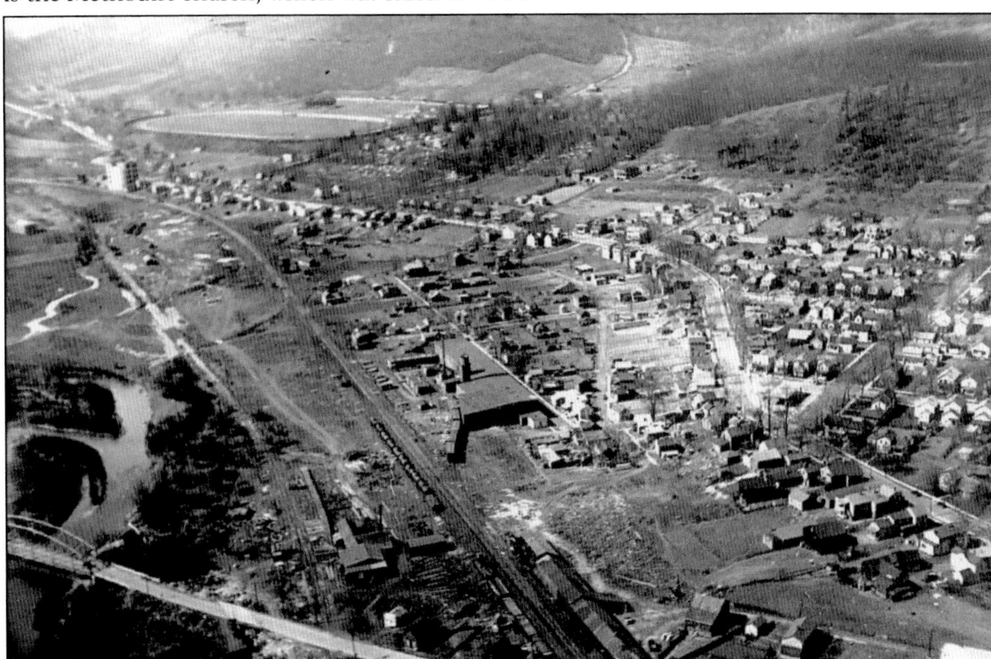

This 1929 aerial view of Titusville's west end shows the Conewango Furniture Company, the Kenneth Rowe lumbermill, and the Alcorn coal and roofing yard. The Conewango Furniture Company (originally the Specialty Manufacturing Company) declared bankruptcy in 1930. Morrison Builders Supply now stands on the former Rowe mill site.

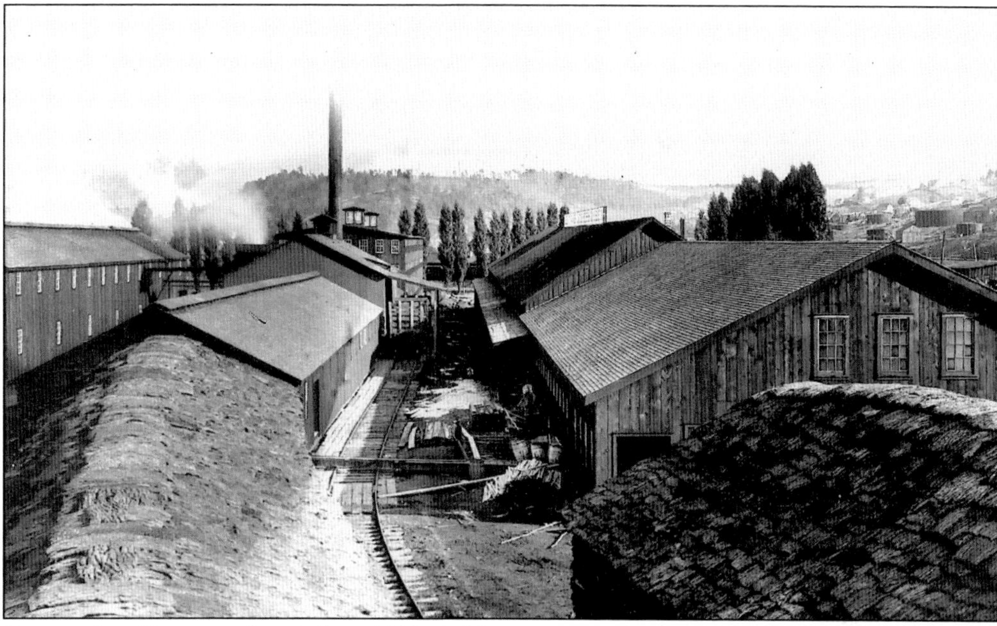

Queen City Tannery, founded in 1889–1890, was once the largest independent sole-leather tannery in the United States. Hides imported from Mexico, Brazil, and Argentina were tanned into leather with tannic acid manufactured on site from locally cut hemlock bark and chestnut wood. Finished sole leather was exported to Britain and Germany. The tannery ceased operations in 1914–1915.

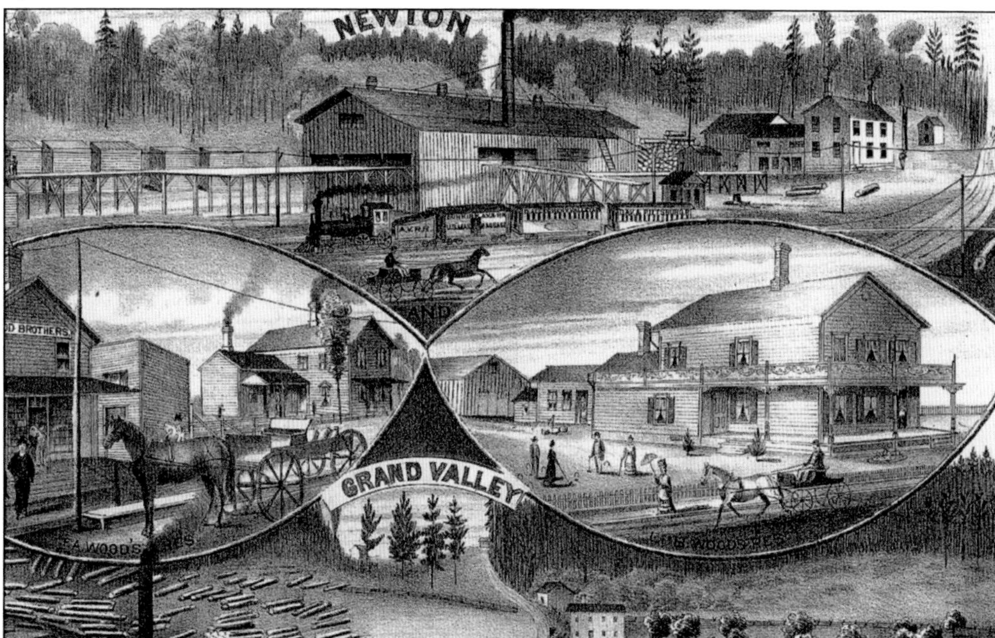

Titusville oil producer David McKelvey was a partner with his brothers-in-law Luman B. and Frank Wood in a lumber operation near Grand Valley, Eldred Township, Warren County. L. B. Wood & Company's mills at Newton Station and Grand Valley could saw 25,000 board feet of lumber per day. The mills operated between 1872 and 1900. (From *Atlas of Warren County*, 1878.)

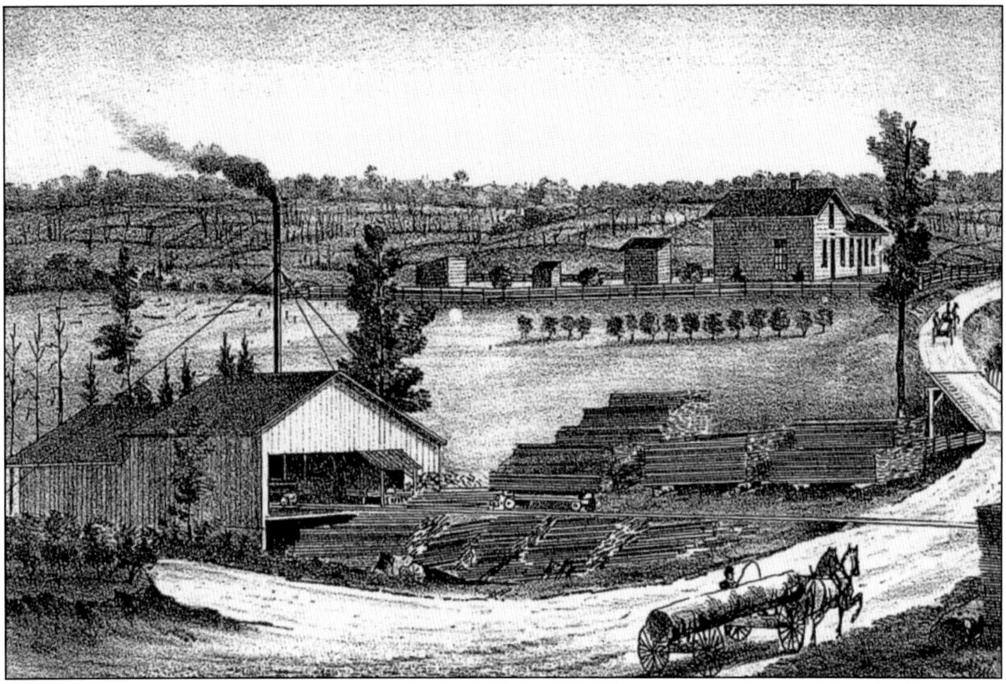

George C. Fish of Athens Township was one of many lumbermen in eastern Crawford County. This 1876 engraving depicts Fish's mill and home. Notice the size of the log on the wagon.

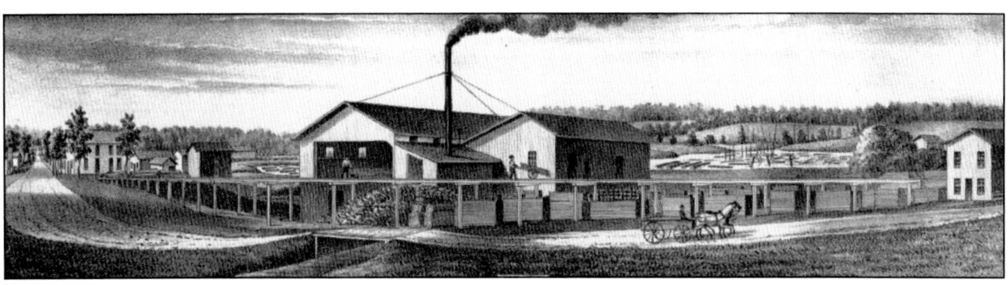

John Waid operated a steam-powered sawmill in Steuben Township, Crawford County. This H. P. Whinnery drawing shows that Waid's mill was a fairly elaborate operation, complete with a log pond. (From *Atlas of Crawford County*, 1876.)

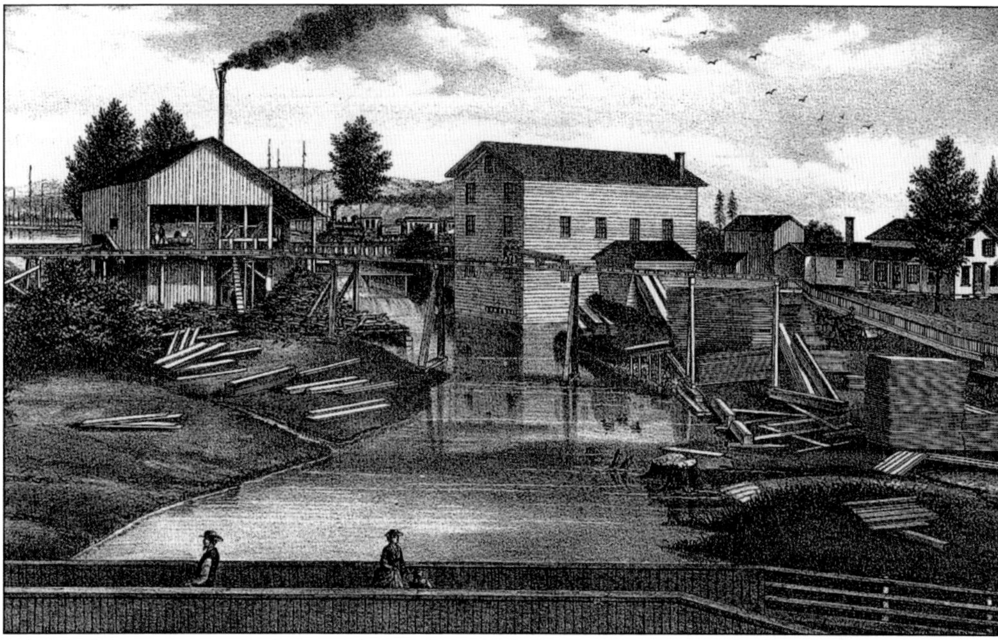

John Jude's operation at Spartansburg, Crawford County, was typical of many early mills near Titusville. Jude's facility contained both sawmill and gristmill structures side by side. The steam-powered mills could also be run by water. Steam was used when the water level was low. Note the Clear Lake Dam and railroad tracks in the background.

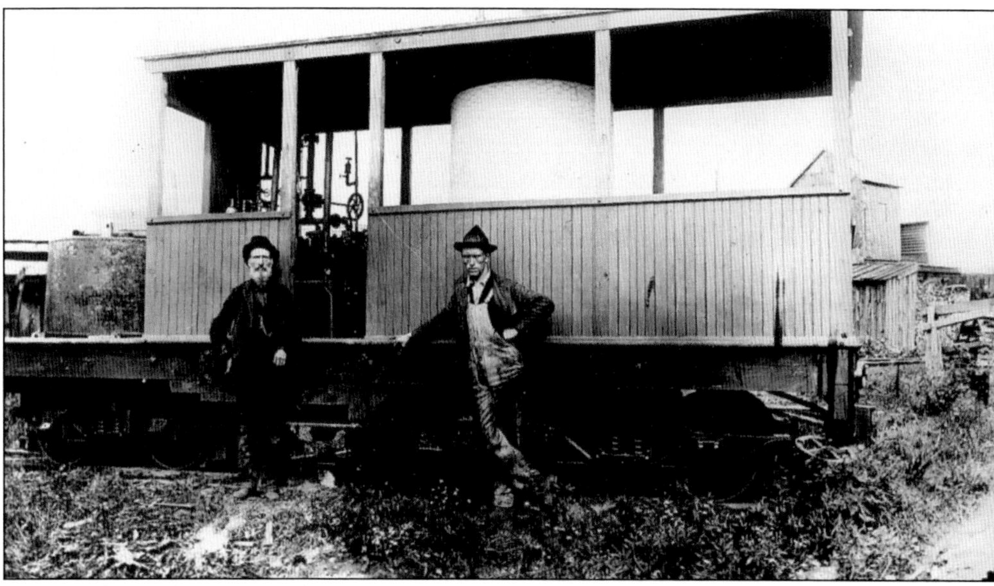

One of the earliest steam logging locomotives was designed by Spartansburg resident and lumberman Charles Scott. His design became the prototype of the locomotive built by the Climax Manufacturing Company of Corry, Pennsylvania. Scott (with a beard) is shown beside a used Climax locomotive after it was sold to the Stephens & Heisman Cooperage in Titusville. Stephens & Heisman manufactured wooden barrels near the present Titusville Middle School site in 1890. Michael Heisman, one of the owners, was the father of John Heisman, the football coach for whom the Heisman Trophy is named.

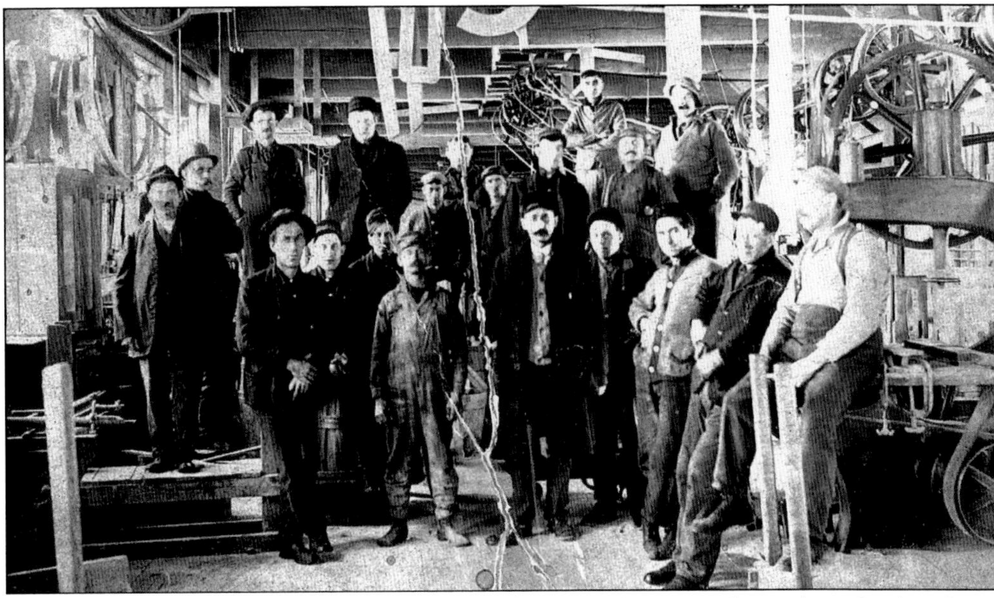

Seen is an interior view of the Specialty Manufacturing Company, located on Garden Street in Titusville, c. 1900. L. T. Gorenflo, D. J. Whitney, Theodore Reuting, and Joseph Seep owned this woodworking plant. Specialty Manufacturing (also known as the Novelty Works) was founded in 1892. It manufactured lawn furniture, ironing boards, stepladders, and other wooden items. John and William Marthaler are the two men on the far right. (Courtesy of the Titusville Herald.)

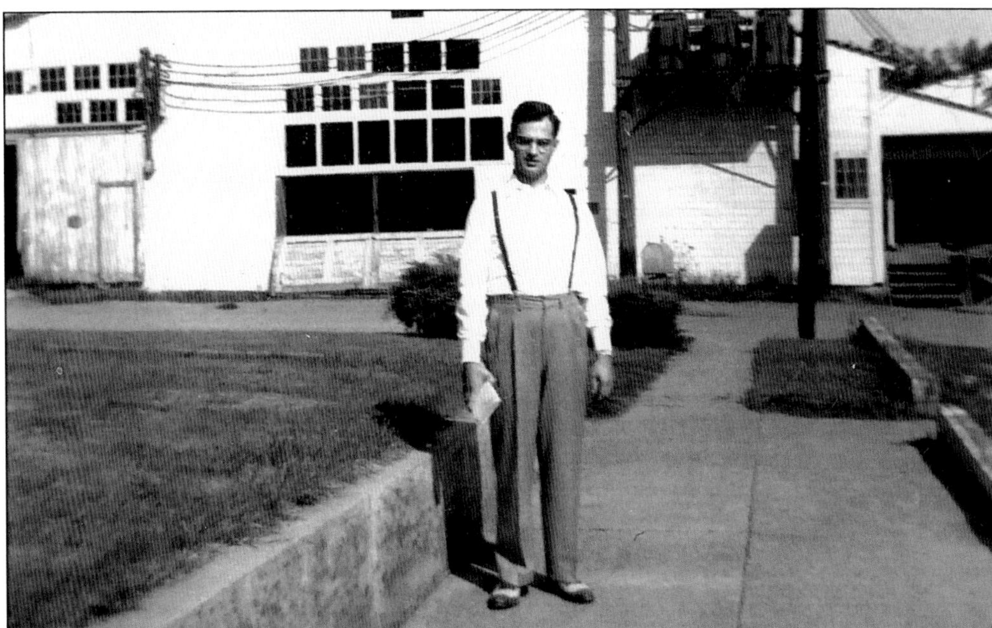

Elmer S. Weber is seen in front of the Fisher & Young mill in 1954. This mill was the largest lumbermill in Pennsylvania during the 1950s. It boasted two 54-inch band saws for cutting high- and low-grade lumber. Weyerhaeuser Choicewoods operates a dry kiln–planing mill facility on this site today.

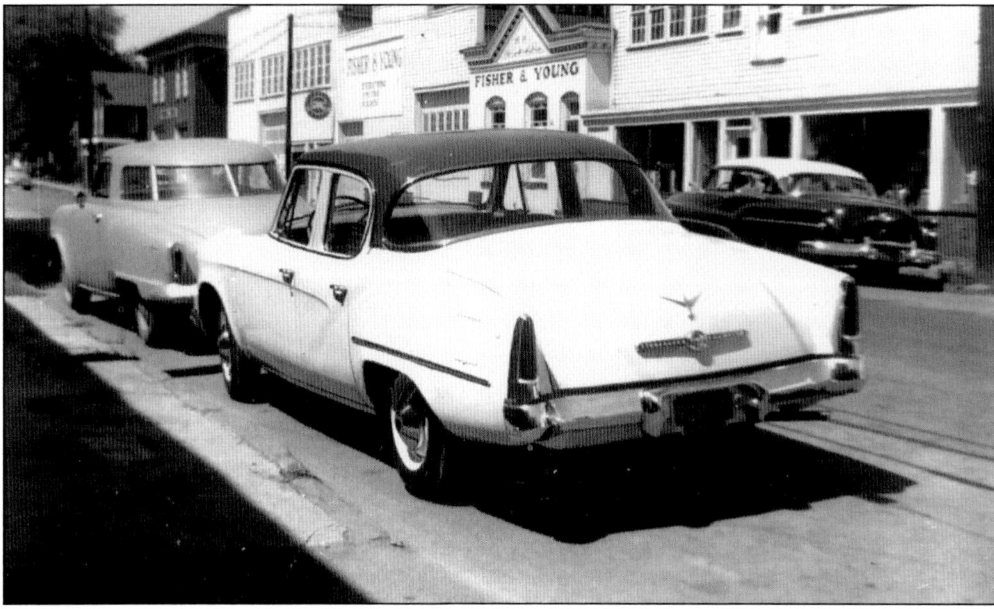

David Olson purchased the Reuting lumber operation in 1919. After Olson declared bankruptcy, his planing mill and retail store were acquired by Fisher & Young in February 1939. The West Central Avenue site was expanded by the new owners, who added a General Motors Corporation truck dealership. The Studebaker automobiles in the foreground were owned by Elmer Weber.

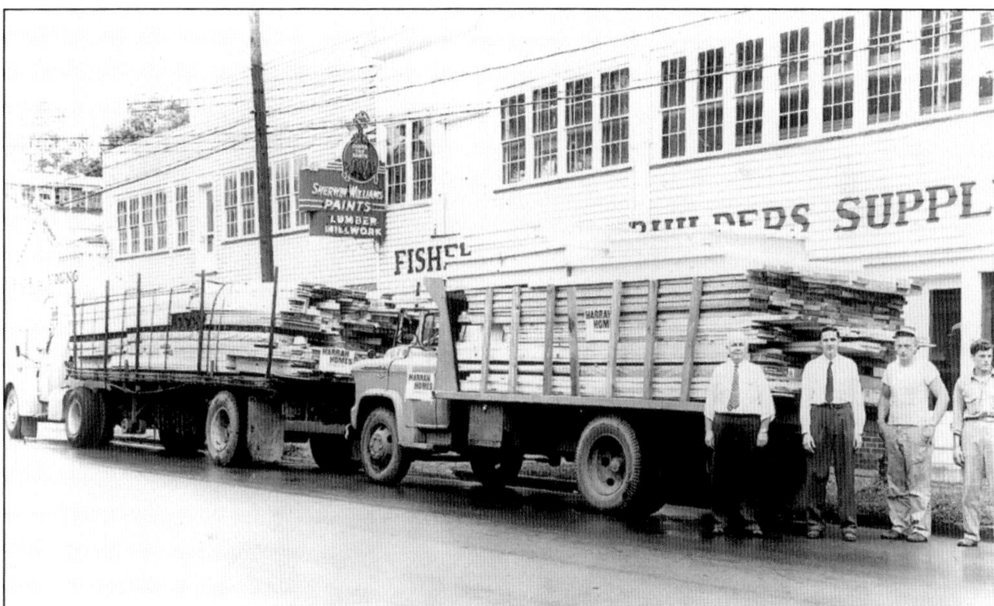

Precut homes designed by Howard Harrah were manufactured at the Fisher & Young millwork plant during the 1950s. This 1955 photograph shows two trucks transferring materials for the home constructed for Elmer Weber and his wife. On the right are Howard Harrah, Jack Ludwick (the mill manager), Richard Hubbard, and Ralph Howe. The Fisher & Young retail store and millwork plant at 324 West Central Avenue ceased operation and were razed in 1965.

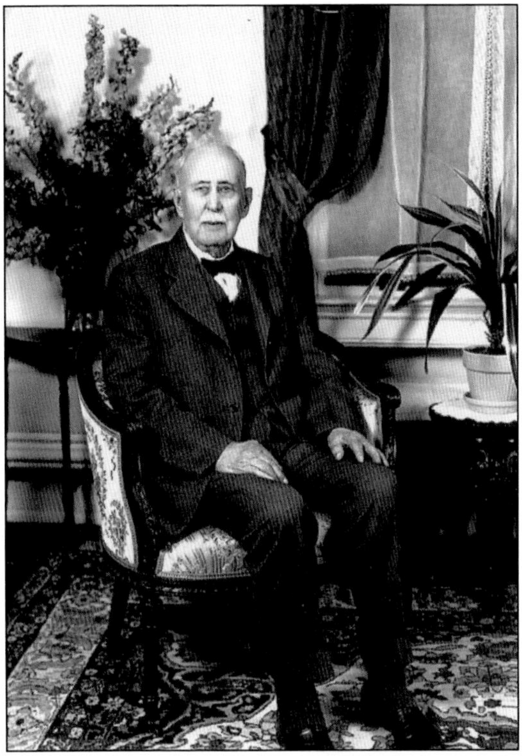

Isaac Shank (1839–1936) was Titusville's grand old man of lumbering. Shank operated a retail lumber business and sawmills until shortly before his death. (Courtesy of the Titusville Herald.)

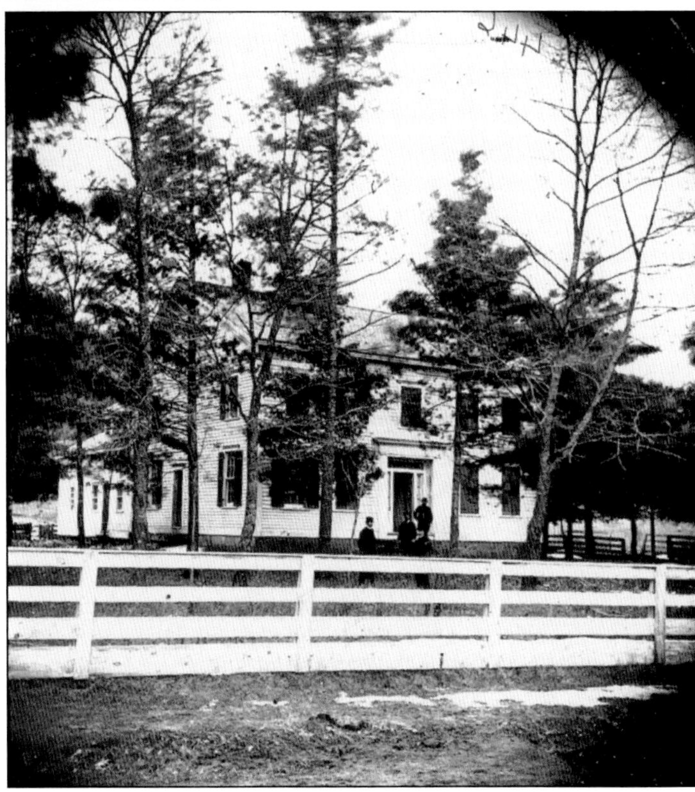

The John Watson home on East Main Street was owned by one of Titusville's earliest lumber manufacturers. John Watson's son, Lewis Findlay Watson, became a lumberman and U.S. congressman from Warren. This house still stands today.

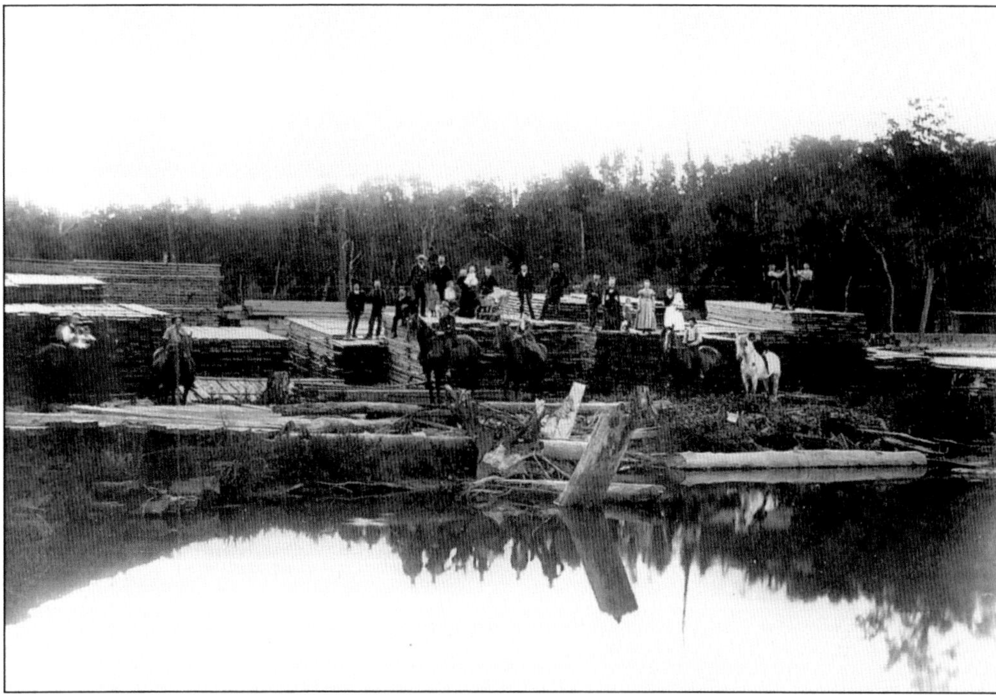

This is an unidentified Titusville-area lumbering site. Horses, men, women, children, and a baby are very much in evidence. (Courtesy of the Drake Well Museum.)

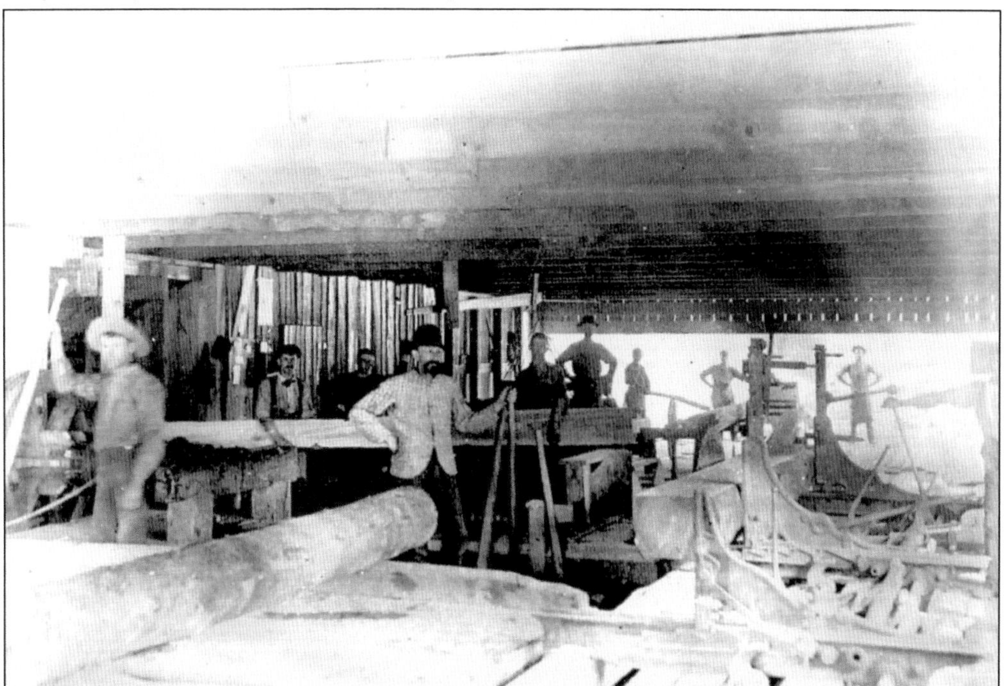

Seen is the interior of an unidentified sawmill in the Titusville area. Note the large timber squared on the saw carriage and that the men on the left have a large slab, or board. (Courtesy of the Drake Well Museum.)

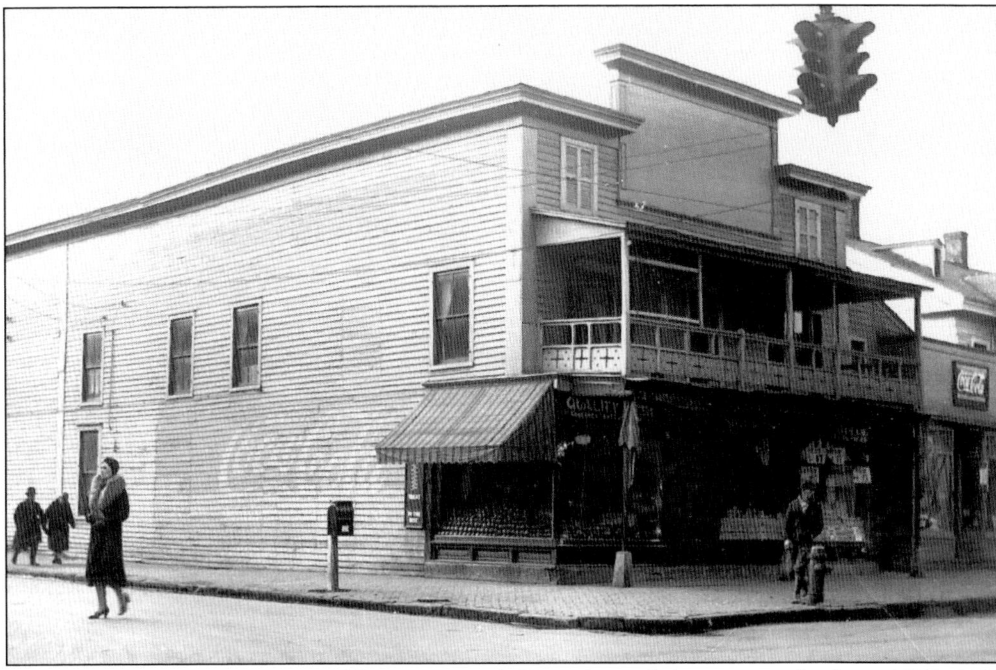

This landmark structure at Franklin Street and West Central Avenue was built in 1853–1854 as the office building and company store for Brewer, Watson & Company, lumbermen. Col. Edwin L. Drake frequently visited the offices while drilling his oil well on the firm's sawmill site. The building later housed wholesale and retail groceries. Notice the Coca-Cola signs in this 1929 photograph. (Courtesy of the Drake Well Museum.)

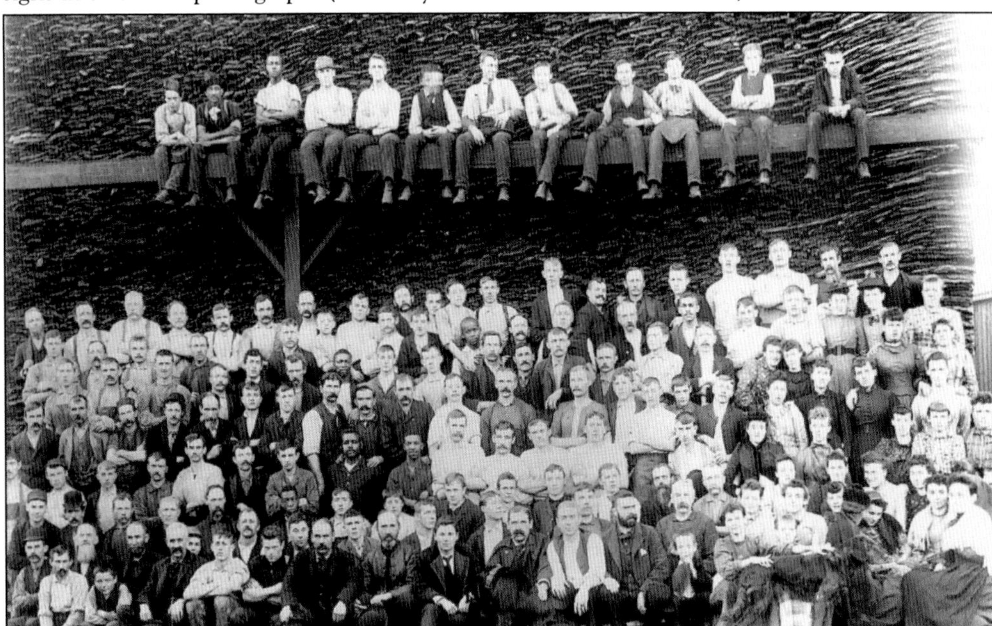

Seen here are employees of the Queen City Tannery in 1894. The workers, many of whom were Swedish immigrants, seem dwarfed by the mammoth bark pile. People of various races and nationalities were employed in the tannery. (Courtesy of the Drake Well Museum.)

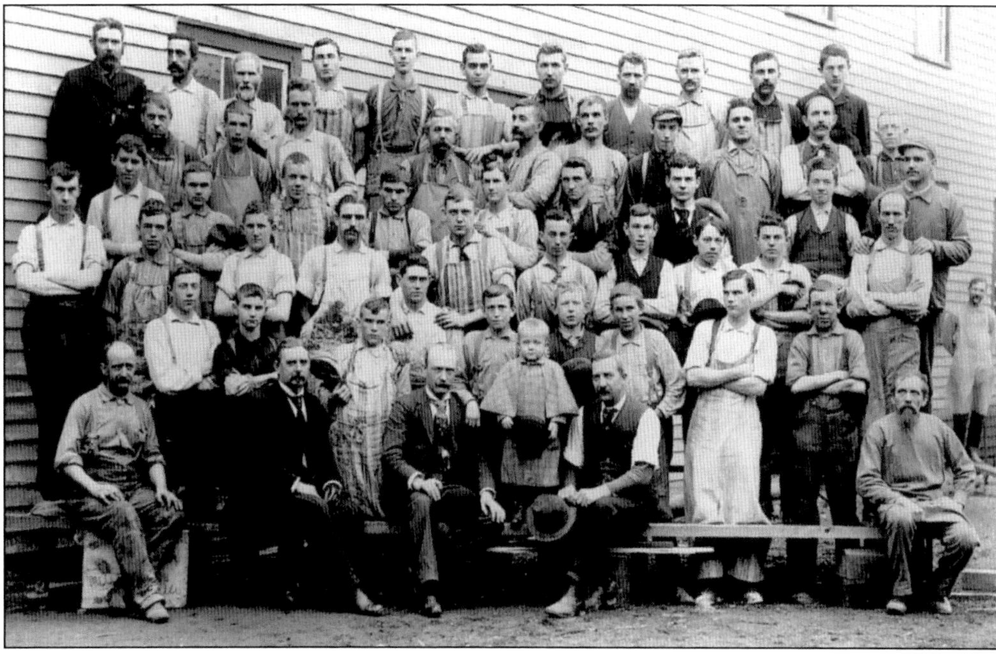

Titusville Elastic Chair Company employees are seen in this *c.* 1895 photograph. This firm later evolved into Marsh Gauge Pole Company Marsh Planing, a successor business, which now operates just outside the Titusville city limits. (Courtesy of the Drake Well Museum.)

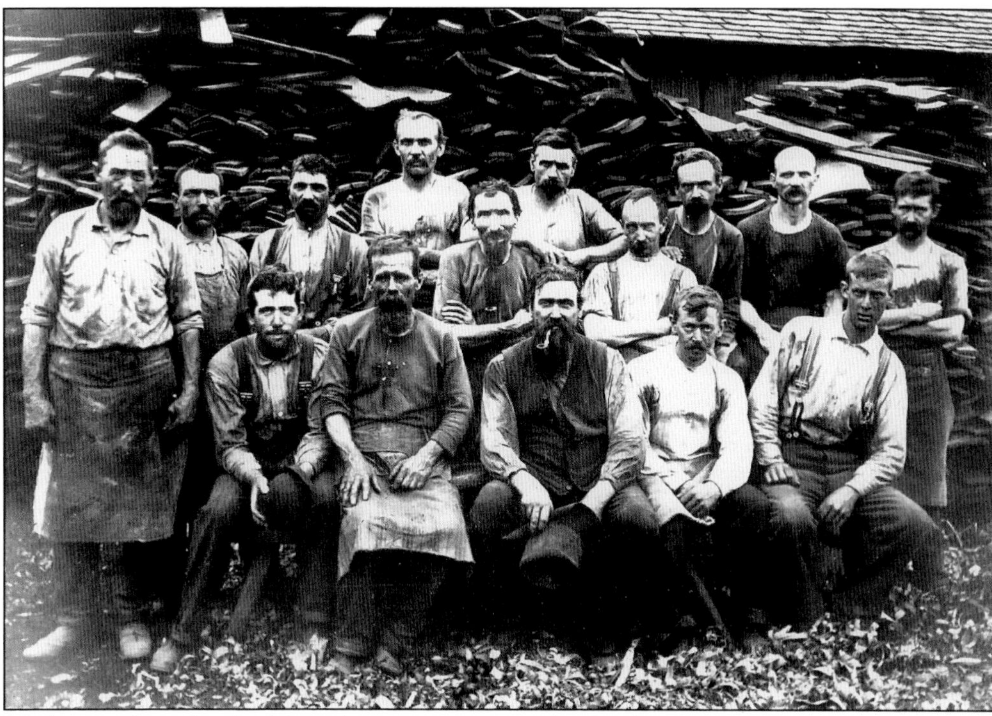

Workers with a pile of oak barrel staves are seen at the Stephens & Heisman Cooperage in the east end of Titusville in 1880. This is a good photograph showing the relationship between the oil and lumber industries. (Courtesy of the Drake Well Museum.)

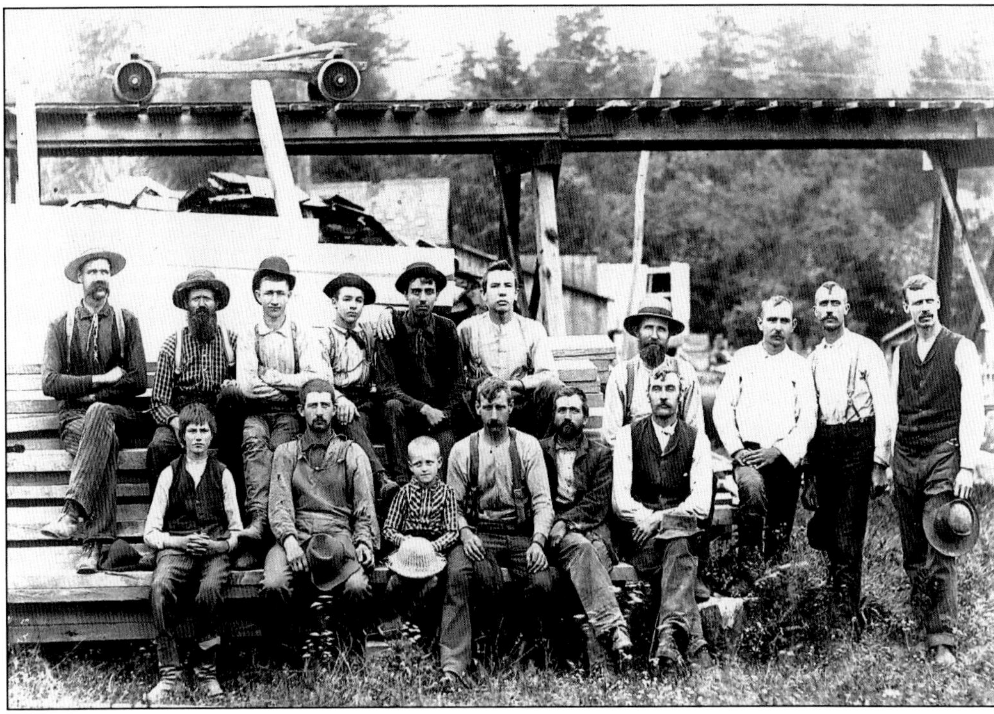

A group of men and boys is pictured at an unidentified Titusville-area sawmill site. The runway for moving lumber can be seen overhead. (Courtesy of the Drake Well Museum.)

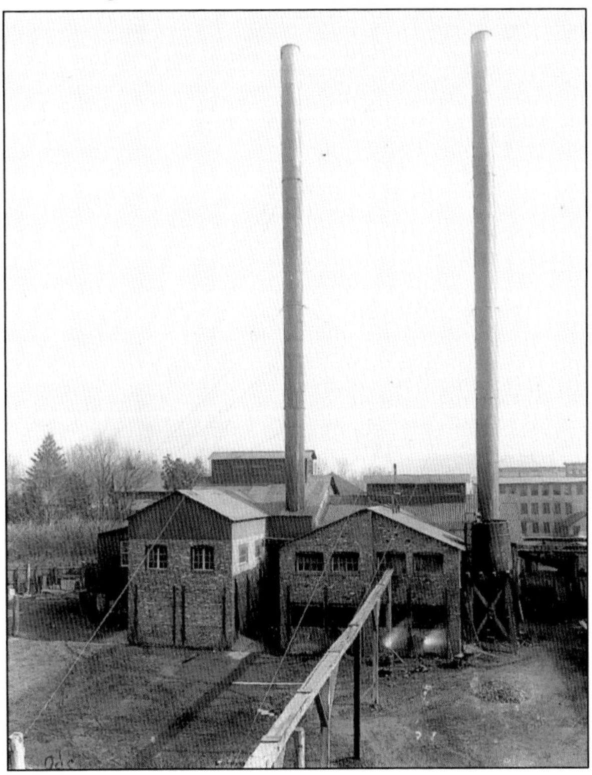

Seen is one of two boiler houses on the Queen City Tannery property. Sawmills and tanneries burned their own wood waste for heat and power. The bark mill and leather-finishing building can be seen in the background. (Courtesy of the Drake Well Museum.)

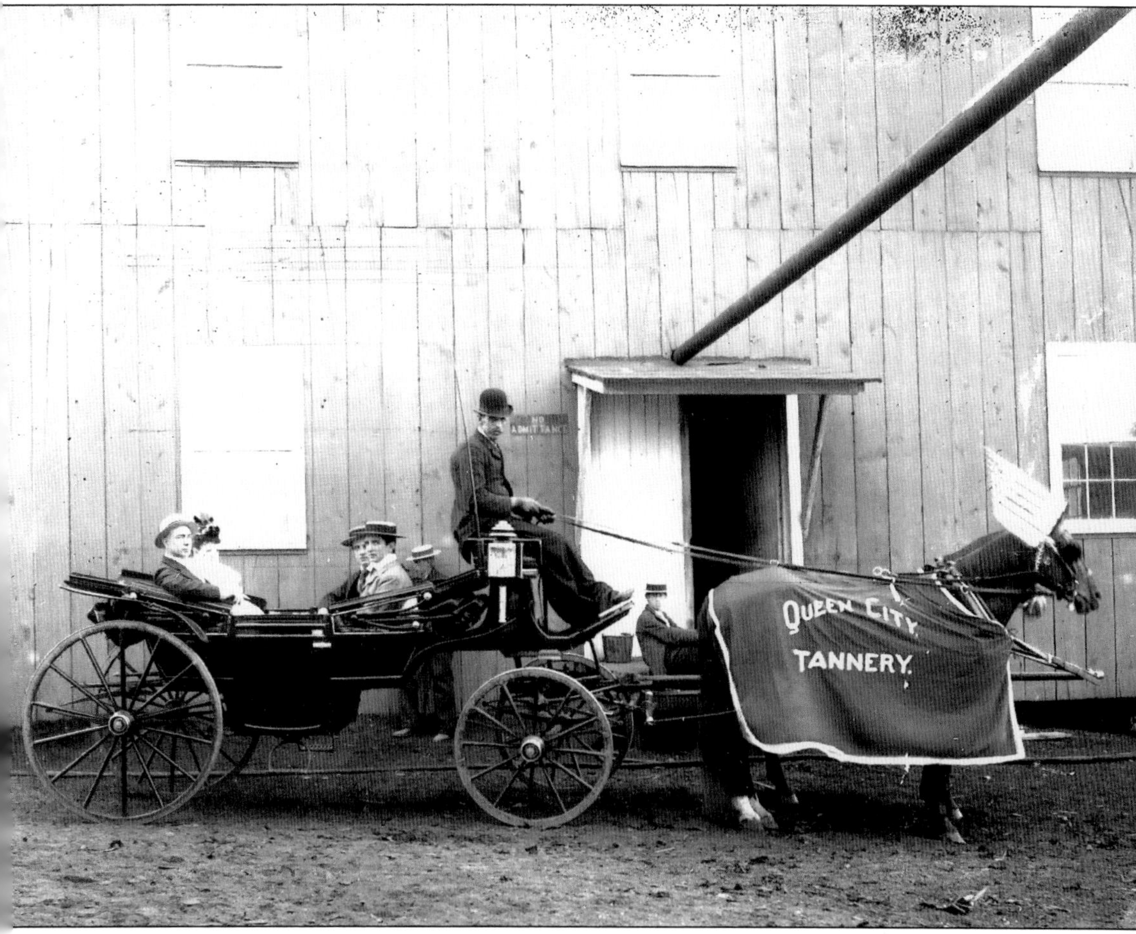

Members of the Queen City Tannery office staff are in a carriage at the plant, possibly for a parade. Samuel Maxwell, tannery superintendent, is in the light-colored hat. (Courtesy of the Drake Well Museum.)

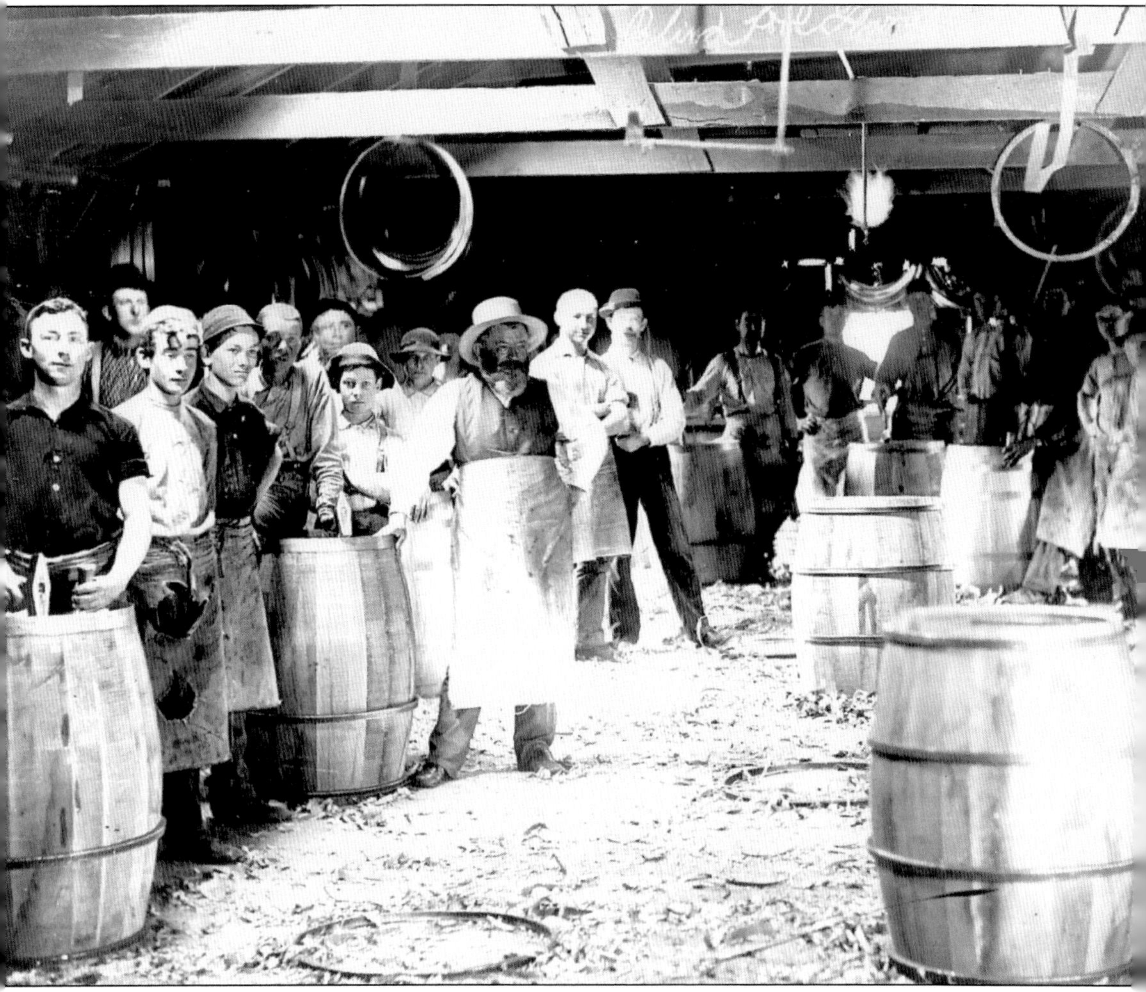

In this 1888 view is the interior of Stephens & Heisman Cooperage, on South Kerr Street in Titusville. Michael Heisman, a German-speaking immigrant from the Alsace region of eastern France, was also a partner in Titusville's American Oil Works. (Courtesy of the Drake Well Museum.)

Two

The Oil Boom
Production, Refining, and Related Industries

Although widely acknowledged to be the petroleum industry's birthplace, Titusville was actually on the Pennsylvania oil region's edge. The Titusville geological quadrangle covers 220 square miles. Only 67 square miles (mainly in Venango and Warren Counties) contain oil sand formations.

The completion of the Drake Well (August 27, 1859) caused Titusville's population to grow from 350 to approximately 8,000 permanent and floating residents by 1865–1866. Titusville became the jumping-off point for nearby oil fields in the surrounding counties.

The world's first machine shop and foundry facility to exclusively produce oil-industry items opened here in 1860. Oil refineries, tank and barrel factories, a nitroglycerine plant, railroads, and an oil exchange soon followed.

Natural-gas production followed local oil discoveries. The world's first true gas well was drilled in Oil Creek Township, Crawford County, in 1872.

Oil production remained one of the mainstays of Titusville's economy well into the 20th century. Refining and the manufacture of oil-field machinery also remained important economic factors until the 1940s and 1950s.

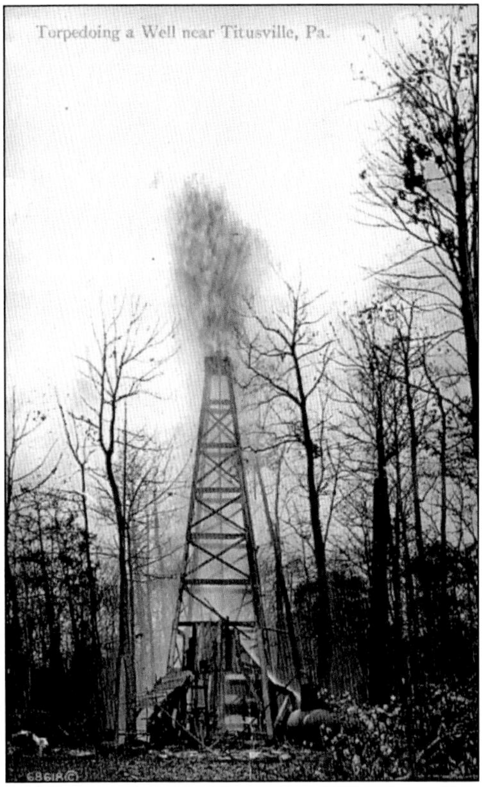

Seen is an unidentified Titusville-area oil well after it was torpedoed with a charge of nitroglycerine. The spray of water, oil, and debris can be seen over the derrick. (Courtesy of Kathryn Newson.)

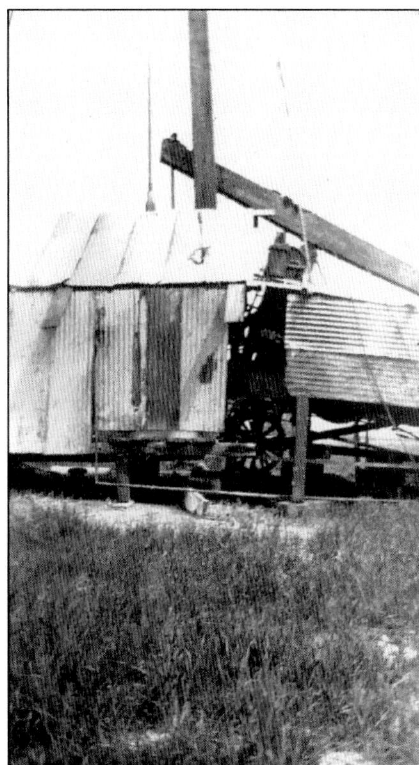

Star drilling rigs were portable, steam-powered units. They replaced standard rigs in the Titusville region c. 1900. This rig was photographed in Oil Creek Township, Crawford County, during the late 1920s. (Courtesy of Myrna Wescoat.)

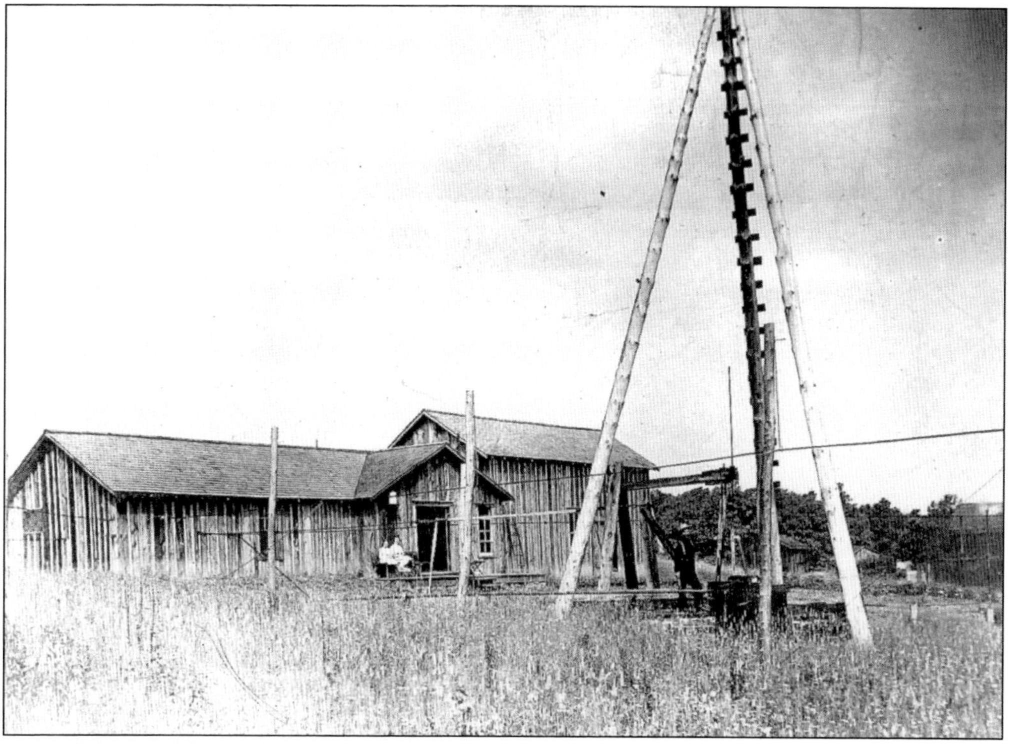

One of the world's first plants for extracting gasoline from natural gas was located on Susan Emery's oil lease southeast of Titusville. It operated from 1903 to 1905. Pumper Anthony Fasenmyer can be seen beside the pumping jack. His daughters are on the left, at the powerhouse door. Note the doll carriage. (Courtesy of the Drake Well Museum.)

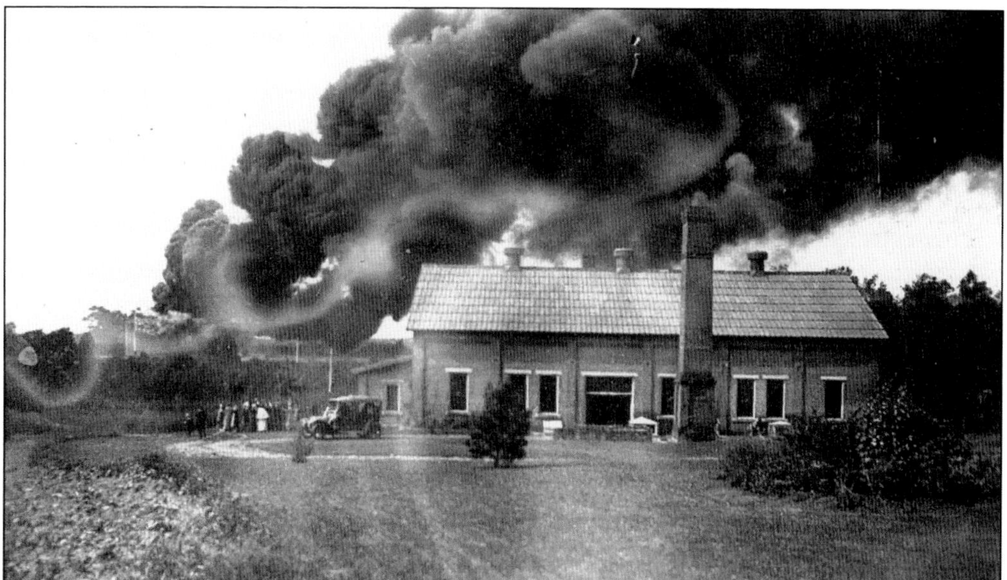

Fire damaged a storage tank at Tidewater Oil Company's Fieldmore pump station in Oil Creek Township, Venango County, in 1915. A large crowd of curiosity seekers can be seen. The pump station was abandoned in 1939 and was converted into a machine shop.

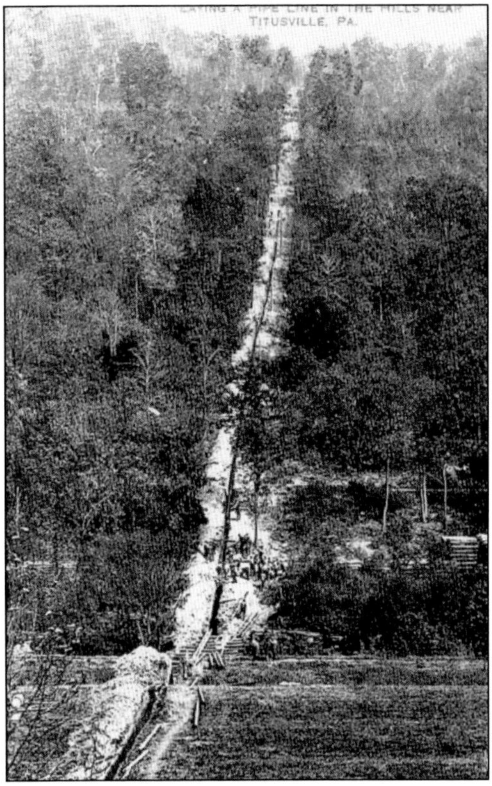

Laborers from Italy, Armenia, and Croatia dug the trenches for the Tidewater pipeline connecting the Illinois oil fields to the Bayonne, New Jersey, refinery. Construction crews stayed in camps near Titusville. Note the trench and sections of pipe. (Courtesy of Kathryn Newson.)

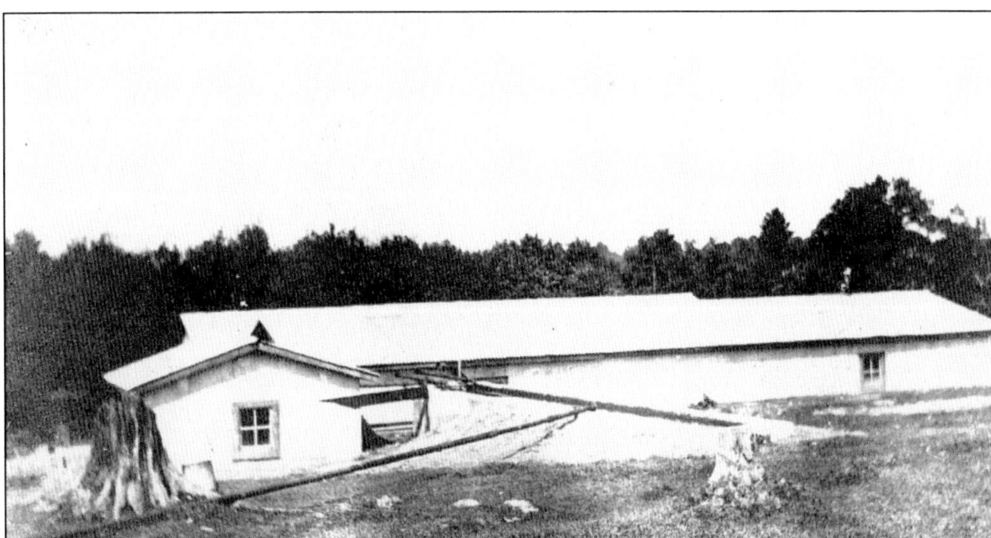

The Bayliss, Bloss and Wege Oil Company owned an oil lease with a natural gasoline plant (Casinghead) in Oil Creek Township, north of Titusville. This 1928 photograph shows the compressor house and water-cooled pipe coils for extracting gasoline from natural gas. (Courtesy of Myrna Wescoat.)

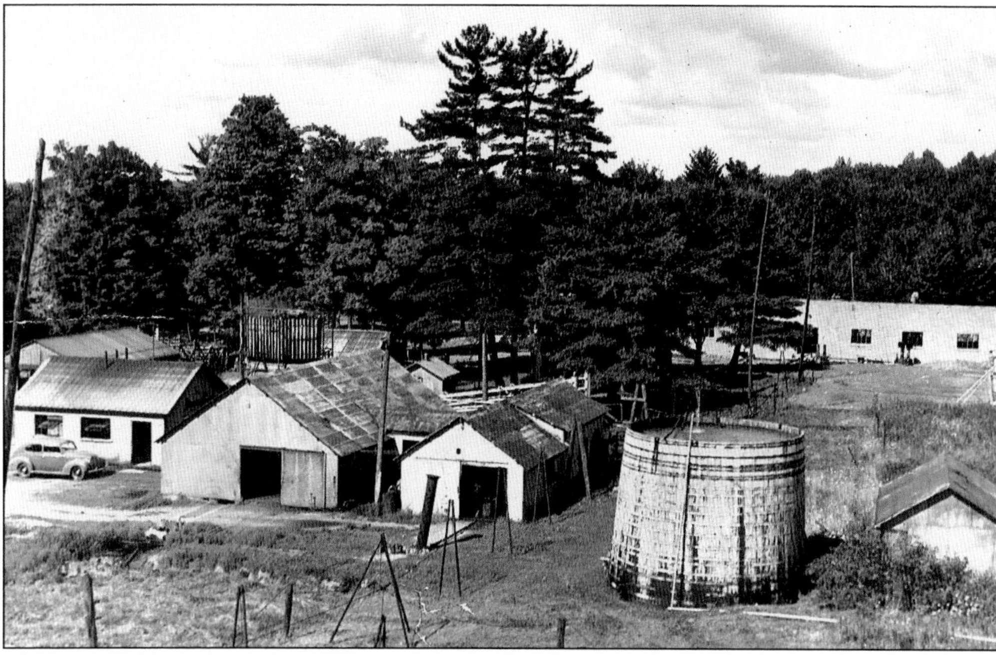

The National Petroleum Corporation was one of the largest oil-production firms in the Titusville region. Owned by the Fertig and Hogg families, National Petroleum operated oil leases with elaborate secondary recovery systems in Warren, Venango, and Forest Counties. The Goodwill Hill (in Southwest Township, Warren County) leases were especially elaborate. The structures in the lower center contained high and low stage compressors for extracting natural gasoline. The building on the far left contained a large compressor for injecting dry gas from the gasoline plant into oil sands to increase production. (Courtesy of the Drake Well Museum.)

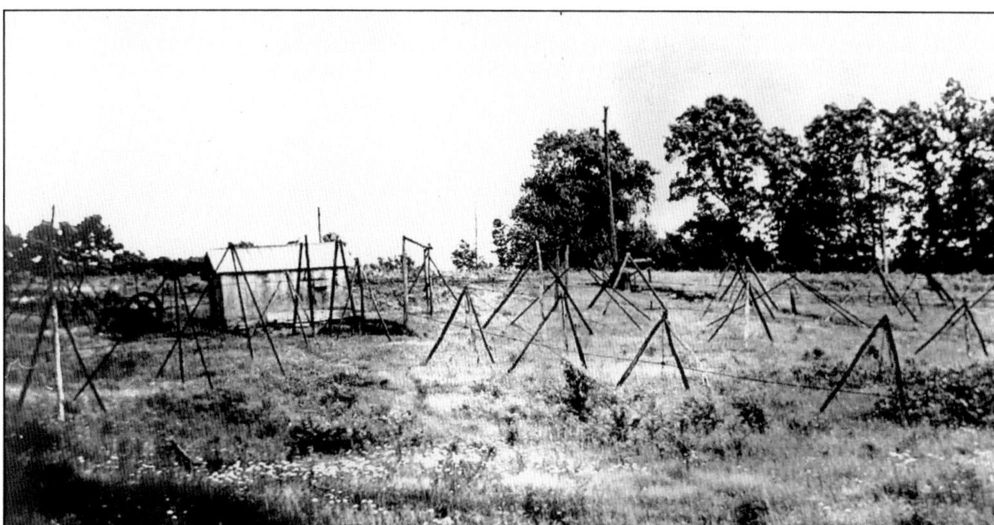

National Petroleum also generated electricity on their properties for pumping oil wells. This 1944 photograph shows a powerhouse at Goodwill Hill, Warren County, converted to run on electricity. The gas engine, which formerly pumped the wells, is on the left. Nearly 20 rod lines can be seen running to the well locations. (Courtesy of the Drake Well Museum.)

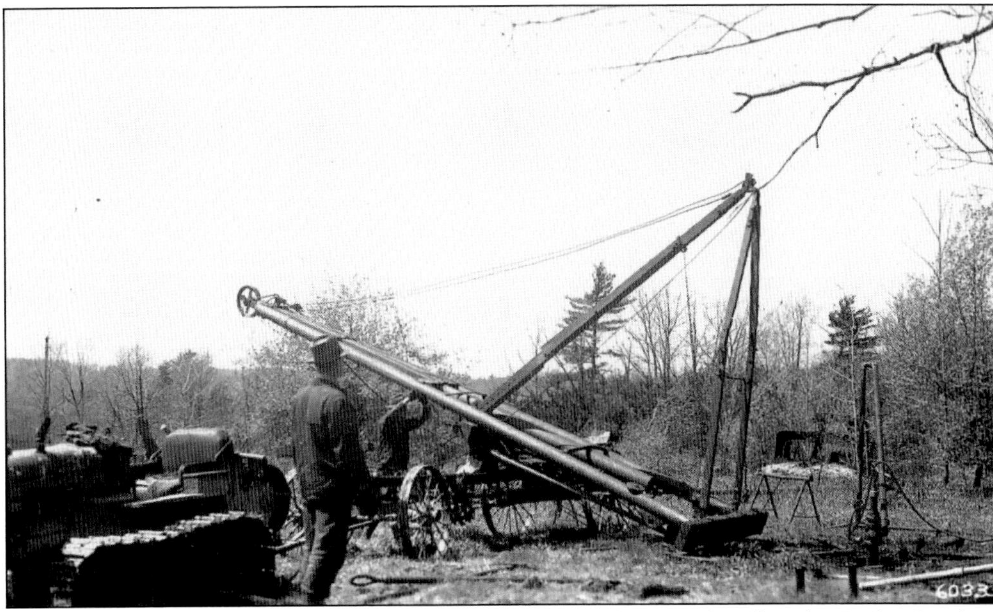

Iron King portable pulling masts replaced derricks at producing oil wells. The Bailey Brothers Wolf's Head lease, near Pleasantville, used a portable mast and Cletrac tractor.

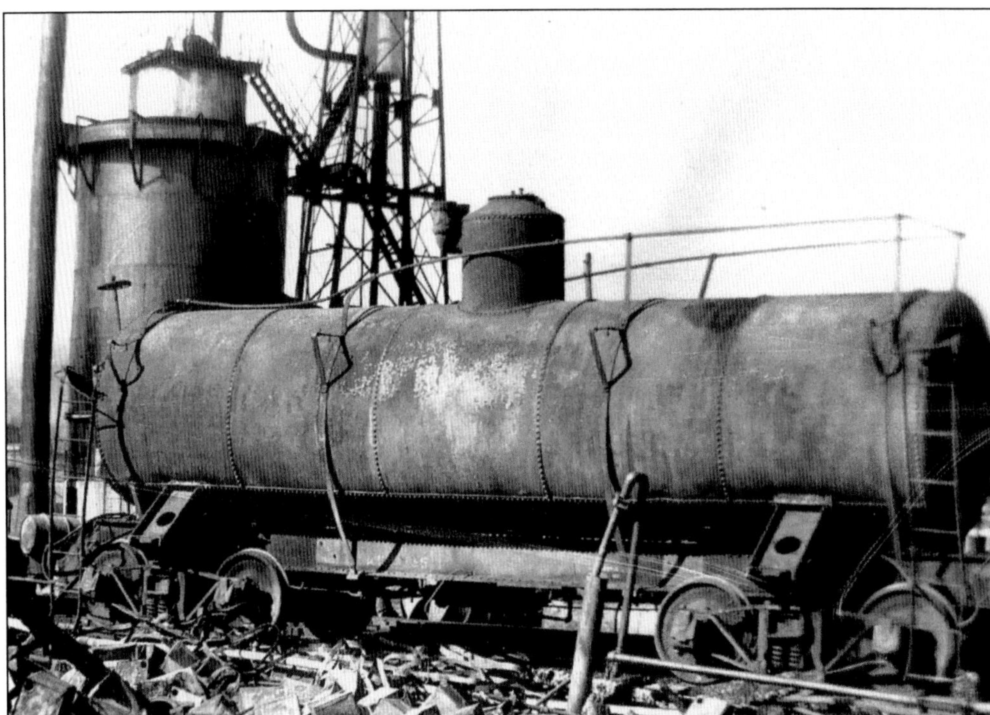

Two serious fires struck the American Oil Works, in 1923 and 1926. Behind the devastation, an early gasoline-cracking unit can be seen. (Courtesy of the Titusville Herald.)

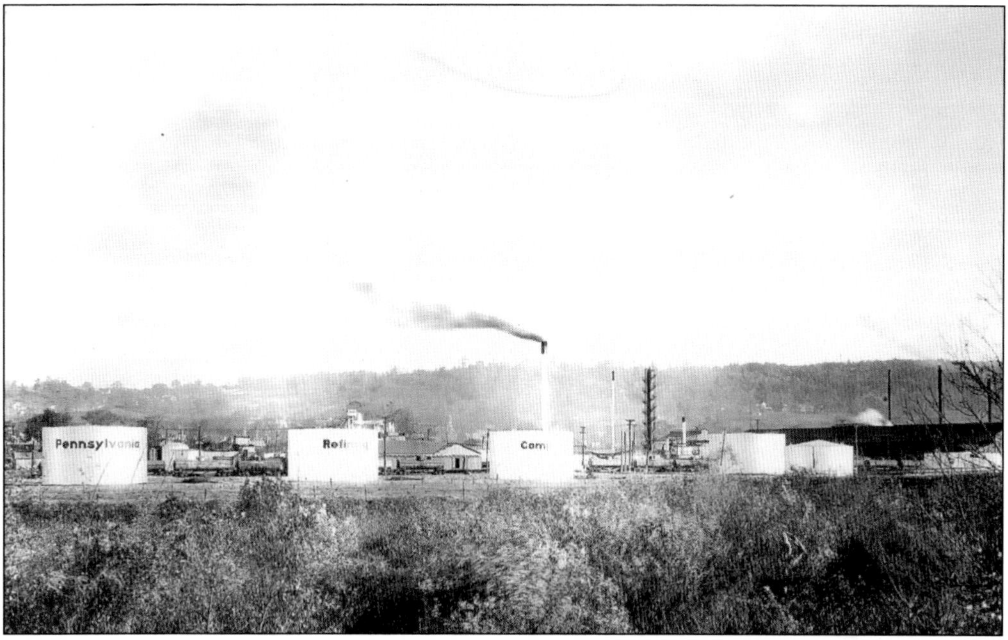

The Pennsylvania Refining Company of Butler and Karns City purchased the American Oil Works in 1926. New facilities including a filter house and fractionating tower were added. This 1933 photograph shows the crude oil–storage tanks, railroad sidings, barrelhouse, and distillation, or fractionating, unit. The Titusville Forge Company is clearly visible on the right.

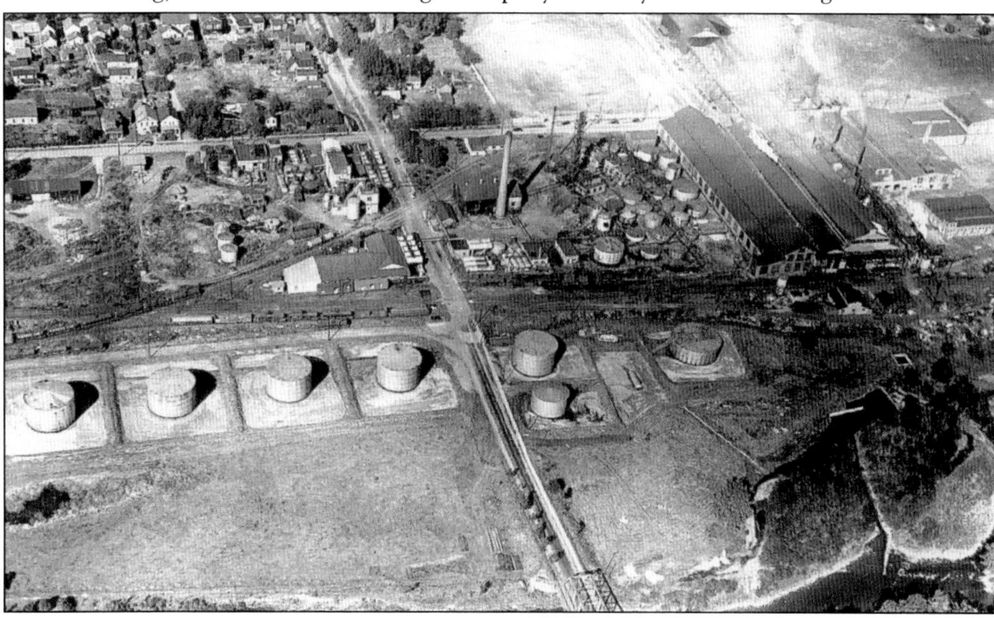

A 1930s aerial view of the Pennsylvania Refining Company (the Penn-Drake refinery) reveals much of Titusville's east end. At the center right is the Titusville Forge Company's building. The structures on the far right housed the American Radiator Company until 1929. Cyclops Steel Company purchased the old radiator plant in 1935. The Pennsylvania Refining Company's Titusville operation closed in 1948. Today, the Titusville Middle School occupies part of this site. (Courtesy of the Titusville Herald.)

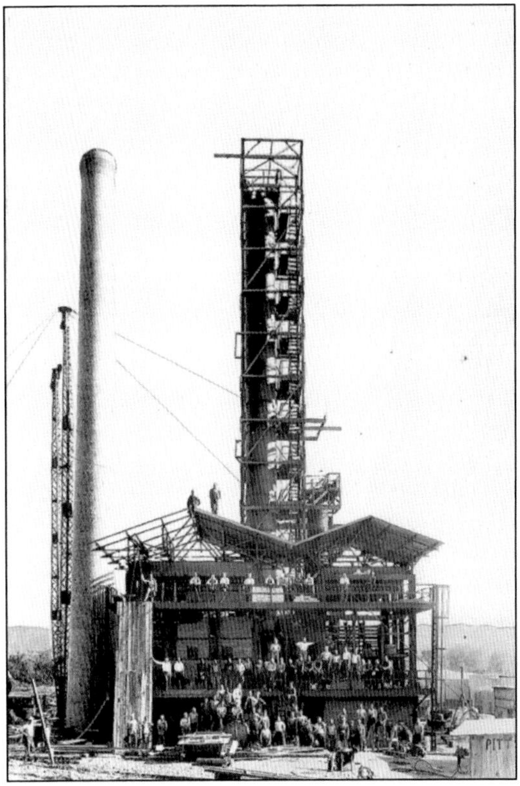

The Crew Levick Company purchased the Pennsylvania Paraffine Works and the adjacent Bessemer Refining Company in 1915. A year later, Cities Service Company acquired Crew Levick. Both Titusville sister refineries were joined into a single unit. New blending and distillation facilities were added, as this 1930 photograph shows.

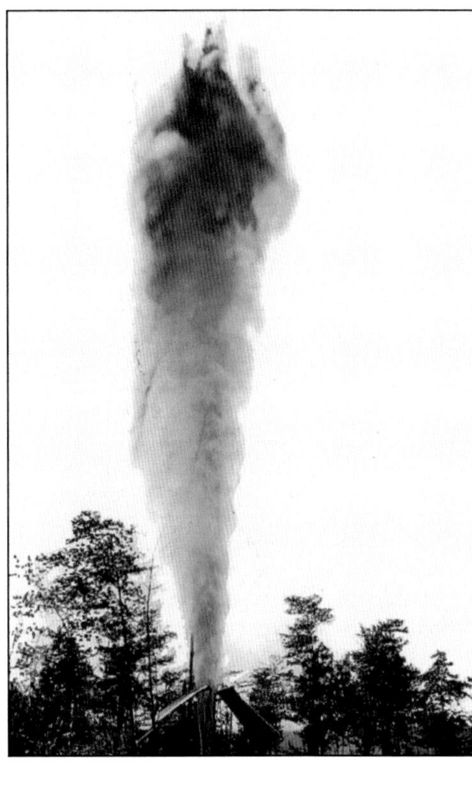

Cities Service operated a pipeline system, which served its Titusville facility. This well, shown being torpedoed with nitroglycerine, was on one of the local leases connected to the Cities Service system.

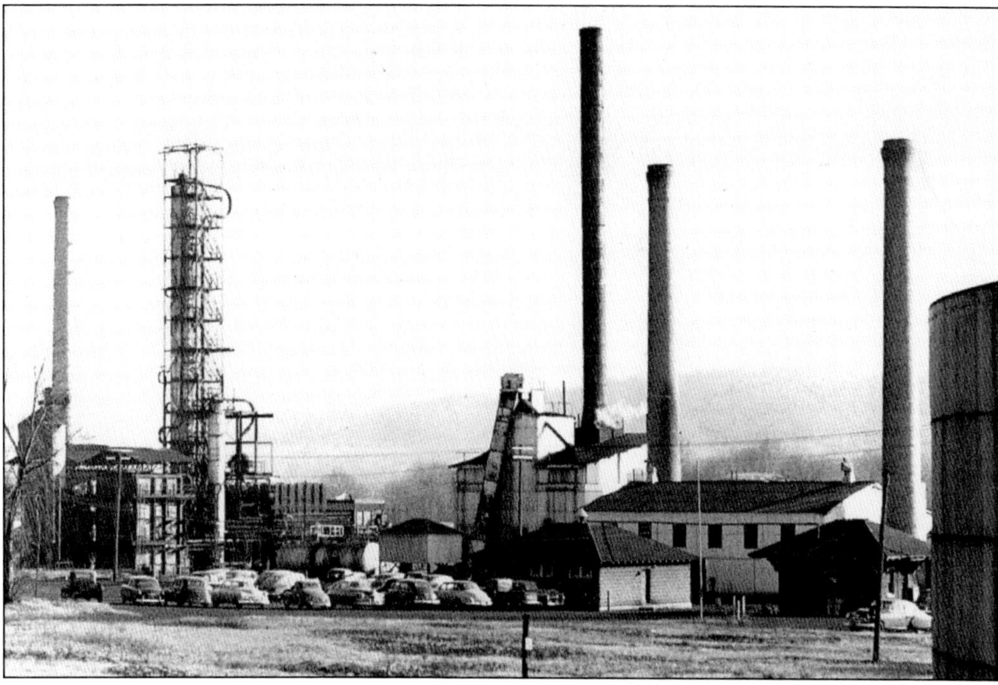

A late-1940s view of the Cities Service refinery shows distillation, or fractionating, units, boiler houses, and other structures. Titusville ceased to be an oil town when this refinery closed in November 1950. Honeywell Industrial Wax occupies the site today. (Courtesy of the Titusville Herald.)

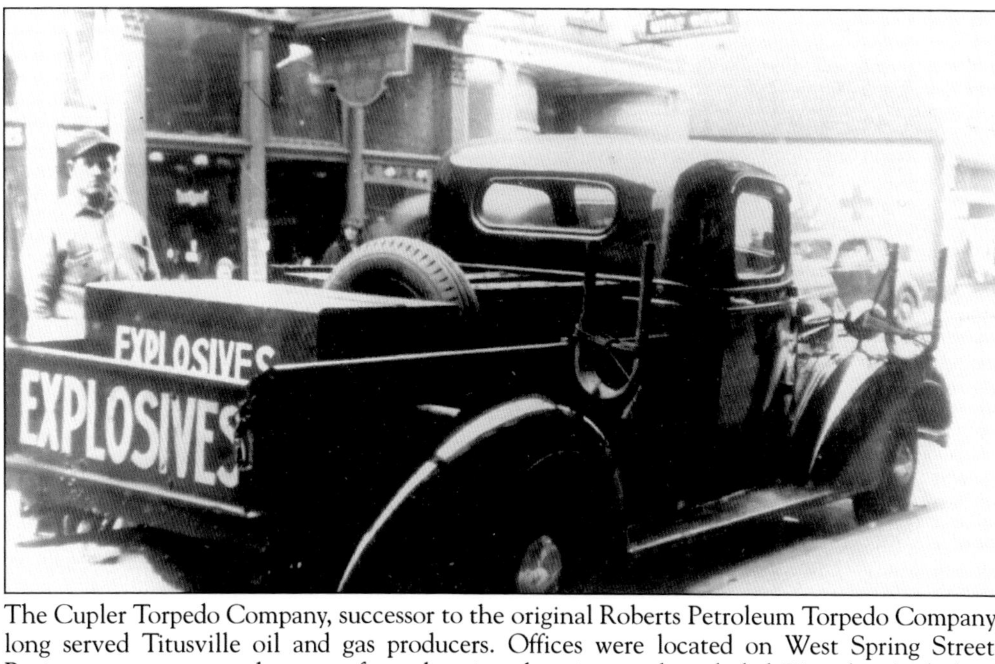

The Cupler Torpedo Company, successor to the original Roberts Petroleum Torpedo Company, long served Titusville oil and gas producers. Offices were located on West Spring Street. Businesses seen across the street from the nitroglycerine truck included Wizenberg's clothing store, the Drake café, and the Johnson clothing store. The "shooter" standing beside the truck (fortunately not carrying a shot) is unidentified in this 1930s photograph.

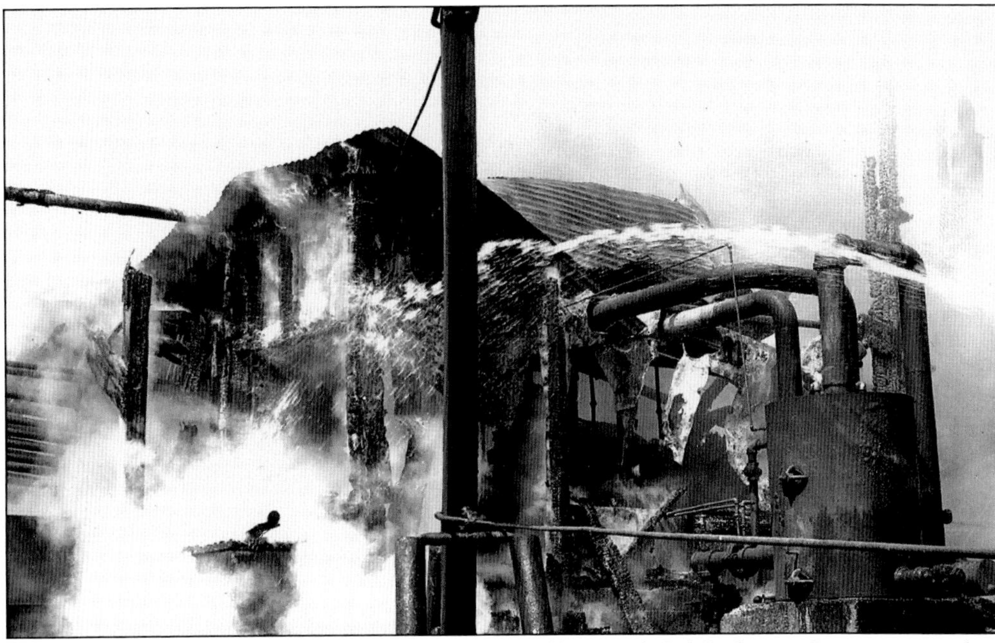

Fire has always been an oil-field hazard. The Wolf's Head Oil Refining Company gasoline plant central powerhouse was destroyed by fire in September 1958. A photograph taken during the blaze clearly shows the rod lines, gasoline-extraction coils, and compressors. Wolf's Head subsequently rebuilt the facilities on this Oil Creek Township, Crawford County, lease. (Courtesy of the Titusville Herald.)

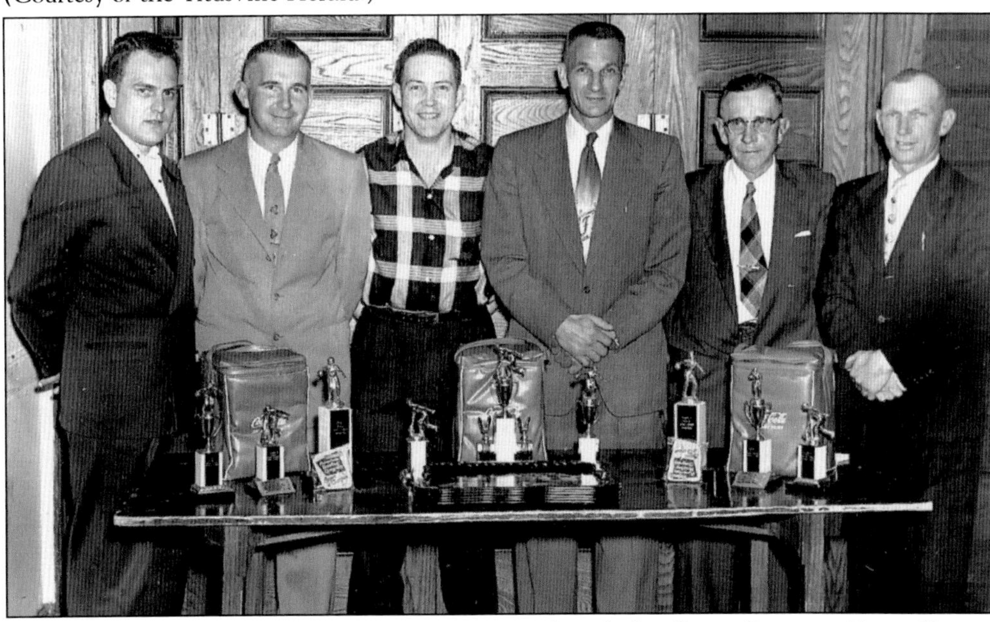

The Quaker State Oil Refining Corporation purchased the Cities Services, Titusville-area pipeline system and oil leases in 1950. The new owners sponsored a bowling team for employees. Of the six Quaker State lease workers with bowling trophies, two—William C. Beers (second from the left) and Cecil Dunham (far right)—can be identified. (Courtesy of the Titusville Herald.)

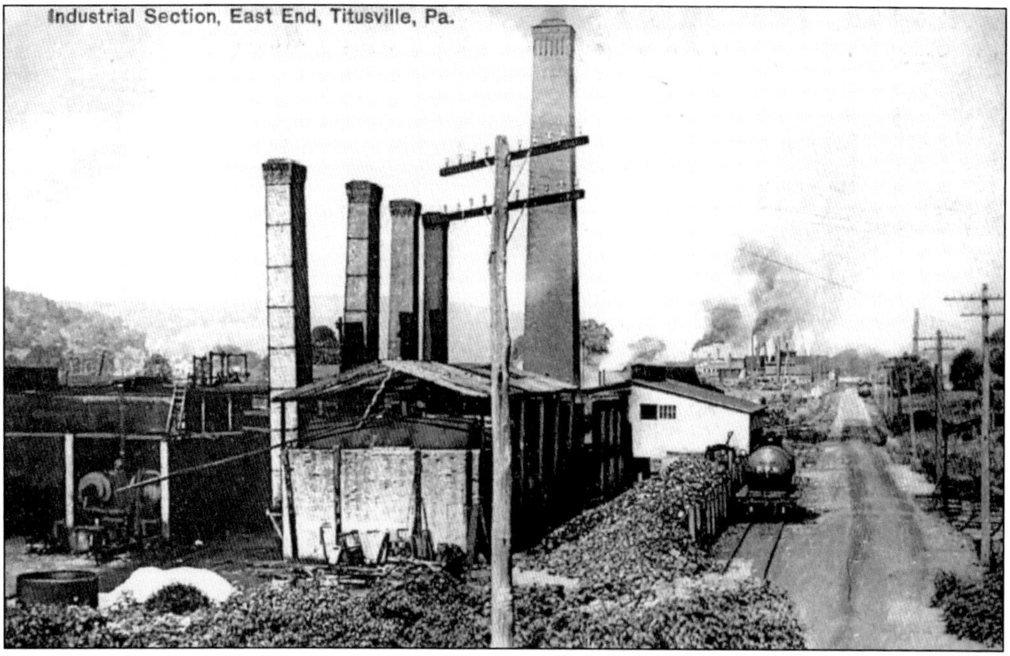

This early photograph of the Pennsylvania Paraffine Works shows much of Titusville's east end industrial section. Facilities of United States Pipe Lines, Cyclops Steel Company, American Radiator Company, Titusville Forge Company, and American Oil Works are visible. Air pollution was very much in evidence. (Courtesy of Kathryn Newson.)

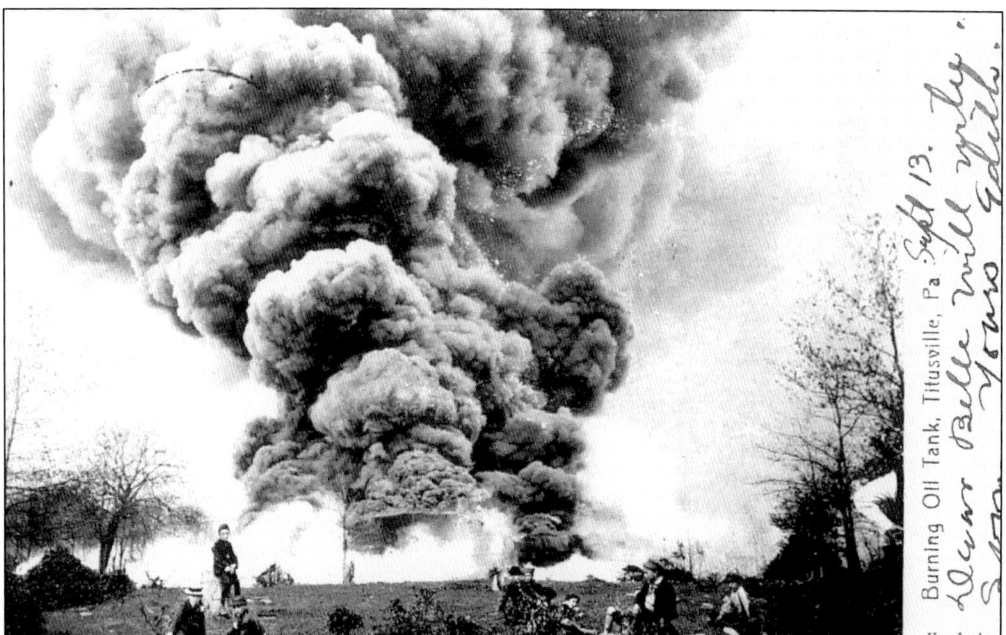

Lightning caused many oil fires. One of the most spectacular occurred near Titusville in 1894. The people in the photograph appear unexcited. (Courtesy of Kathryn Newson.)

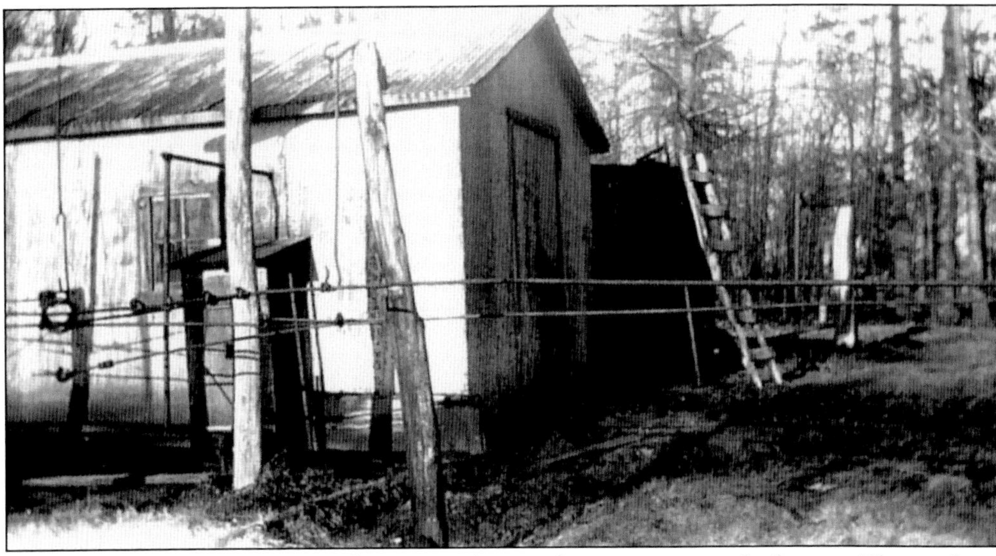

The Bayliss, Bloss and Wege Oil Company's powerhouse was typical of many. This undated photograph shows the powerhouse, which used a Titusville Iron Works gas engine to pump 20 oil wells. (Courtesy of Myrna Wescoat.)

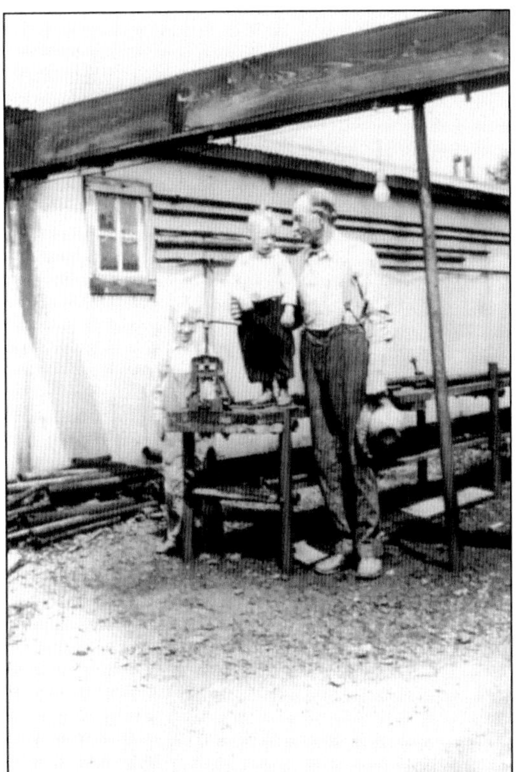

Ben Wescoat was the pumper of the Bayliss, Bloss and Wege lease. He is shown with his sons, Dillon and Melvin, in this 1930s photograph. Note the electric light. (Courtesy of Myrna Wescoat.)

Three

Steel Production and Defense Contracting

Titusville, in addition to being the birthplace of the oil industry, has also been a center of steel production and defense contracting. Local manufacturing plants have been part of "the arsenal of democracy" several times since 1900. They helped put man in space and also dashed totalitarian dreams of tyrants from Kaiser Wilhelm II to Saddam Hussein.

Prof. Charles Eames started an iron-puddling mill in Titusville in 1879. Col. John Carter loaned English-immigrant Charles Burgess, a steelmaker, funds to convert the Eames Petroleum Iron Works into the Cyclops Steel Company in 1884. Cyclops later produced the world's first high-speed tool steel and nickel-chromium stainless steel.

The Titusville Iron Works Company shareholders, desiring a local source of steam and gas-engine crankshafts, helped finance the Titusville Forge Company in 1897. This shop would later manufacture many key defense-related items for World Wars I and II.

Cyclops, the Titusville Iron Works, the Titusville Forge, and other area shops helped create the military industrial complex. They also spawned technology used in production of heavy machinery and civilian goods. Employees of these shops later struck out on their own and started businesses that have perpetuated the local industrial base.

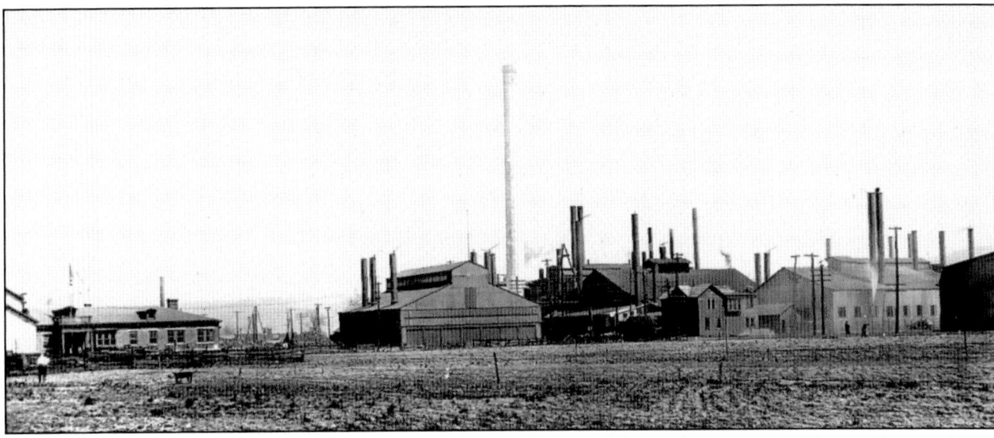

Eames Petroleum Iron Works opened an oil-fueled puddling furnace in Titusville in 1879. Englishman Charles Burgess, an immigrant steelmaker, purchased the bankrupt Eames plant in 1884. He renamed the facility Cyclops Steel Company and converted it to produce tool steel. Burgess invented the first high-speed and self-hardening tool steels. Carl Boker & Sons, New York steel dealers, purchased the Cyclops Steel Company in February 1916. New facilities, including larger crucible furnaces, a 10-inch rolling mill, and a new boiler house with a 175-foot chimney, were added to the Titusville mill. This 1920s photograph shows facilities added for World War I defense contracting. Note the man working his garden. Several oil wells can also be seen.

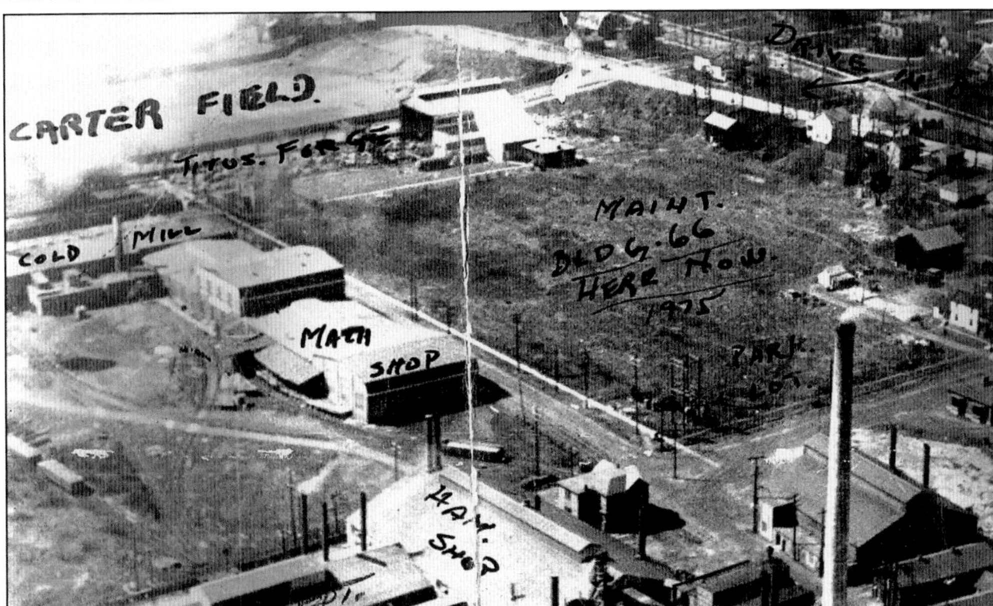

The Cyclops Steel Company declared bankruptcy in 1923–1924. The Universal Rolling Mill Company, a Bridgeville steel manufacturer, acquired the Titusville shops with financial backing from area residents in 1926. Over the next two years, the wooden plant buildings were replaced with steel and sheet-metal structures. Adjacent industrial sites of the American Radiator Company (purchased by Cyclops in 1935) and Titusville Forge Company are visible in this early-1929 aerial view. Compare this view with the other photograph of same complex. Most of these buildings remain standing and are now part of the Titusville Opportunity Park.

The Universal-Cyclops Steel Company was Titusville's largest employer for many years. This 1950s photograph shows the 10,000-pound hammer (made by the Erie Foundry Company) in use. Ingots were forged into tool steel bars or broken down into billets for the rolling mills. Notice the hammer operator and crew of six helpers. Hammer shop work was hot and extremely dangerous.

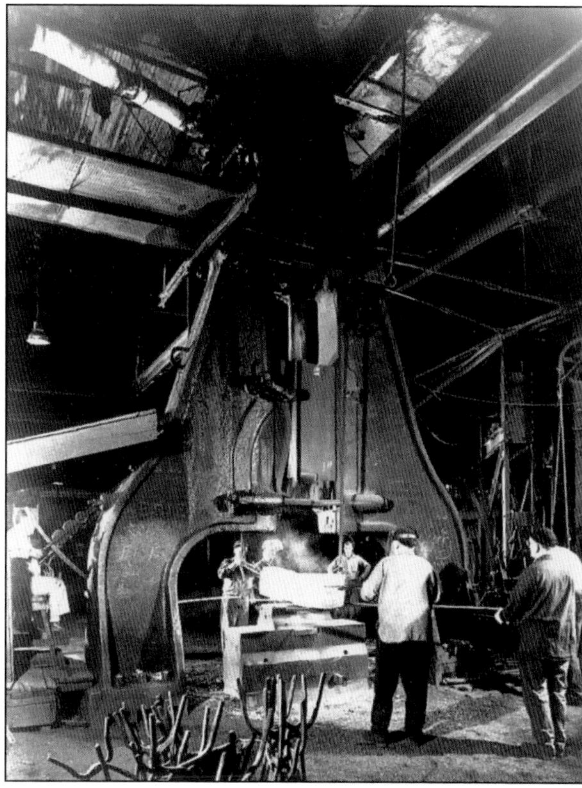

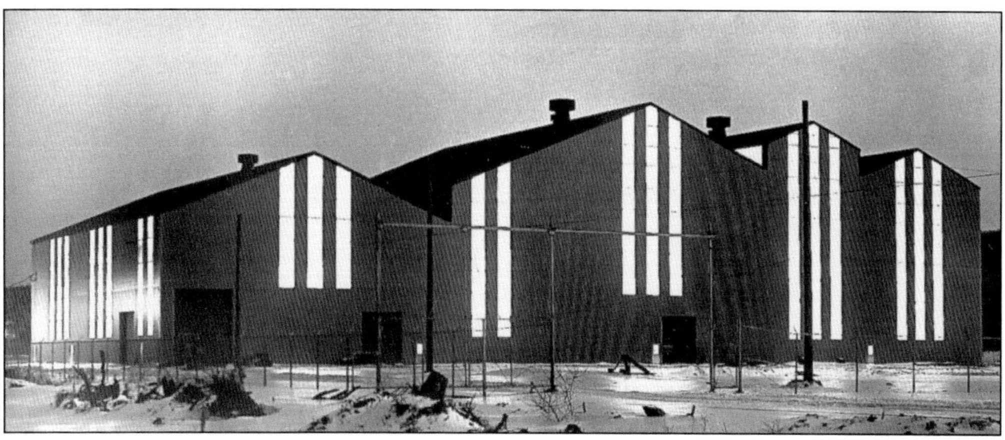

Seen is the "Cyclops cathedral" at night in December 1968. During 1968, the Universal-Cyclops Steel Company constructed a large four-bay building at East Titusville. It housed the world's largest electric, vacuum-induction melting furnace with a capacity of 60,000 pounds per heat. The facility, nicknamed the "Cyclops cathedral" by area residents, produced high-temperature alloy steel for the aerospace industry for a quarter century. ESM Group, a rebuilder, or remanufacturer, of continuous casting molds for the steel industry, now occupies this industrial landmark. The electric furnace was removed and sold in 1996–1997. (Courtesy of the Titusville Herald.)

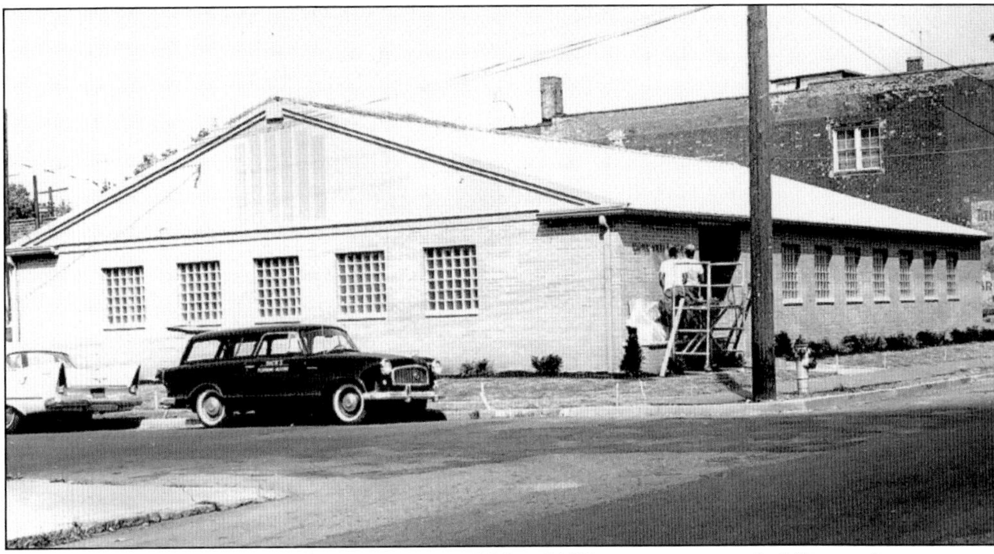

The United Steelworkers of America Local No. 3052 met at several different locations in Titusville. Union hall facilities were constructed for the steelworkers at West Spring and Monroe Streets in 1958. In this photograph, contractors can be seen placing the sign at the entrance. The station wagon belonged to a plumbing contractor. Drake Printing now owns and occupies the former Steelworkers' Union Hall. (Courtesy of the Titusville Herald.)

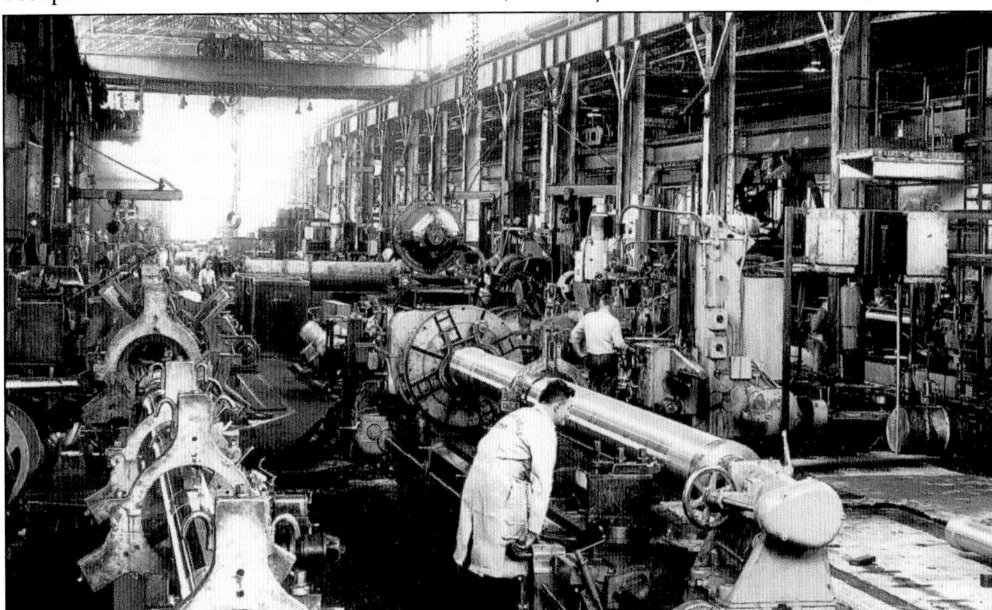

John T. Dillon Sr., with financial backing from Titusville Iron Company (Titusville Iron Works) shareholders, founded the Titusville Forge Company in 1897. Sold to Bethlehem Steel Corporation in 1913, the forge was expanded to manufacture defense-related items. Dillon, who had subsequently purchased the Titusville Iron Works, reacquired the Titusville Forge in 1919. This 1950s view of the forge's No. 1 machine shop reveals the size of the jobs performed there. Naval propeller shafting, steel mill machinery, and engine crankshafts were among the products. (Courtesy of the Drake Well Museum.)

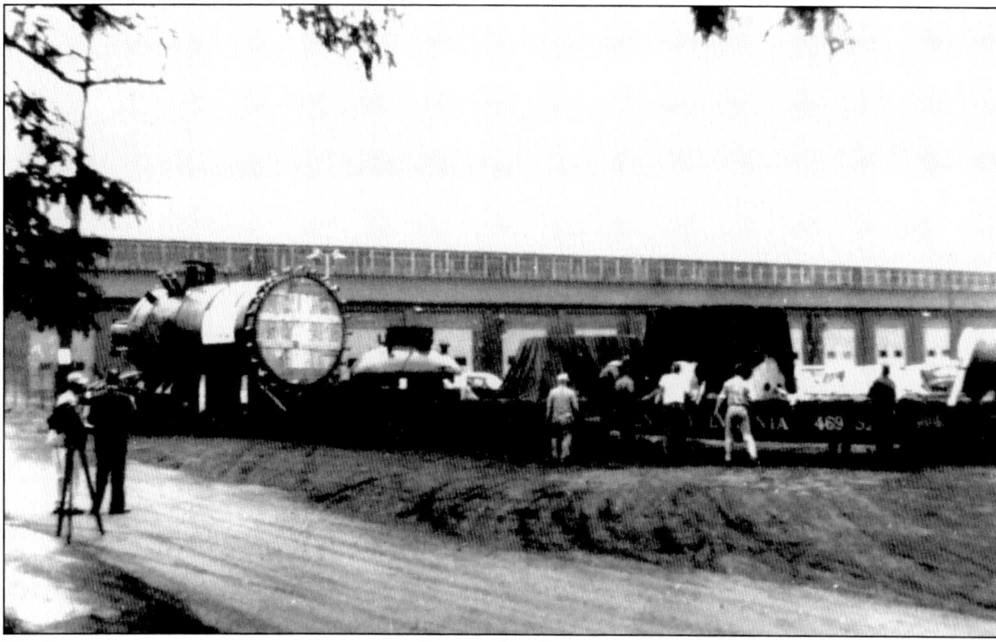

Nuclear reactor components were manufactured at the Titusville Forge in 1958. Plant employees helped secure the heavy items on railroad flatcars.

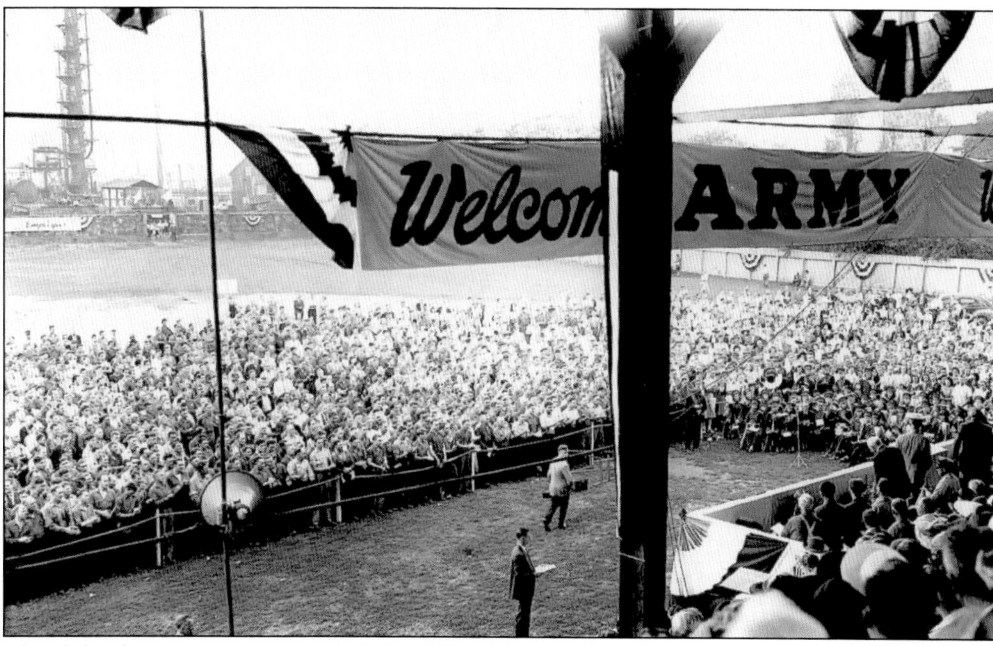

The federal government awarded the Titusville Iron Works and Titusville Forge plants of Struthers Wells Corporation the Army-Navy E Award on September 9, 1942. Items produced at the Titusville plants played key roles in the U.S. Navy's victory at Guadalcanal and the British 8th Army's victory at El Alamein. KDKA Radio, Pittsburgh, broadcast the ceremony. Employees of both plants can be seen filing onto Carter Field for the ceremony. The Titusville High School band can be seen at the center right. Distillation units of the Penn-Drake refinery are visible in background.

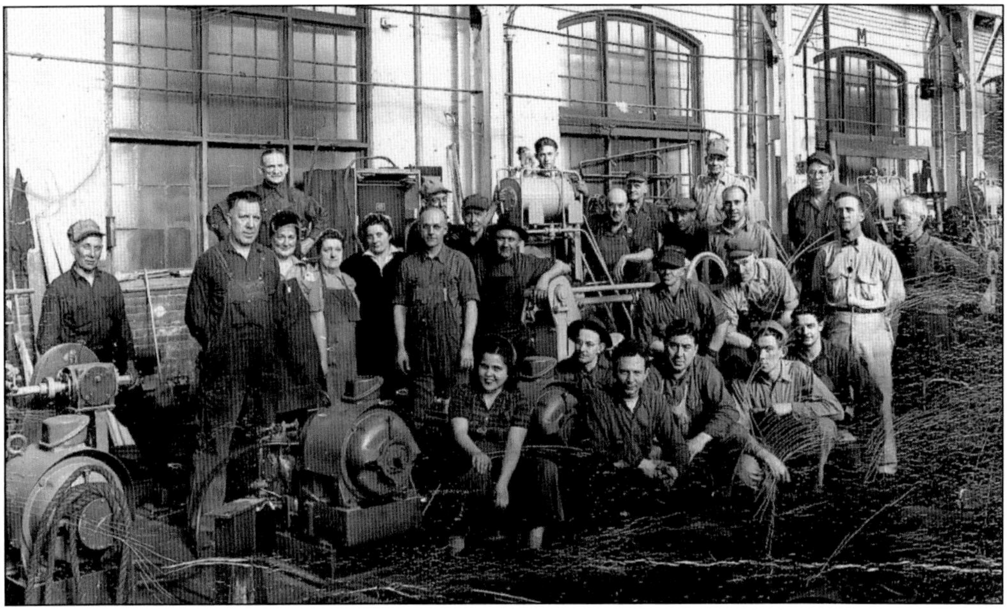

Items produced at the Titusville Iron Works during World War II included naval steering gears, capstans, and windlasses. Women were hired to replace men drafted into the armed services. A group of male and female ironworks employees can be seen with steering gears in the process of construction. (Courtesy of the Titusville Herald.)

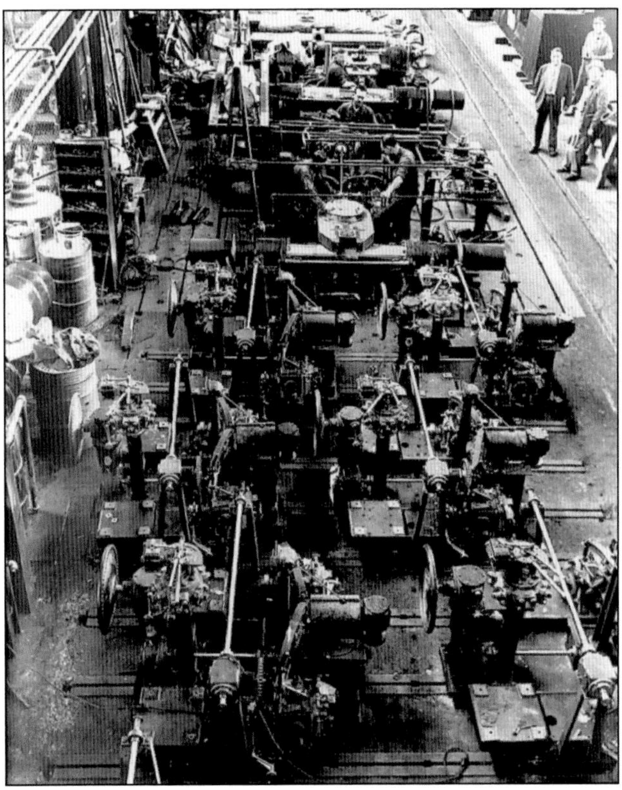

An overhead view from the crane reveals the scope of the Titusville Iron Works naval steering gear and anchor windlass manufacturing capability. During World War II, buildings originally used for producing steam and gas engines were utilized for defense contracts. (Courtesy of the Drake Well Museum.)

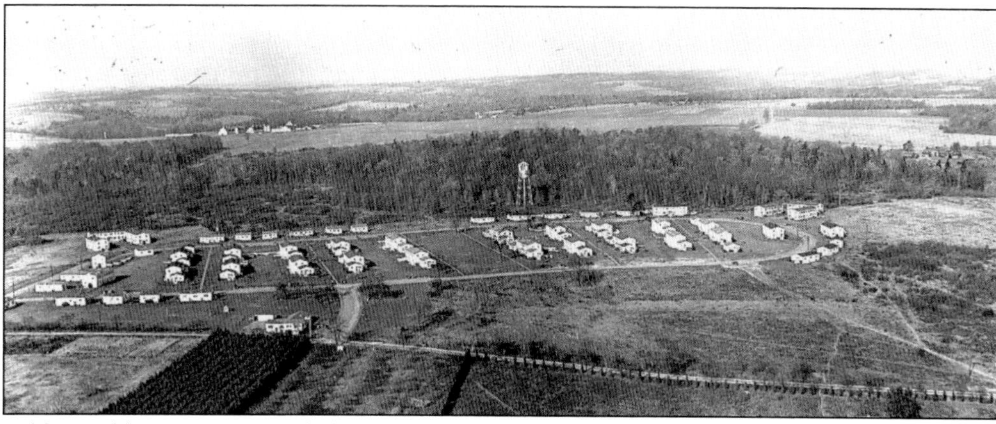

Additional housing was needed in Titusville for the defense workers. The federal government, in 1940–1941, purchased a farm at the Titusville city limits. A war workers' housing project called Sunset Heights was constructed. Many of these military barracks-style housing units remain in use today.

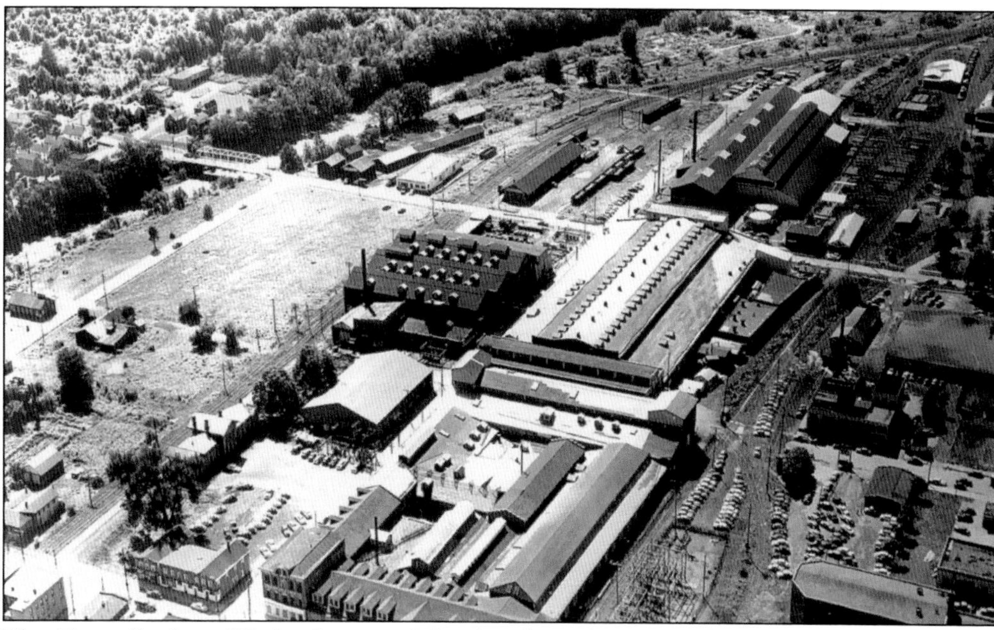

The Titusville Iron Works dominated local industrial activity for an entire century. This 1950s aerial view clearly illustrates the size of the ironworks plant. The buildings in the lower foreground housed office, storeroom, and machine shop facilities. Behind them were structures that housed maintenance, power plant, and boiler shop departments. In the upper center is a structure built during World War II to house forge shop facilities for artillery shells and naval gun barrels. It was later converted into a heavy welding, assembly, and testing facility. Structures surrounding the ironworks complex included, clockwise from the left, the Pennsylvania Railroad passenger depot, the Titusville Handle Factory, the Smedley welding shop, the United Hardware & Supply Company, the Pennsylvania Railroad freight house, the former Titusville Oil Works barrel house, the Grange League Federation feed mill, the National Supply Company's store, Robinson's wallpaper warehouse, and the Titusville Dairy Products Company. Most of the former ironworks buildings have been converted to other uses and remain today.

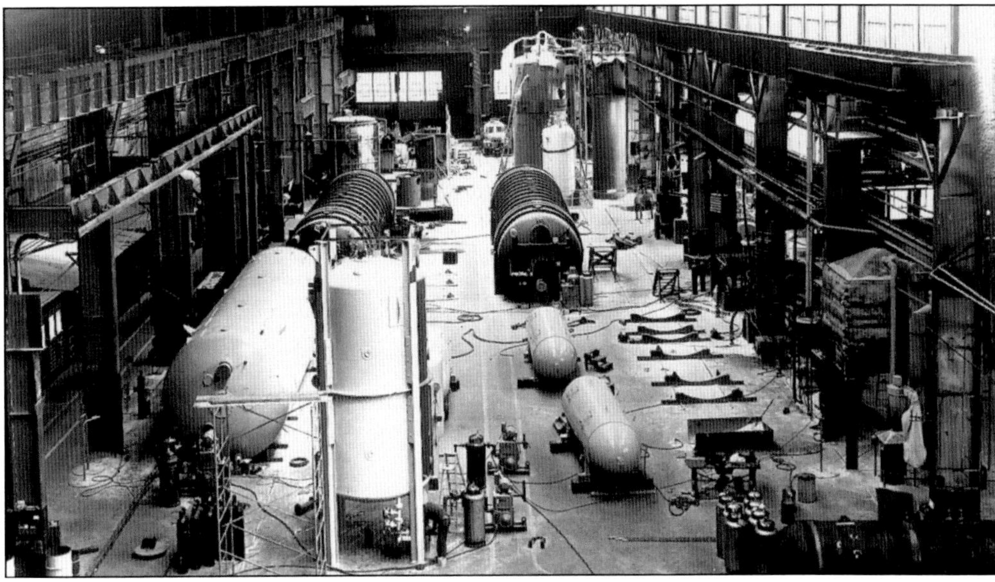

The Titusville Iron Works, Titusville Forge, and Warren plant of the Struthers Wells Company were under common ownership after 1920. Defense-related orders integrated the three factories into a single unit. Intercontinental ballistic missile (ICBM) silo production during the cold war exemplified this relationship. Outer missile silo shells were built by the ironworks, and inner liners were built by Struthers Wells in Warren in 1960. Final assembly and testing took place at the Titusville Forge's welding shop. (Courtesy of the Drake Well Museum.)

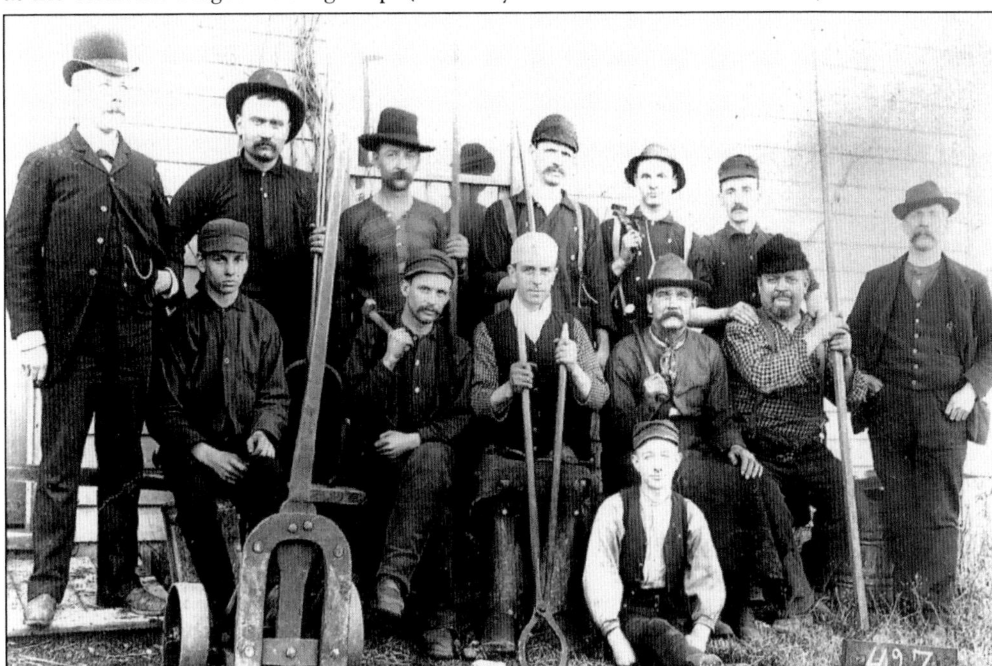

This is an early photograph of Charles Burgess (left, in a derby) and some of his Cyclops Steel Company employees. These men were said to have been superstitious, and production halted if a dog wandered into the mill. (Courtesy of the Drake Well Museum.)

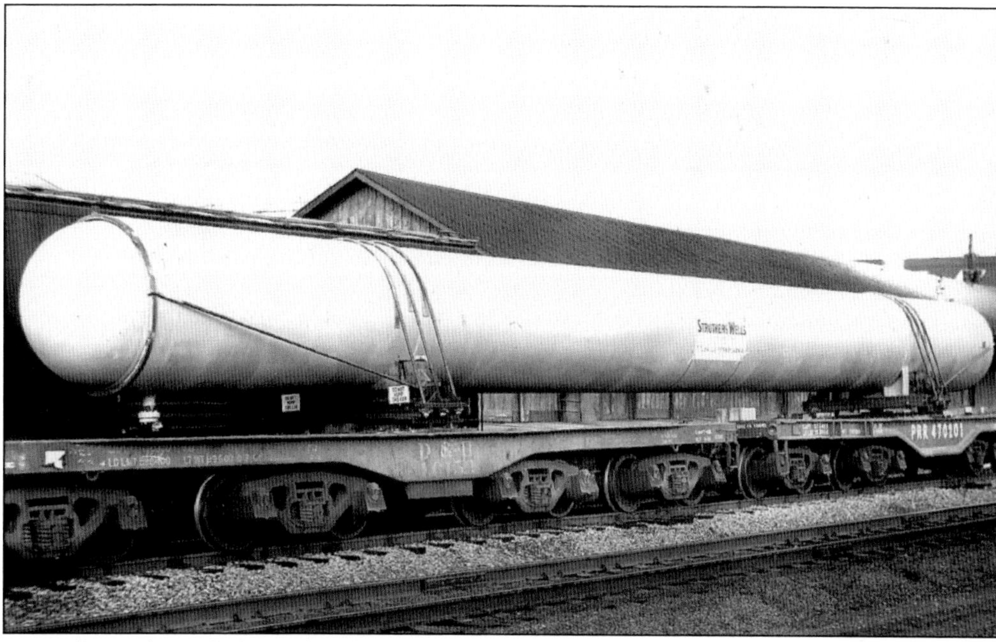

Titusville's industrial plants also played important roles in the U.S. space program. Underground rocket-fuel storage tanks were fabricated in the Titusville Iron Works boiler shop in 1964. This order was one of the last for the historic plant. (Courtesy of the Titusville Herald.)

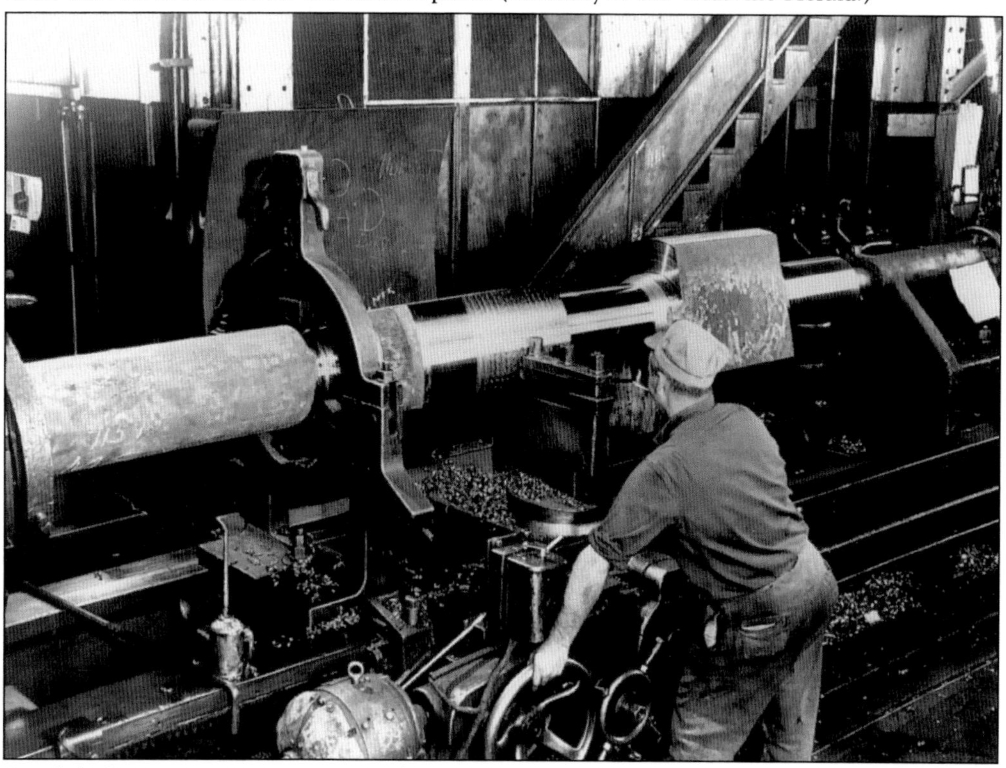

Crankshafts were a major segment of Titusville Forge's output. A crankshaft is shown being rough turned on a lathe. Crankshaft production ceased in June 1963.

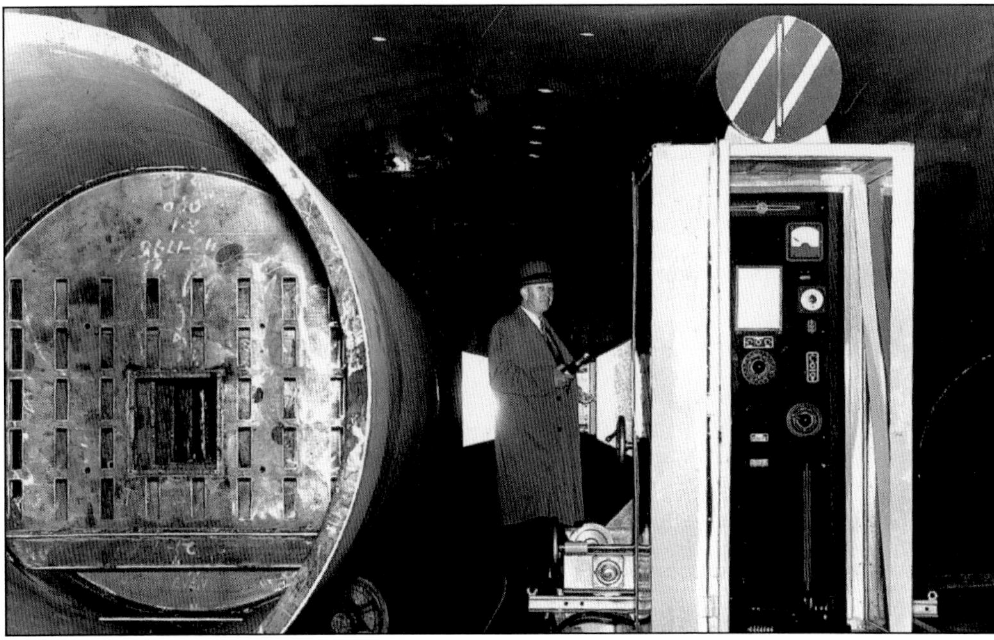

Stanford "Pete" Johnson, works manager of the Titusville Forge Division plant, inaugurated the weldment department's X-ray machine in the 1950s. The forge division's welding shop was actually interchangeable with the ironworks division's boiler shop. (Courtesy of the Drake Well Museum.)

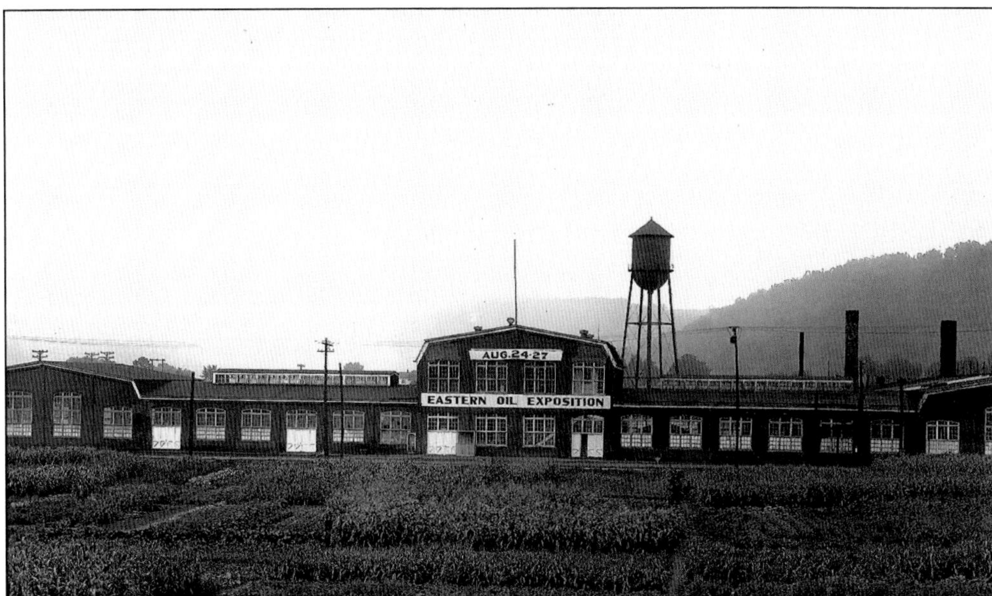

The former American Radiator Company shops were used for the Eastern Oil Exposition during the Diamond Jubilee of Oil, which took place on August 24–27, 1934. The Cyclops Steel Company purchased the vacant industrial facility one year later. Precision rolling facilities installed here made items for ship turbines and airplane engines during World War II and the Korean War. Universal Stainless and Alloy Products now operates this facility, known to many area residents as "the Cold Mill Department." (Courtesy of the Titusville Herald.)

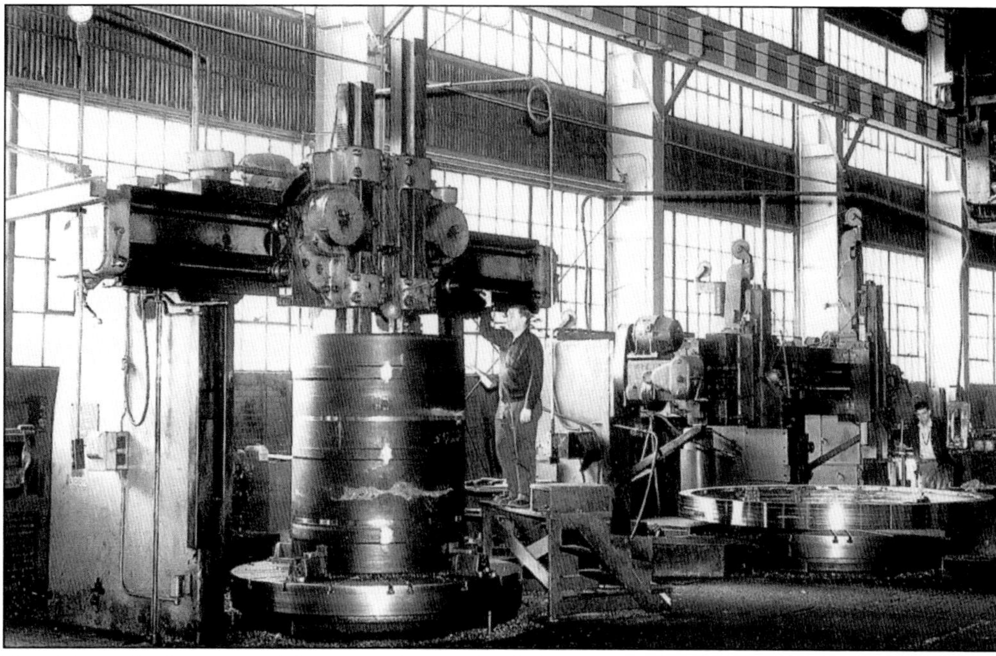

The Titusville Forge used large machines for defense-related production, such as the drill-press and boring mill shown here. Both machinists in this 1958 photograph are unidentified. (Courtesy of the Drake Well Museum.)

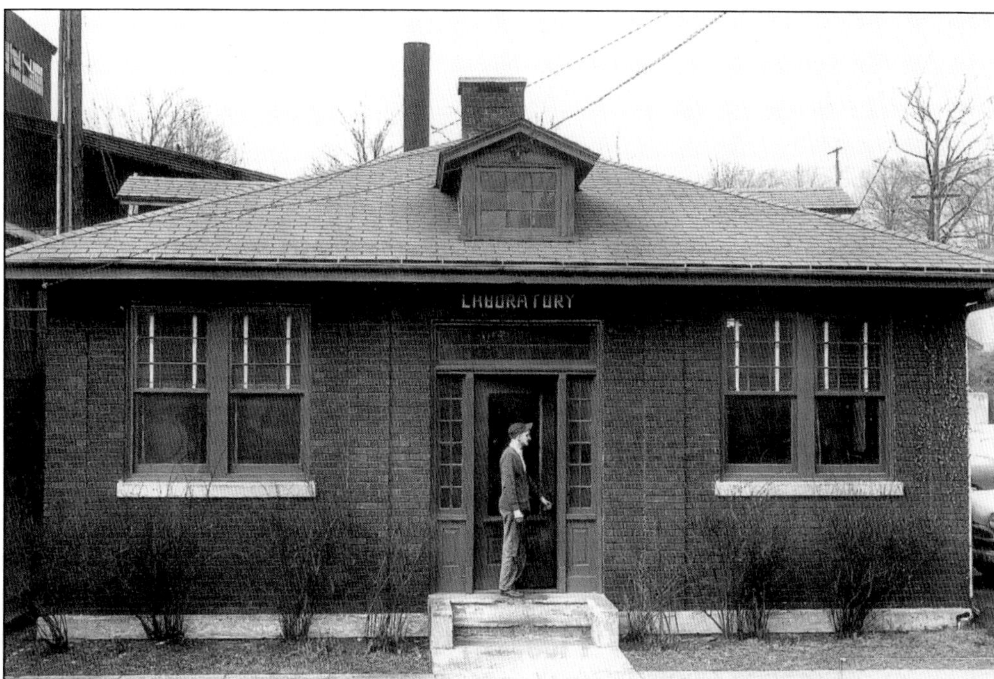

Robert Hotaling enters the laboratory building of the Titusville Forge plant in April 1958. (Courtesy of the Drake Well Museum.)

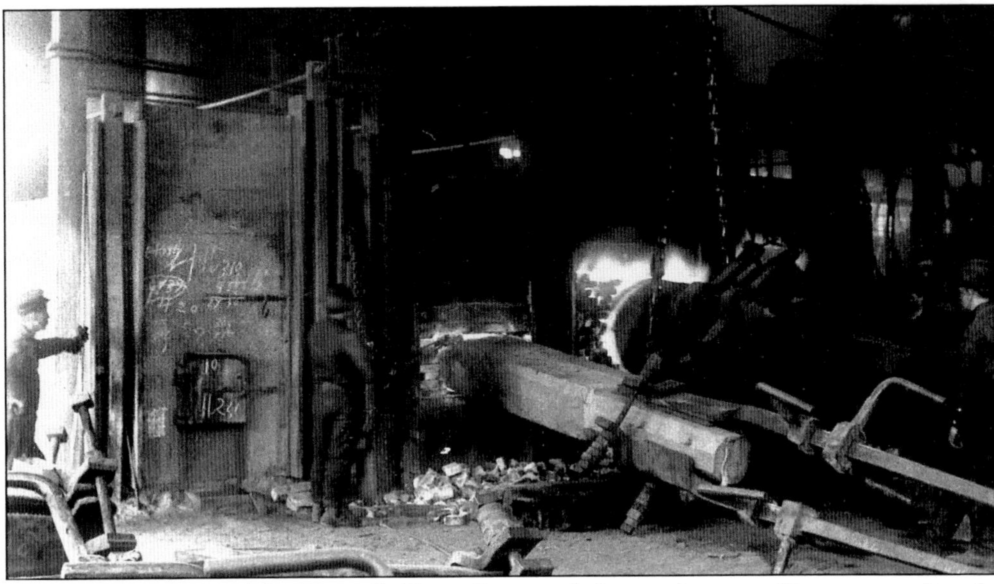

This is an early view of the Titusville Forge Company's forging furnaces. The men tending the furnace are nearly dwarfed by the massive ingot.

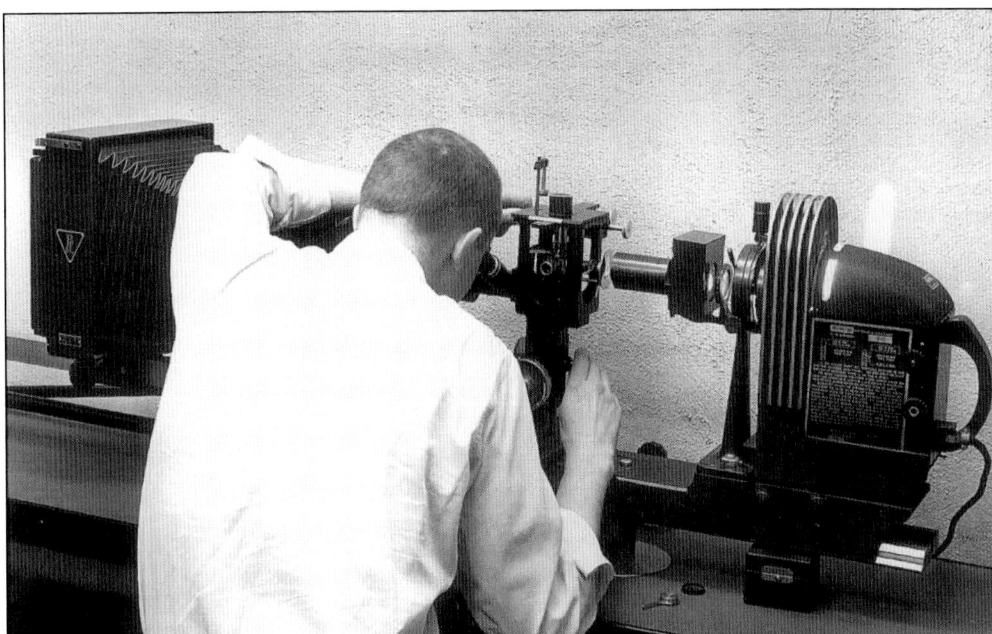

High-powered microscopes were used in the forge's testing and metallurgical laboratory. The technician seen in this April 1, 1958, photograph is unidentified. (Courtesy of the Drake Well Museum.)

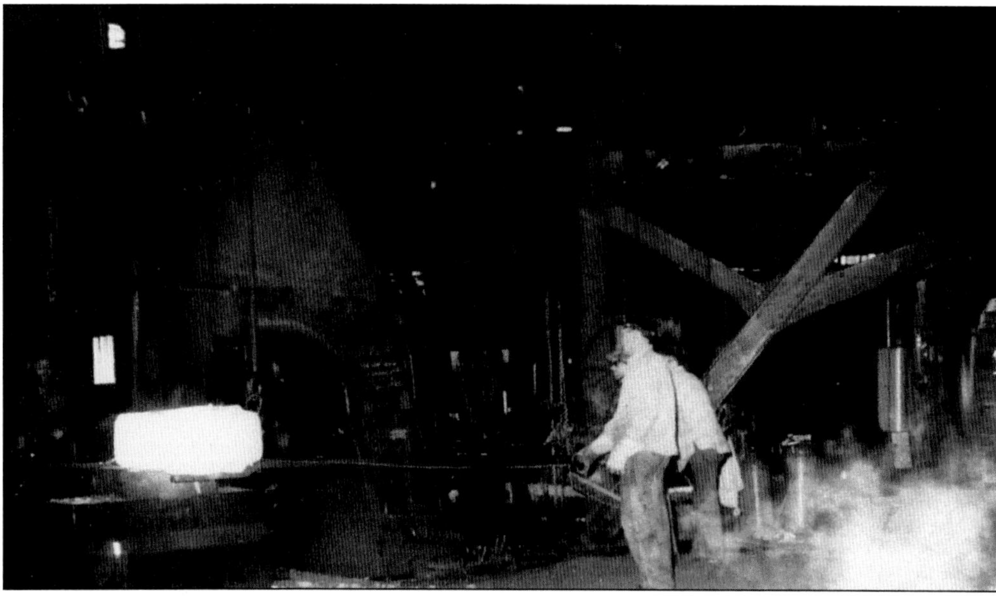

One of the smaller Universal-Cyclops Steel hammers is seen in operation here. Noise from the steam-powered hammers could be heard five miles away.

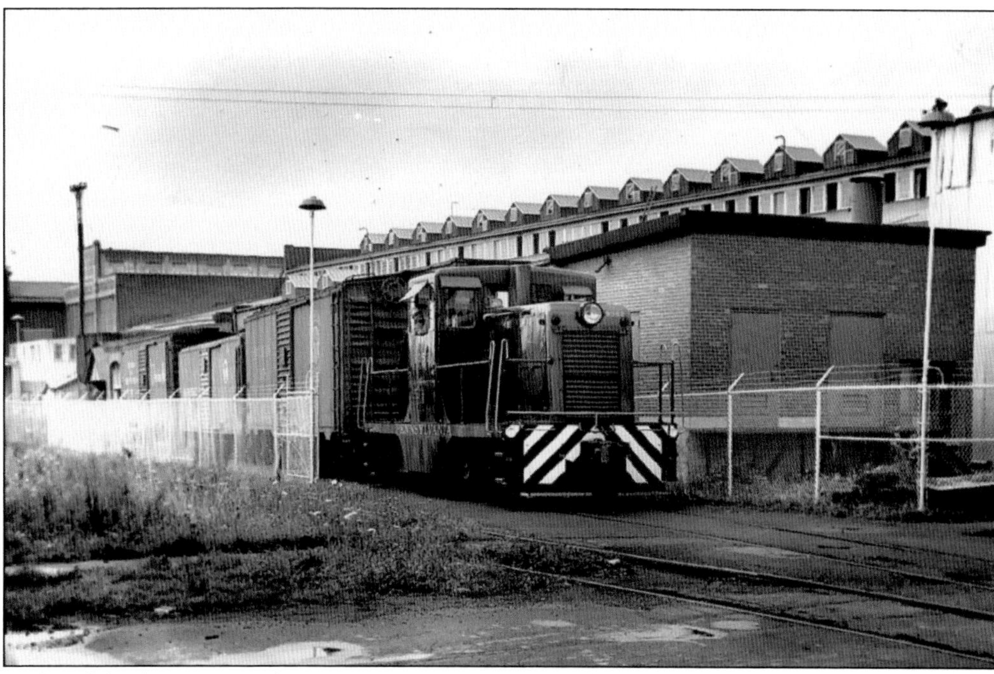

Railroad facilities were of paramount importance for shipment of defense-related items from Titusville factories. For moving cars between the ironworks and forge plants, the Pennsylvania Railroad used this diesel-powered switch engine. The Titusville Iron Works boiler shop buildings can be seen in this photograph, taken along South Perry Street. (Courtesy of the Titusville Herald.)

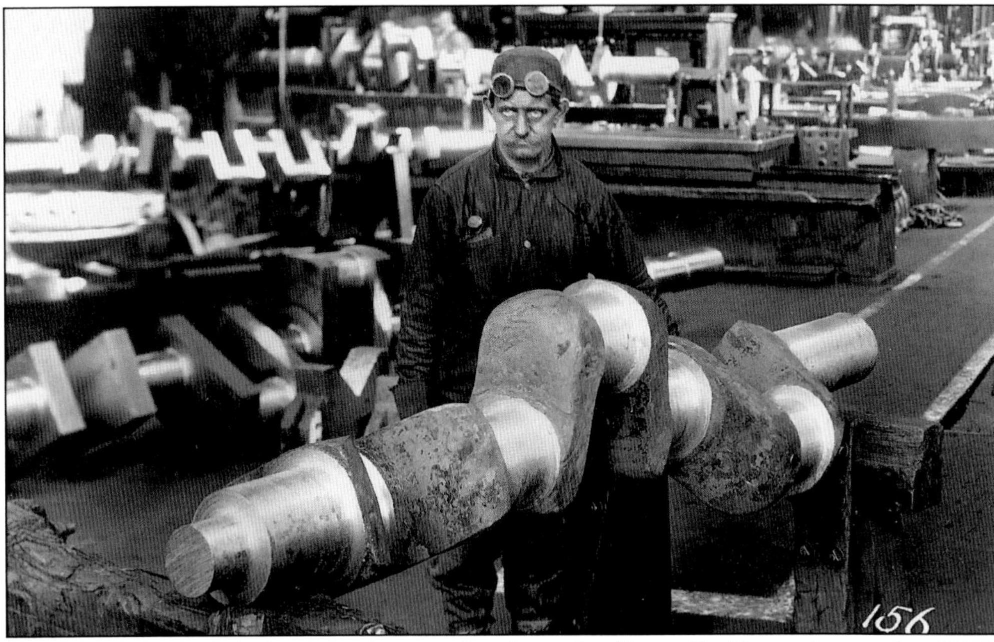

Diesel engine crankshafts were first produced at the Titusville Forge during the 1920s. An unidentified forge employee is shown with several finished cranks. (Courtesy of the Drake Well Museum.)

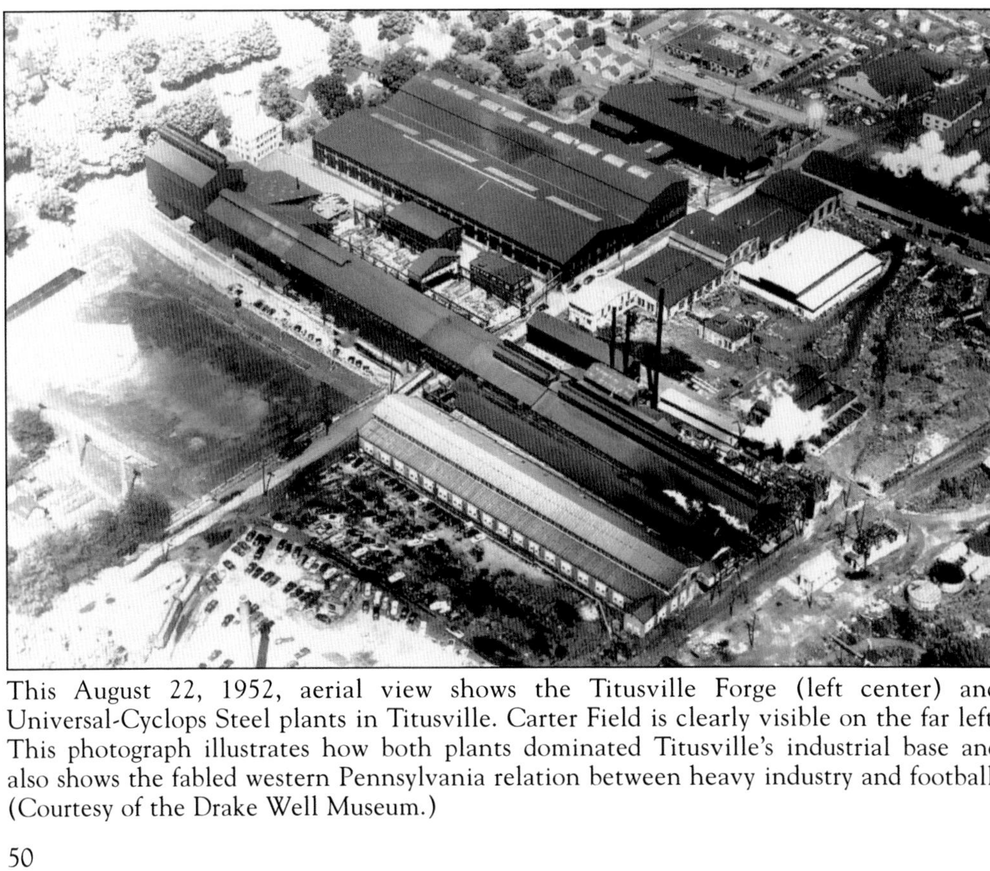

This August 22, 1952, aerial view shows the Titusville Forge (left center) and Universal-Cyclops Steel plants in Titusville. Carter Field is clearly visible on the far left. This photograph illustrates how both plants dominated Titusville's industrial base and also shows the fabled western Pennsylvania relation between heavy industry and football. (Courtesy of the Drake Well Museum.)

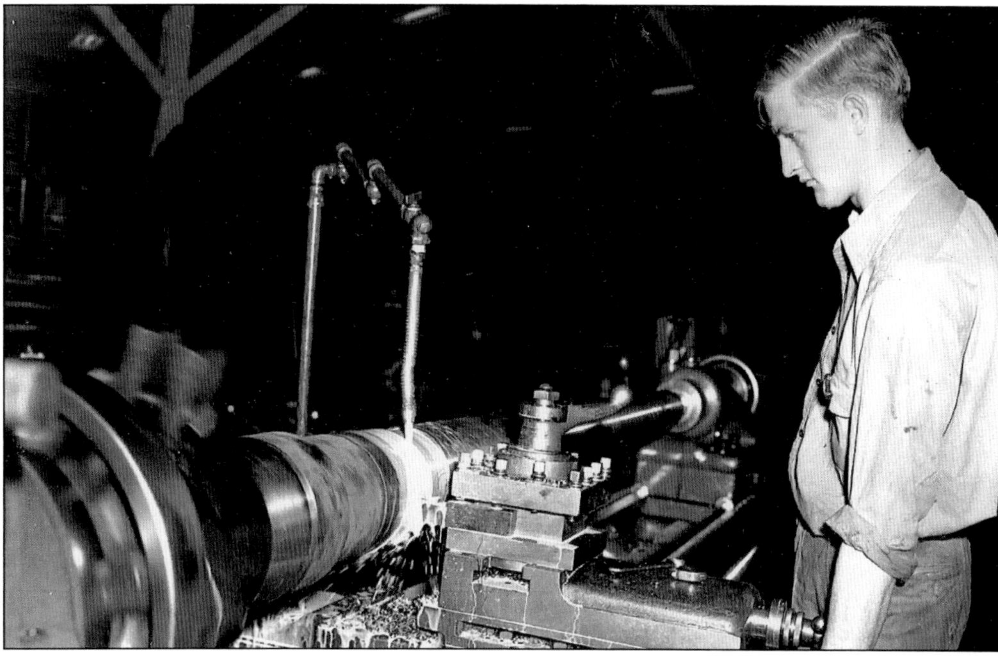

An unidentified Titusville Forge employee finishes turning a shaft on one of the facility's numerous lathes. (Courtesy of the Drake Well Museum.)

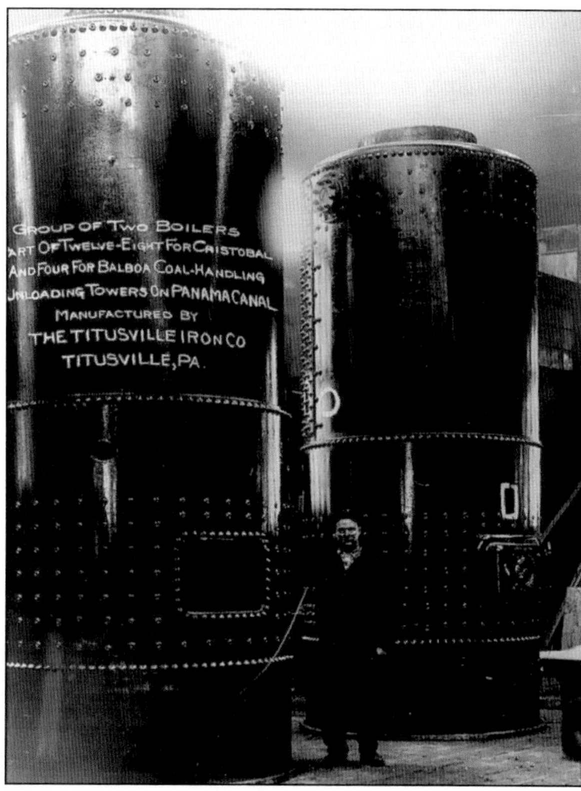

Titusville's industrial plants manufactured items for military bases and other American installations in the Panama Canal zone. This *c.* 1912 photograph, taken in the Titusville Iron Company (Titusville Iron Works Company) boiler shop, shows two of the boilers, for coaling stations at Cristobal and Balboa, Panama. An unidentified workman stands beside the boilers.

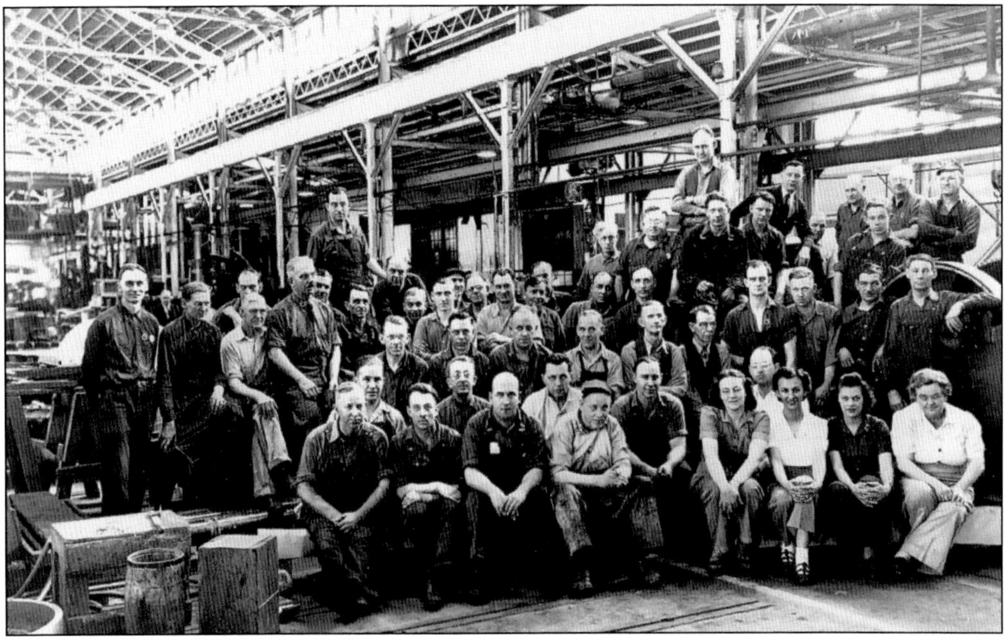

Floor, clerical, shipping, and bench workers at the Titusville Iron Works machine shop and assembly floor posed for this 1944 photograph. Alfred Hunt, a longtime ironworks employee who also owned oil wells near the Drake Well site, is standing on the far left in the third row. (Courtesy of the Drake Well Museum.)

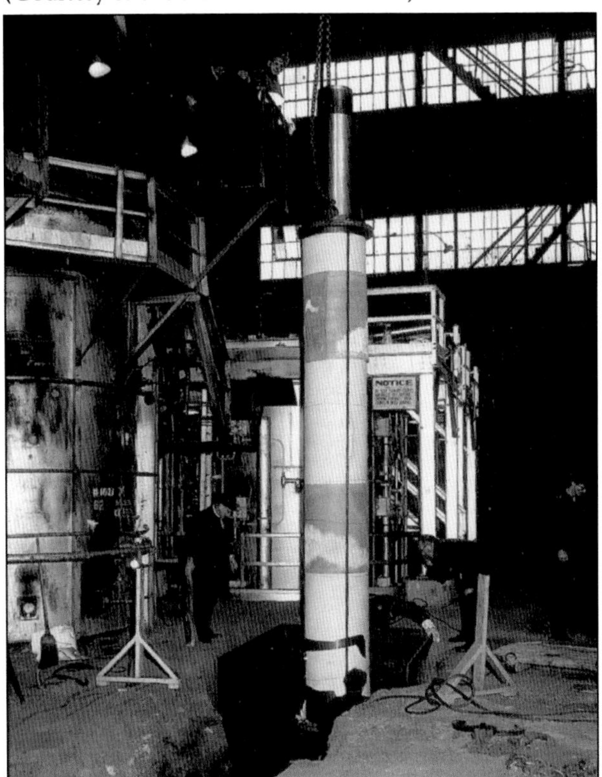

The Struthers Wells Corporation closed the Titusville Forge and much of the Titusville Iron Works from April to June in 1963. The forge's annealing, heat treat, and machine shops reopened as Titusville Crankshaft and Machine Company in 1964. The National Forge Company subsequently purchased the plant and ran it until July 1970. This 1967 photograph shows a naval propeller shaft being lowered into a soaking pit chamber. (Courtesy of the Drake Well Museum.)

Four

General Industry and Business

Titusville has long been a Pennsylvania industrial and commercial town with connections to the rest of the state (and nearby New York and Ohio). Industrial and business occupations traditionally associated with Erie, Pittsburgh, Philadelphia, Scranton, Johnstown, and other Pennsylvania cities have also existed in Oil Creek Valley.

Trends leading toward a diversified economy started in the 1880s and 1890s, when wealthy oil barons, lumbermen, and merchants provided capital for starting new industrial plants. Some of these firms had national recognition.

Products ranging from heating boilers and radiators to switchblades and Hula-Hoops have been manufactured in Titusville. Textile (ribbon) mills, harness shops, breweries, bakeries, soap factories, carriage and wagon shops, a canoe and boat factory, electronics plants, and a patent-medicine firm have provided jobs at one time or another.

Service industries have long been significant in the region. These have included wholesale groceries, a wholesale hardware and industrial supply warehouse, banking and financial institutions, and a once renowned mail-order wallpaper retailer. Products and services from these firms benefited Titusville's retail stores.

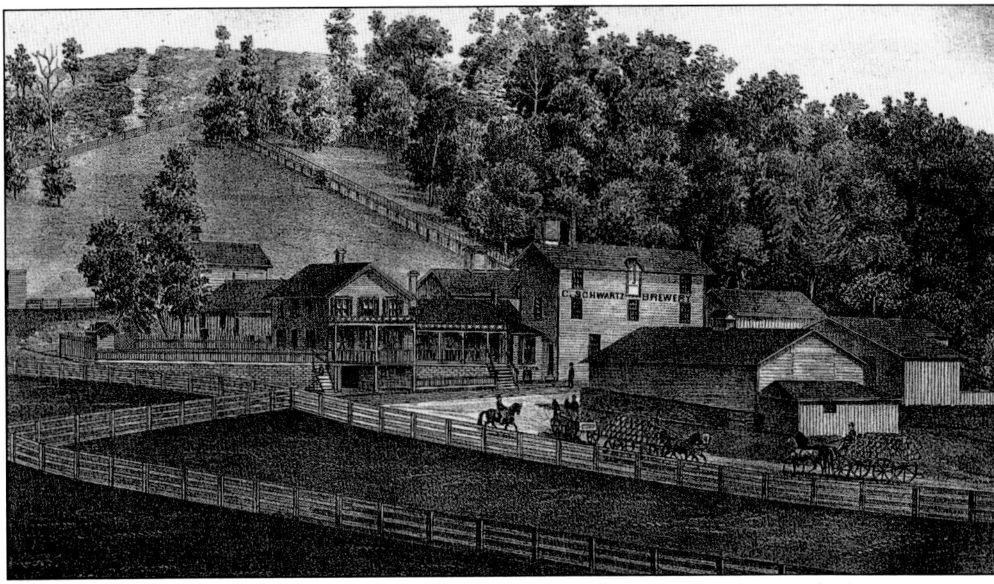

Charles Schwartz operated the Titusville Spring Hill Brewery in the west end of town in 1876. Schwartz's operation manufactured its own malt, unusual for a small brewery. Fire destroyed the operation in 1905. (From *Atlas of Crawford County*, 1876.)

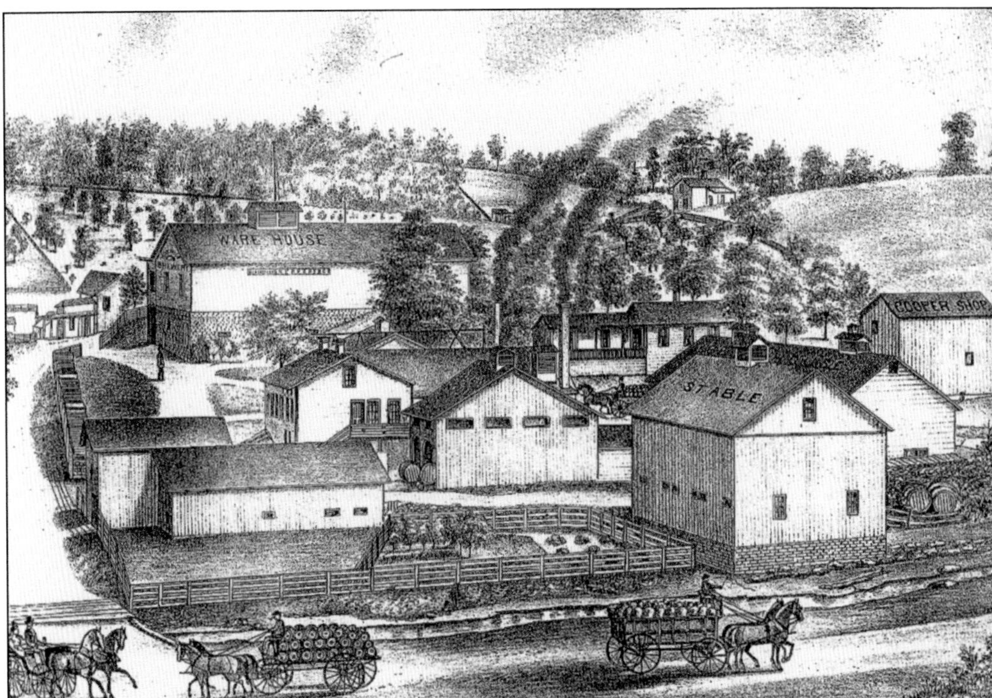

In 1876, Joseph Hoenig, Peter Theobald, and John Theobald operated the Titusville City Brewery, located at South Franklin and South Streets. This family-owned brewery had an ice pond and also shipped beer in a refrigerated railroad car. Charles Roessner later bought the City Brewery from the John Theobald family. Prohibition brought about its demise. (From *Atlas of Crawford County*, 1876.)

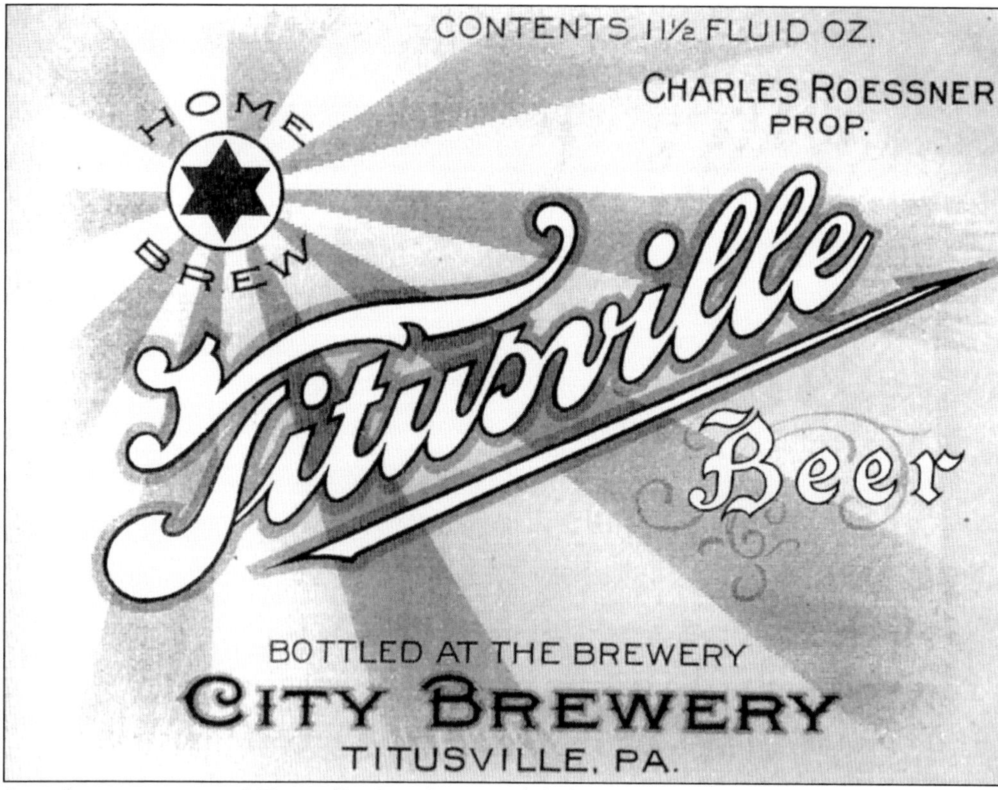

Seen here is an actual Titusville City Brewery label. Beer brewing has recently resumed in Titusville with the establishment of a microbrew pub. (Courtesy of Kathryn Newson.)

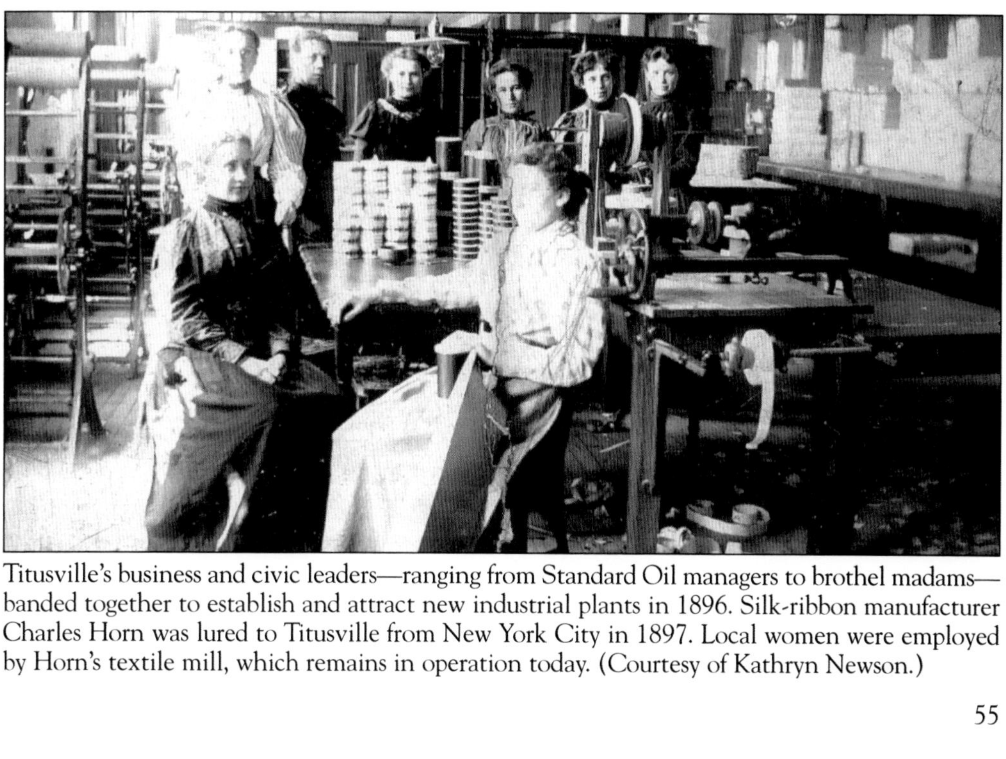
Titusville's business and civic leaders—ranging from Standard Oil managers to brothel madams—banded together to establish and attract new industrial plants in 1896. Silk-ribbon manufacturer Charles Horn was lured to Titusville from New York City in 1897. Local women were employed by Horn's textile mill, which remains in operation today. (Courtesy of Kathryn Newson.)

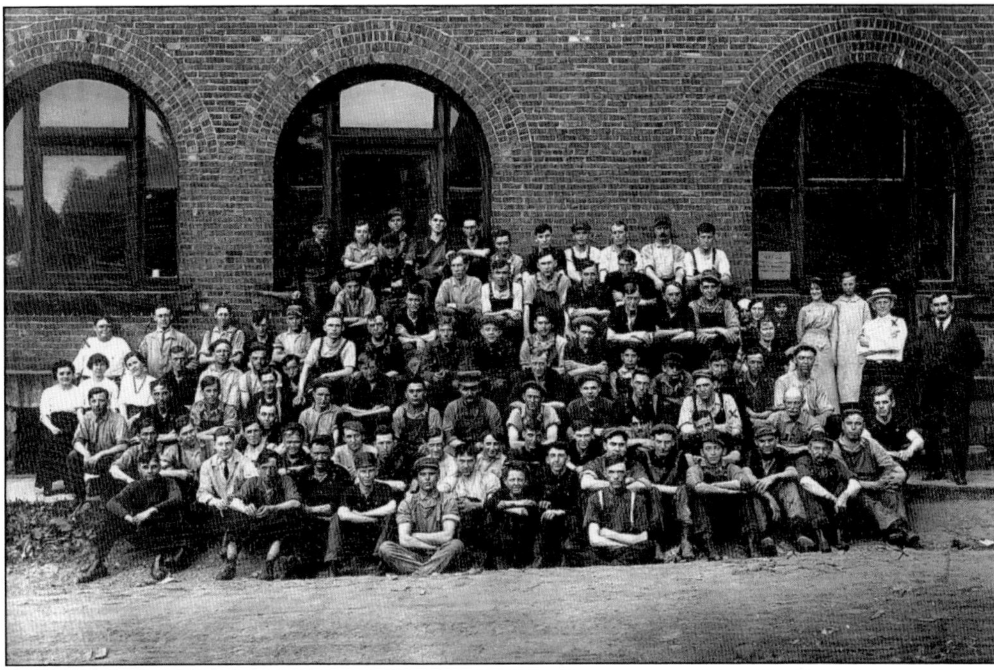

Seen are employees of the Schatt & Morgan Cutlery Company on May 29, 1914. Many of these workers were German, Swedish, and English immigrants. Others were from the Seneca Iroquois reservation at Cattaraugus, New York. An abundance of natural gas for operating furnaces and machinery was essential to the plant's operation. Knives manufactured in Titusville have been sold and used throughout America. (Courtesy of the Titusville Herald.)

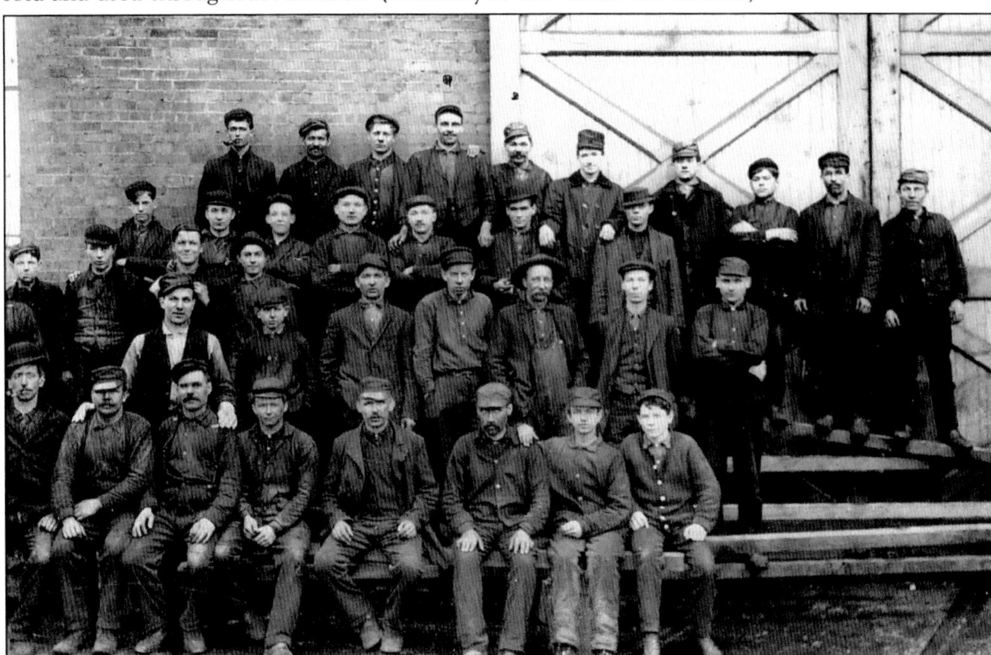

Titusville Iron Works boiler shop workers are seen in this c. 1907 view. Many of these men were Polish immigrants.

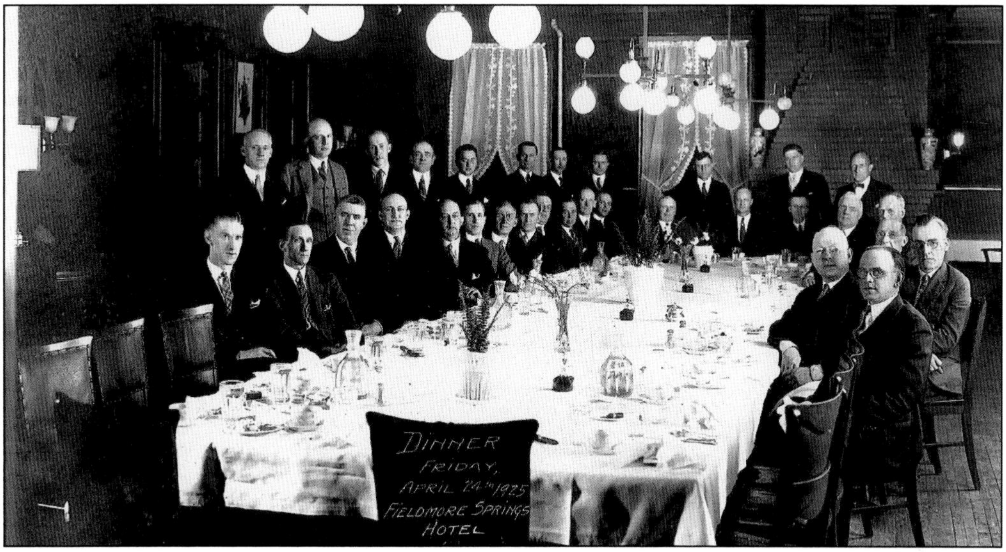

John T. Dillon Sr. (1860–1934), former superintendent of the Erie Forge Company, founded the Titusville Forge Company with backing from Titusville Iron Company (Titusville Iron Works Company) shareholders. Dillon became principal owner of the Titusville Iron Works Company in 1919 and the Struthers Wells Company in 1920. Titusville Iron Works officers, management, and supervisors gave a dinner for Dillon at the Fieldmore Springs Hotel on Friday, April 24, 1925. John T. Dillon Jr. (1884–1958), who succeeded his father as head of the three plants, is on the far right. (Courtesy of the Titusville Herald.)

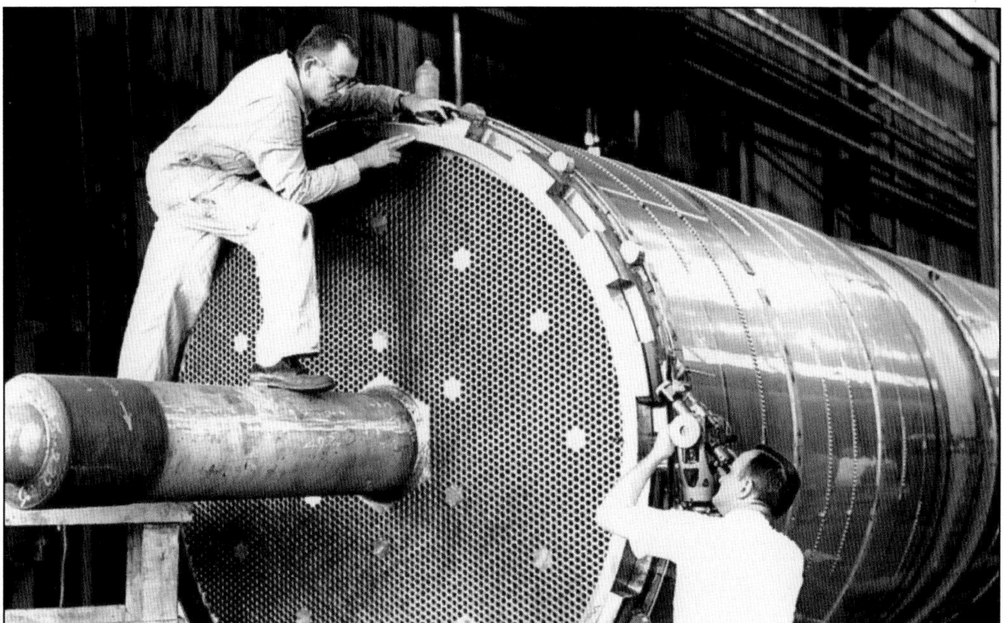

Inspectors are seen in the Perry Forge welding, assembly, and test facility in the 1950s. Seams of large welded vessels had to be examined to detect structural defects. Both men are unidentified.

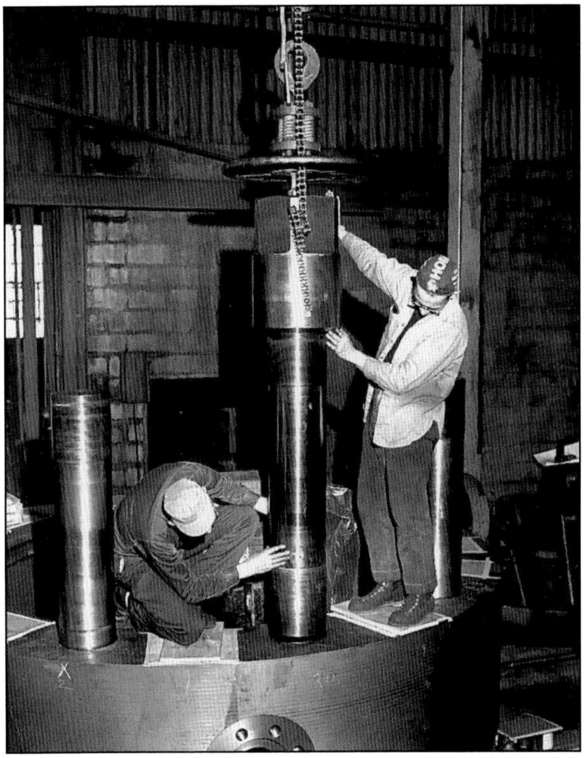

Fitters are at work in the Titusville Iron Works-Struthers Wells Corporation Perry Forge welding shop. A pit used for welding and testing large vessels was installed in this facility, which expanded the ironworks boiler shop, in 1947–1948. The men in the photograph are standing atop a large weldment placed in this pit. Charter Plastics, present owners of the former Perry Forge department, recently filled in this section of the building.

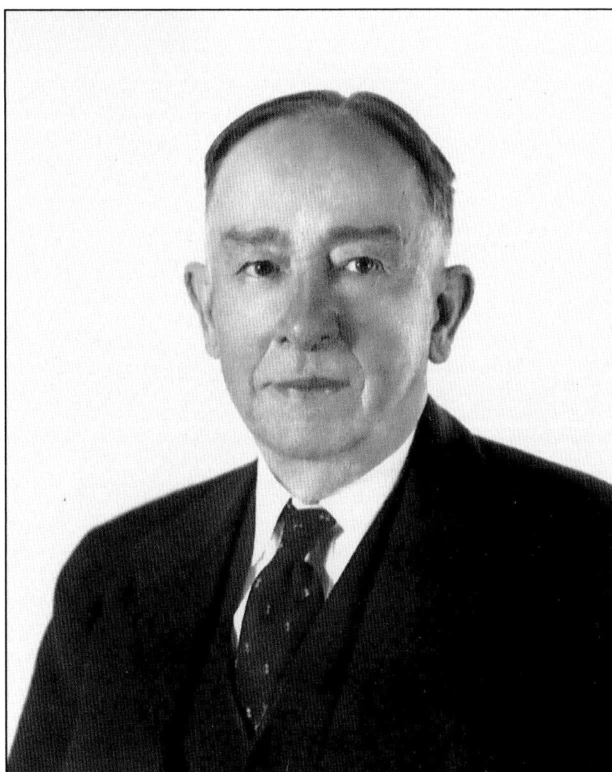

Samuel S. Bryan (1862–1947) owned several wholesale and retail businesses in Titusville, Oil City, and Erie, including S. S. Bryan Hardware, United Hardware & Supply Company, Seep Hardware, and Palace Hardware Company. He also owned oil and gas properties in five states and was active in the Titusville Chamber of Commerce. (Courtesy of the Titusville Herald.)

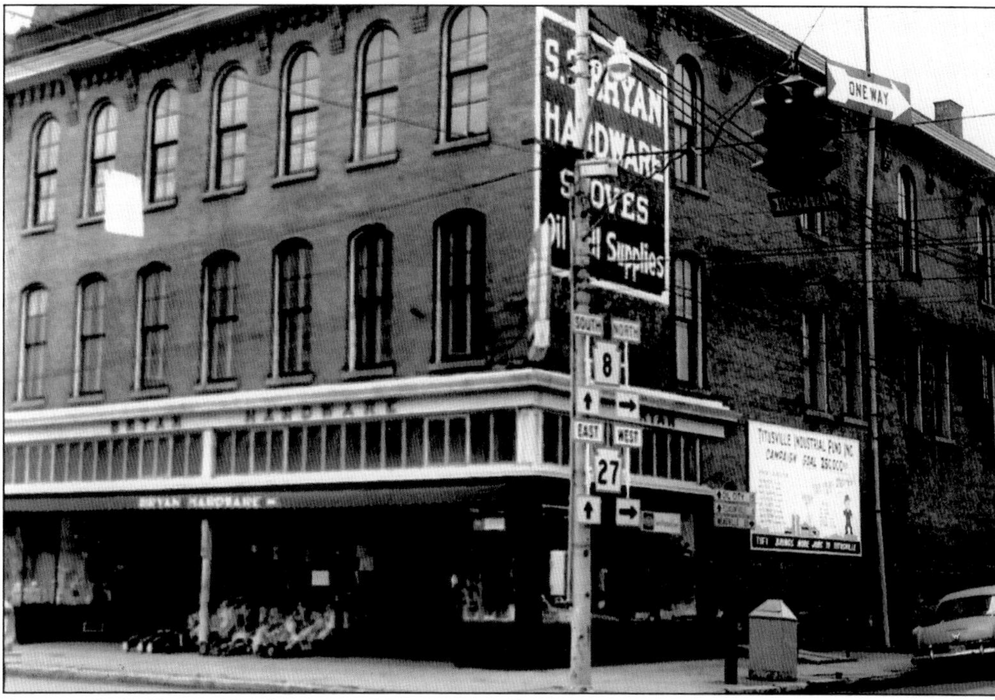

Seen is S. S. Bryan Hardware, on West Central Avenue and Franklin Streets, in 1965. This business has had numerous owners over the years. (Courtesy of the Titusville Herald.)

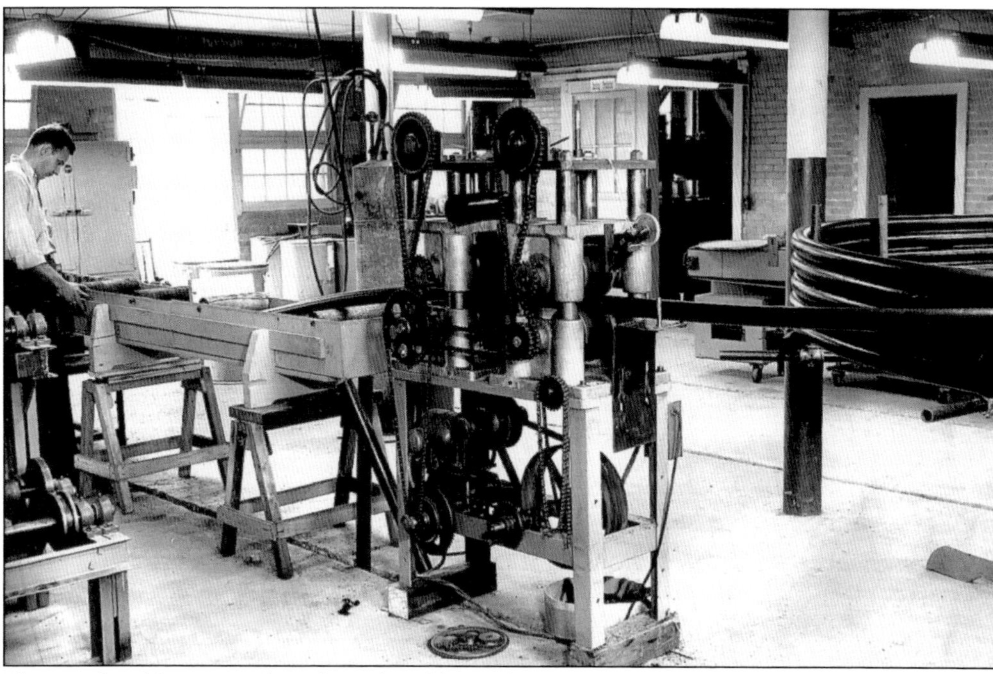

Plastic-related businesses have brought additional recognition to Titusville. Noel Poux moved his Meadville plastic-extrusion firm, Skyline Industries, to the Titusville area in 1947. Skyline set up shop in the former Oakwood Farm dairy barn. Charles Poux, Noel's cousin, is shown operating the plant's first extruder for production of plastic pipe. (Courtesy of Charter Plastics.)

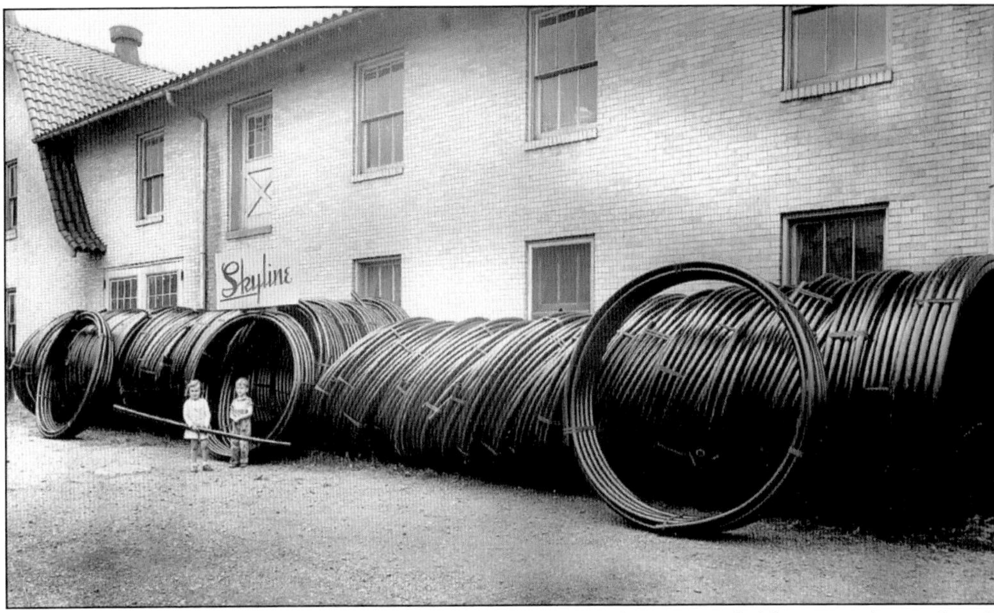

Titusville's plastic plants have perpetuated themselves. These two children are shown beside pipe coils at Skyline Industries *c.* 1953. The little girl holding the pipe section is Charles Poux's daughter, Charlene. Charles Poux and several partners started Oil Creek Plastics in 1972. Charlene Poux Ruot worked at both Skyline Industries and Oil Creek Plastics. She is now part owner of Charter Plastics. (Courtesy of Charter Plastics.)

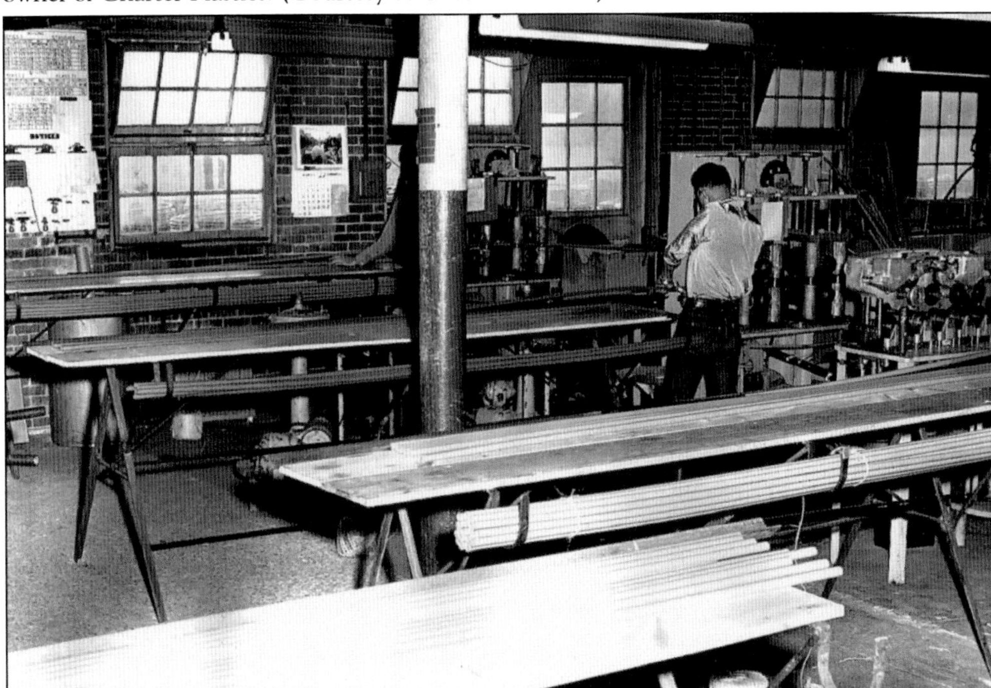

Skyline Industries achieved notoriety for manufacturing 60 percent of the original Hula-Hoops. Skyline supplied plastic tubing to Wham-O Industries in 1958–1959. Two employees are shown extruding and bundling straight lengths of tubing. (Courtesy of the Titusville Herald.)

Cynthia Yingling of Titusville is shown with her Hula-Hoop in action in September 1958. This hoop was probably made from tubing produced by Skyline Industries. (Courtesy of the Titusville Herald.)

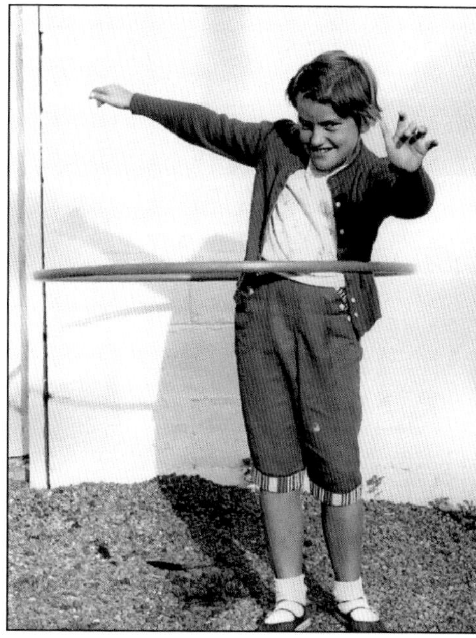

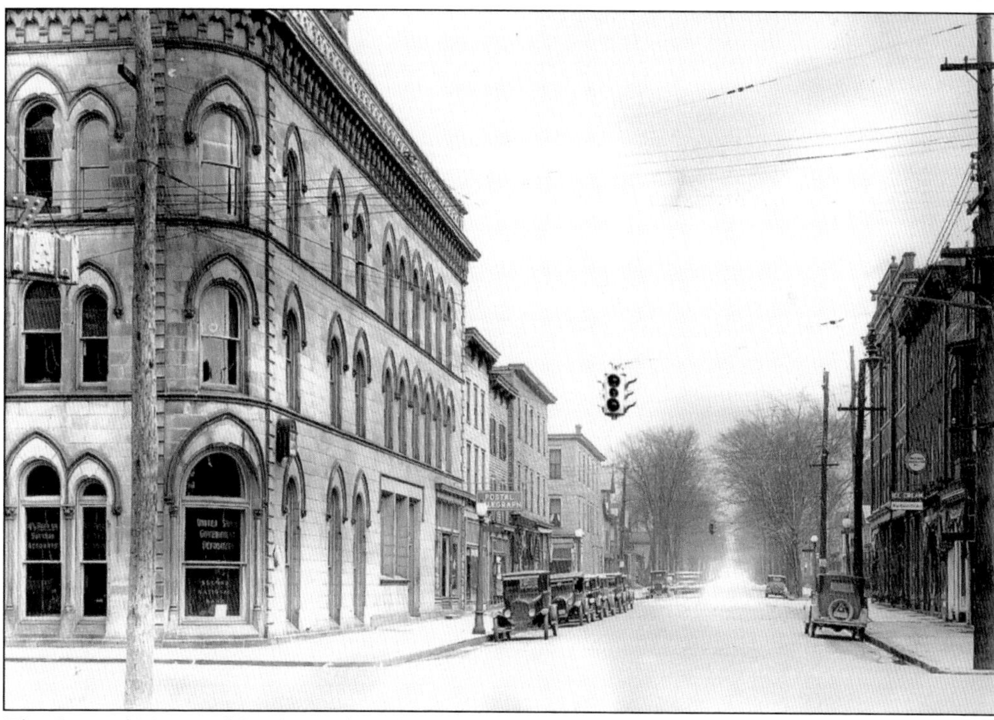

The Second National Bank was long known as the "old bank on the corner." Founded in 1865 by area lumbermen and oil producers, the bank was a two-story brick building. The building was expanded and remodeled in 1872. Expansion into adjoining structures took place three times between 1905 and 1917. Shortly after this 1929 photograph was taken, buildings surrounding the bank were razed to create Scheide Park. The former bank building remains in use as an office complex. The buildings on the opposite side of Washington Street also remain today. (Courtesy of the Titusville Herald.)

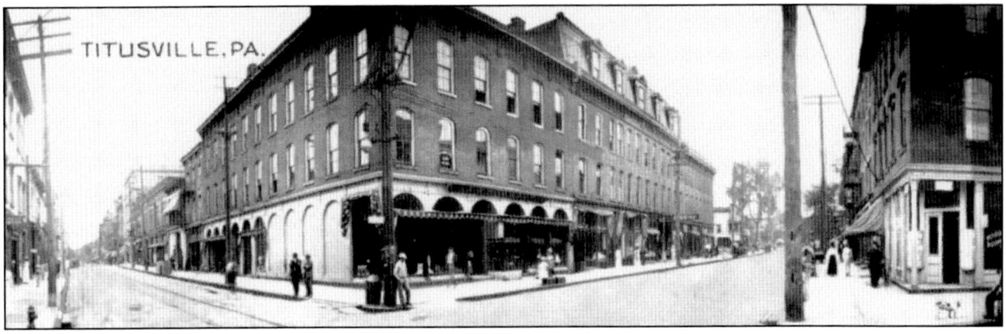

Titusville's downtown business district was long the town's heart. This 1910 panorama (half of which appears below) shows the entire area on both sides of North Franklin and Spring Streets. Most of the buildings on the left (above) remain standing; those on the right (below) have been demolished.

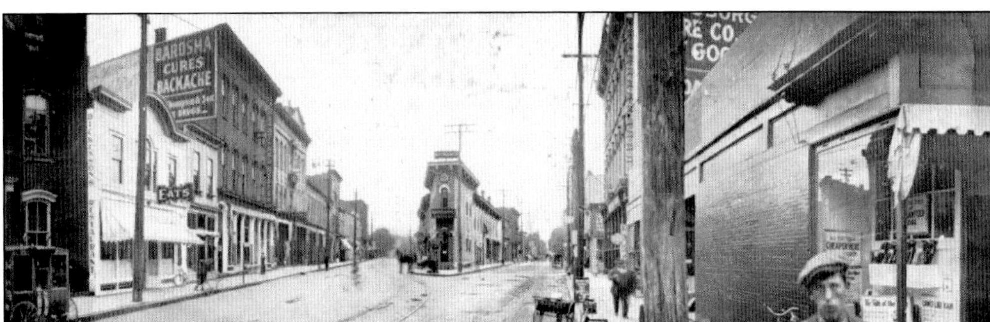

The Flatiron Building (the Citizen's Bank and Barber and Cooley building), although an unusual-looking structure, actually had limited uses. Erected in 1872, the landmark primarily housed offices and a tailor shop. It was demolished in 1966.

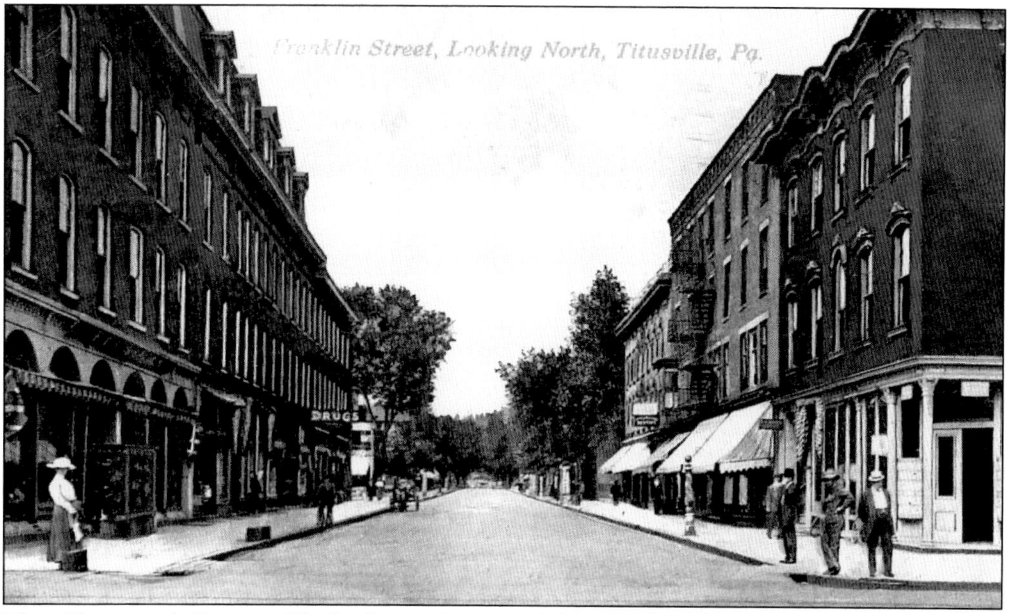

The Chase and Stewart Blocks have dominated North Franklin Street's west side since 1870–1871. Businesses in this retail and commercial complex have included the Bennett Davis clothing store, Thompson's drugstore, and the Thompson Medical Company. Thompson's drugstore still operates at this location. The Thompson Medical Company, manufacturers of patent medicines, ceased operations in 1945. (Courtesy of Kathryn Newson.)

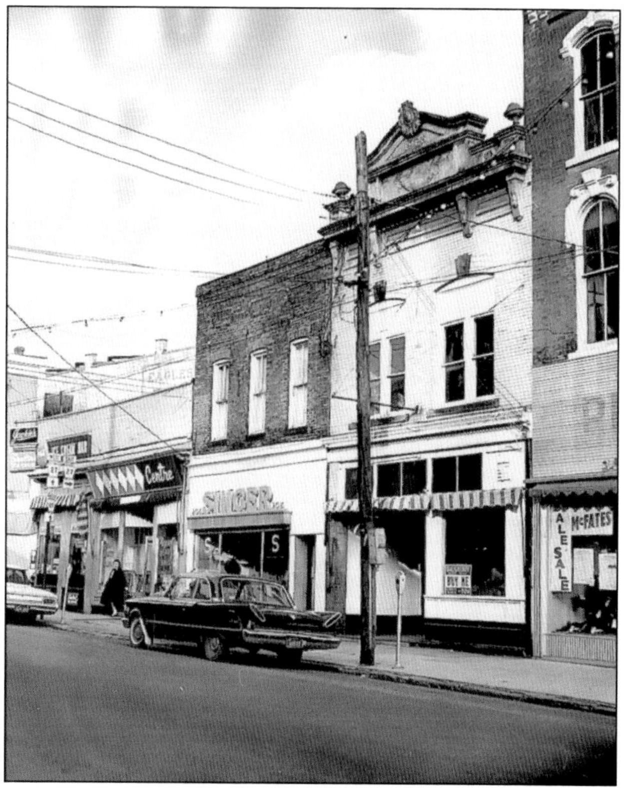

An early-1960s view of South Franklin and East Spring Streets shows Jackie's Ice Cream Bar (also known as the Central Cigar Store), Maysel's Beauty Salon, a Singer sewing machine store, the former Palace Café, and the McFate clothing store. These structures were demolished in 1966. (Courtesy of the Titusville Herald.)

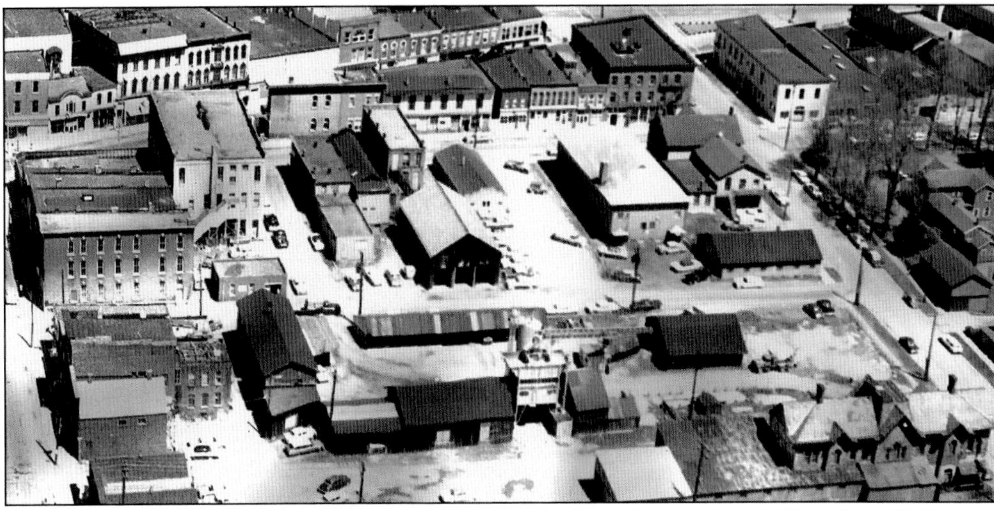

Titusville's Better Days urban renewal project took place during the 1960s. This 1963 aerial view shows the district bordered by South Franklin, Spring, Diamond, and Martin Streets that was condemned and razed. Among these structures were the Titusville Supply Company, Altman's Farm Service (the former New York Central Railroad passenger depot), and the Mitchell insurance agency (in the Flatiron Building). Many of these buildings contained safety hazards. (Courtesy of the Titusville Herald.)

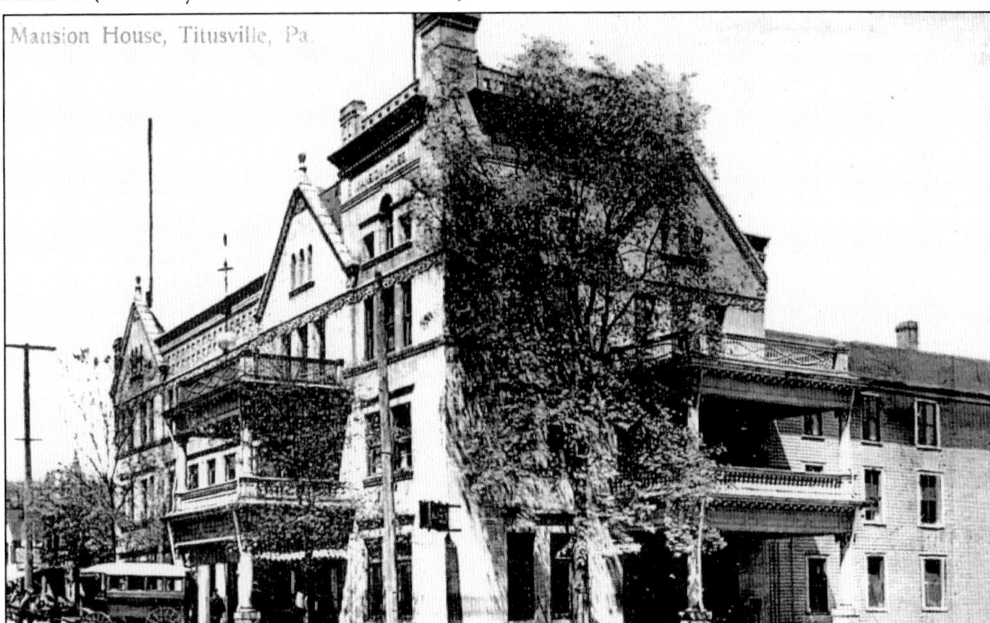

Although not Titusville's earliest or largest hotel, the Mansion House (later known as the Colonel Drake Hotel) was the longest lived. The original wooden hotel began operating in 1864. A brick Romanesque structure was erected using part of the original wooden structure's foundation and framework in 1897. Numerous ownership changes occurred before the hostelry was renamed the Colonel Drake Hotel. The remaining wooden wing was razed and replaced with a modern brick addition in 1946–1948. Little remained of the original structure when the entire complex was demolished in 1998. (Courtesy of Kathryn Newson.)

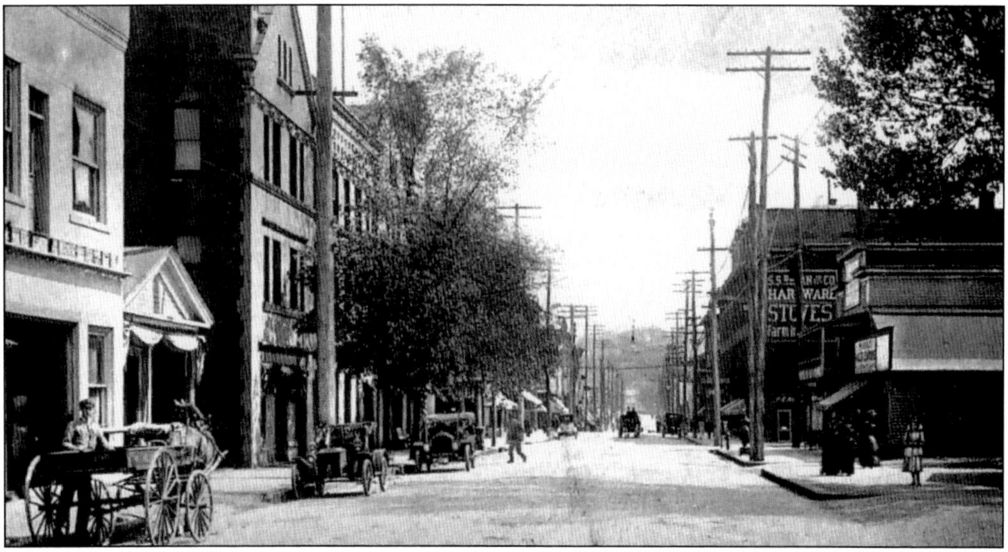

This 1910–1920 view of North Franklin Street shows a side view of the Mansion House. On the far left are the Lambert automobile garage, Keystone Automobile and Garage Company, and Maxwell B. Chick insurance and real-estate agency. Anton Schreck's cigar store, the Reid and McGraw grocery store, S. S. Bryan Hardware, the United Hardware & Supply Company, and the E. K. Thompson drugstore and Thompson Medical Company are on the right. Both automobiles and horse-drawn wagons are in evidence. Times were changing. (Courtesy of Kathryn Newson.)

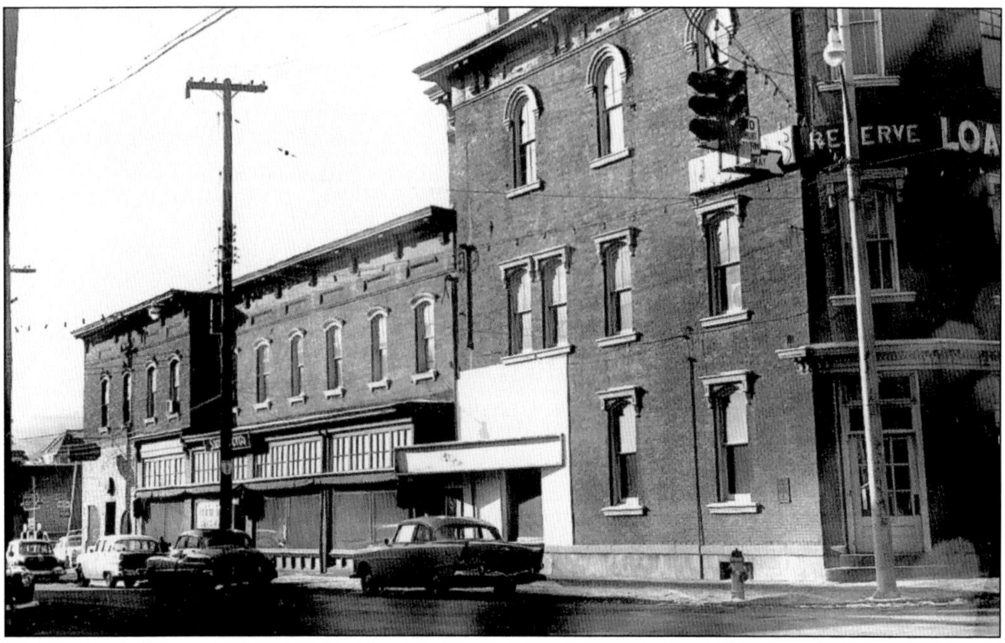

Jacob B. Goldstein's New York Bazaar dry-goods store was located on the southwest side of Franklin and Spring Streets. Evan Swanson purchased the Goldstein store in 1945. He operated the department store at this site until 1957, at which time the business was moved to East Central Avenue. Other occupants of the block were the Scott dry cleaning and tailoring business and the Reserve Loan Company. (Courtesy of the Titusville Herald.)

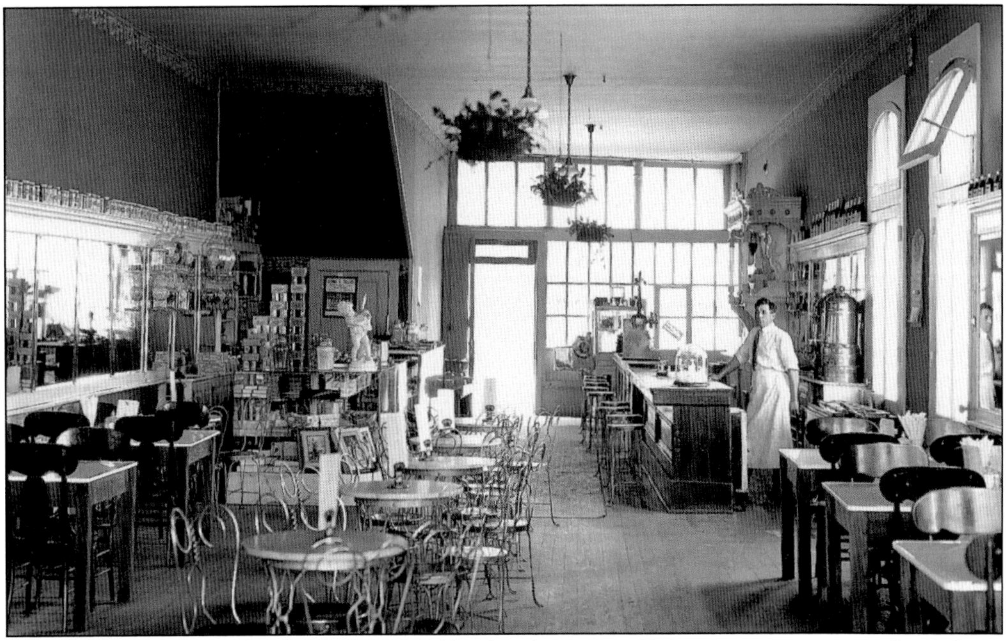

Restaurants and candy businesses operated by Greek immigrants were once common throughout western Pennsylvania. Nick Armatas owned the Liberty Confectionery, a store and restaurant at Diamond and Martin Streets in Titusville in 1922–1923. Armatas is seen inside his shop on May 1, 1922. (Courtesy of Millia A. Sullivan.)

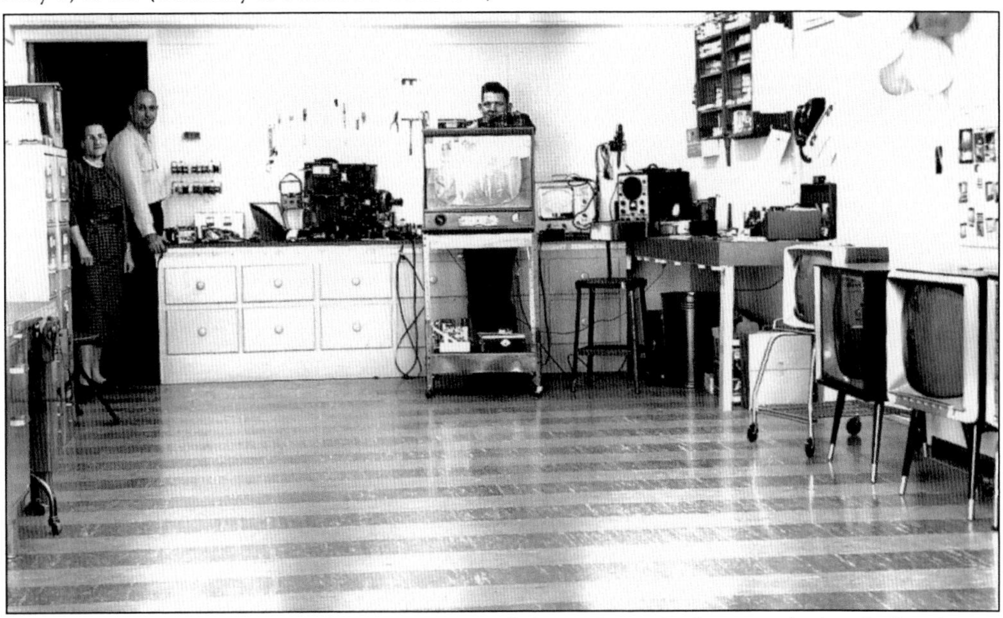

Fred Collins (1912–1991) was for many years a Philco radio and television dealer. Collins began repairing radios while still in high school. Following U.S. Army service in World War II, he began selling television sets. This 1958 photograph shows the Collins radio and television shop in its new quarters on the West Central Avenue Extension in Oil Creek Township, Crawford County. Fred Collins and his wife, Mae, are on the left. Notice the television in front of the workbench. (Courtesy of the Titusville Herald.)

Five

Agriculture

Farming has been important in the Titusville region since the time of the earliest settlement. In 1798, the Holland Land Company in Oil Creek Township, Crawford County, operated a gristmill.

Buckwheat and potatoes were important crops during the early 19th century. Additional gristmills were constructed throughout the region, including one erected on South Franklin Street in Titusville in 1849. It remained in operation for 85 years.

The oil boom actually stimulated local agriculture. Although many families sold their farms after oil had been found on these sites, others (over two-thirds of the Titusville region was barren of producing oil sands) continued to raise buckwheat, potatoes, and livestock. Titusville's wholesale groceries helped supply produce to numerous boomtowns.

Agriculture soon united with petroleum wealth. Oil barons invested in elaborate farming operations. A fairground including a horse track existed near Titusville's west end until 1931.

Buckwheat flour and dairy products were shipped from the Titusville region by rail. Although buckwheat flour milling has passed from the scene, dairying remains to this day.

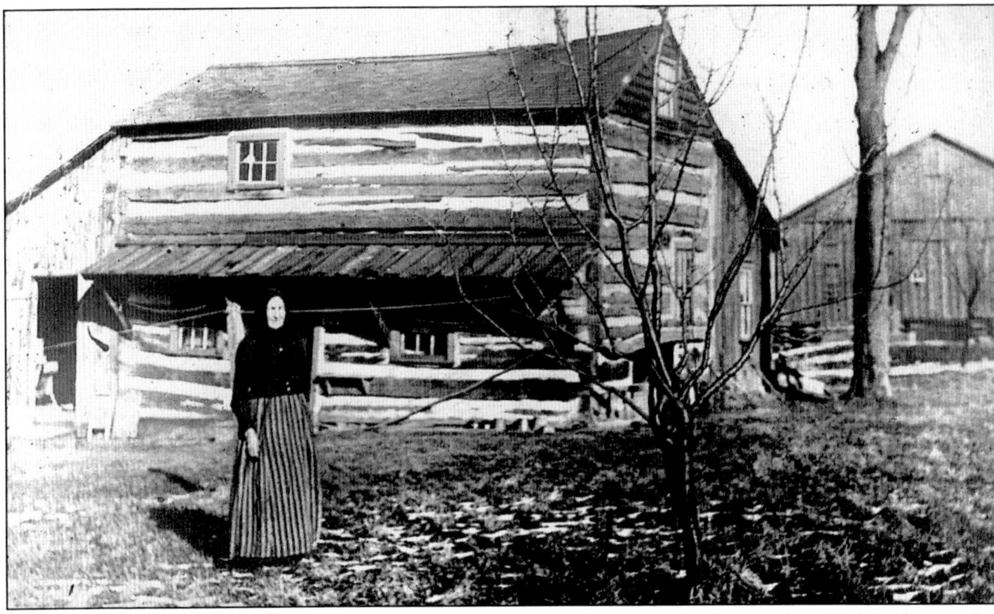

The earliest farmhouses were log cabins. Margaret Ann Hamilton Lamb still lived in a log house in Cherrytree Township, Venango County, *c.* 1900. Although Lamb's cabin was razed long ago, the barn in the photograph stands today. (Courtesy of Kathryn Newson.)

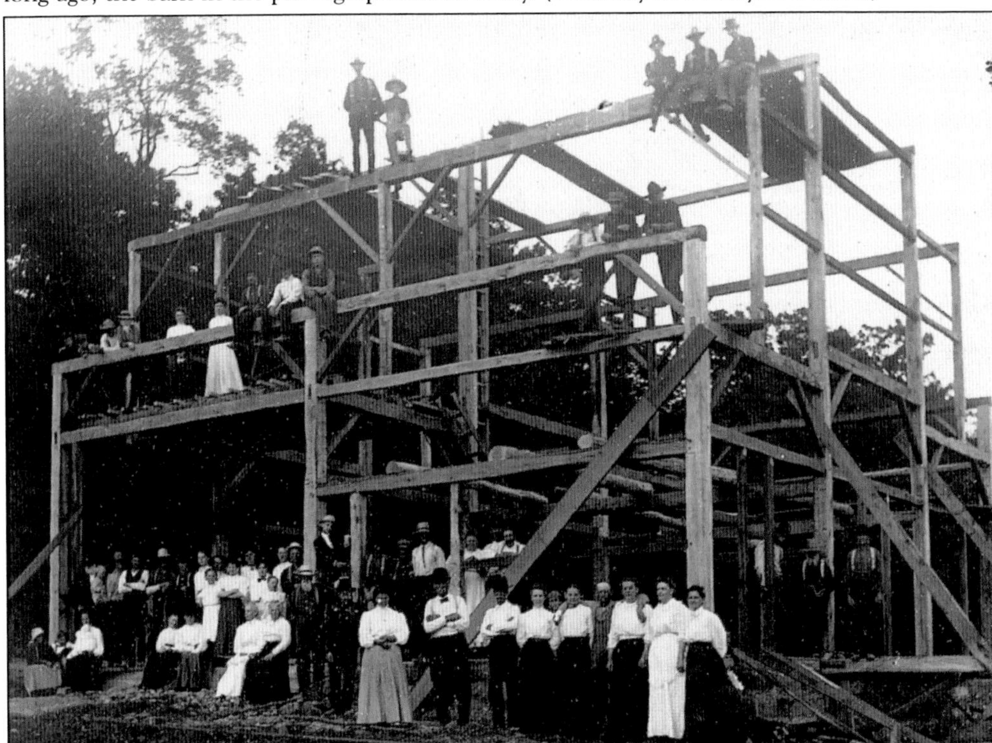

Barn raisings were not only construction projects, but also social events. The erection of the Fleming-Strawbridge-Hamilton Farm barn in Cherrytree Township took place prior to 1900. (Courtesy of Kathryn Newson.)

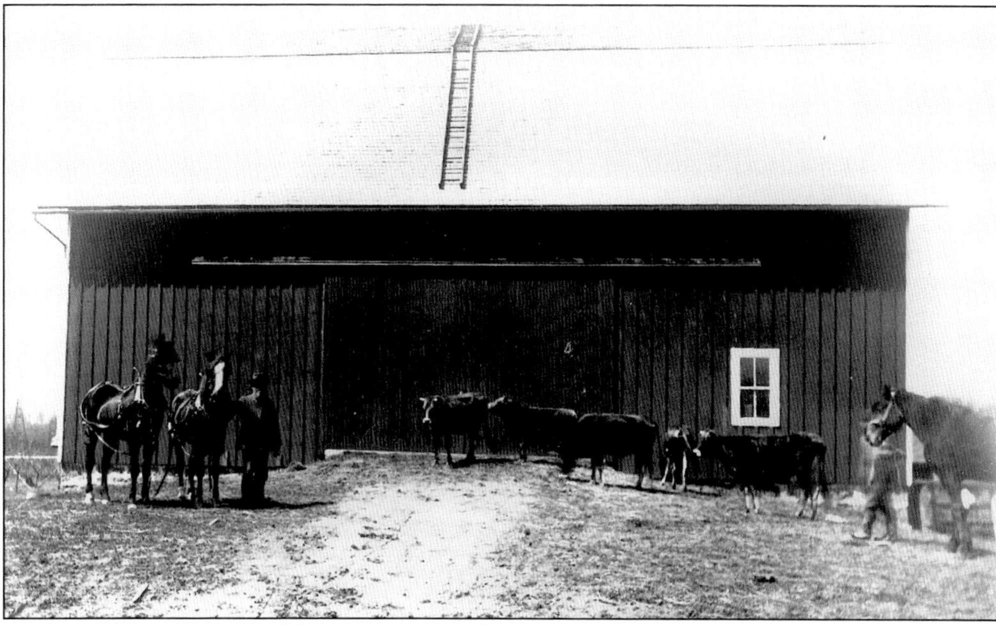

Dairy cattle and teams of horses stand in front of a Titusville area barn. Oil wells in the background indicate the location could have been in Oil Creek Township, Venango County. (Courtesy of the Drake Well Museum.)

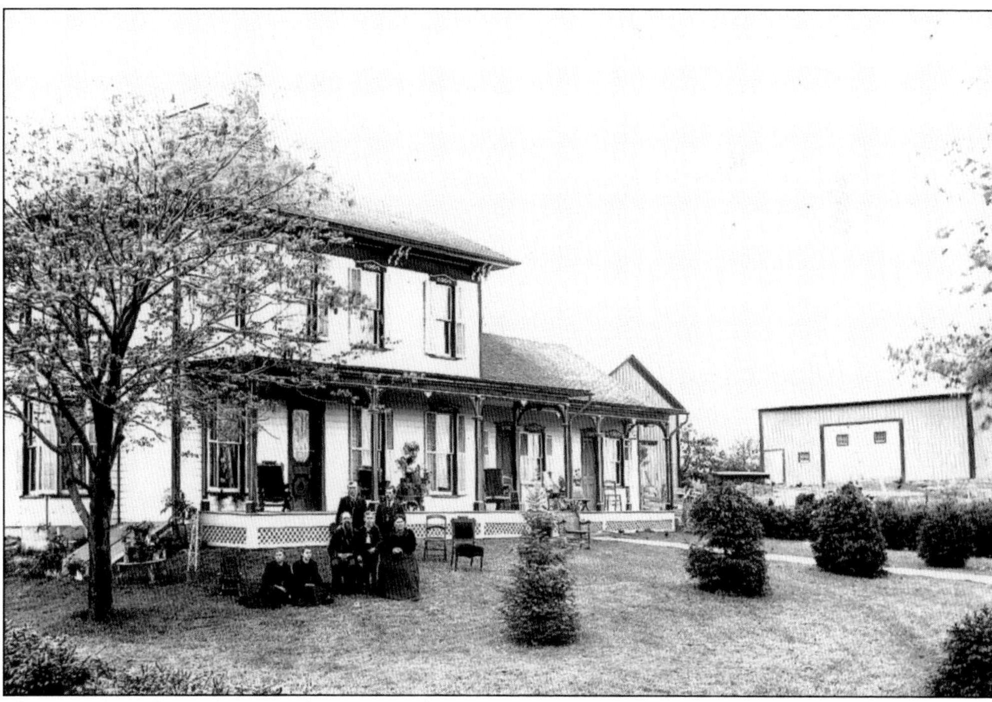

The Lanctot farm was in Plum Township, Venango County. The family was photographed seated before the farmhouse. Two barns and several chickens can be seen on the right. (Courtesy of the Drake Well Museum.)

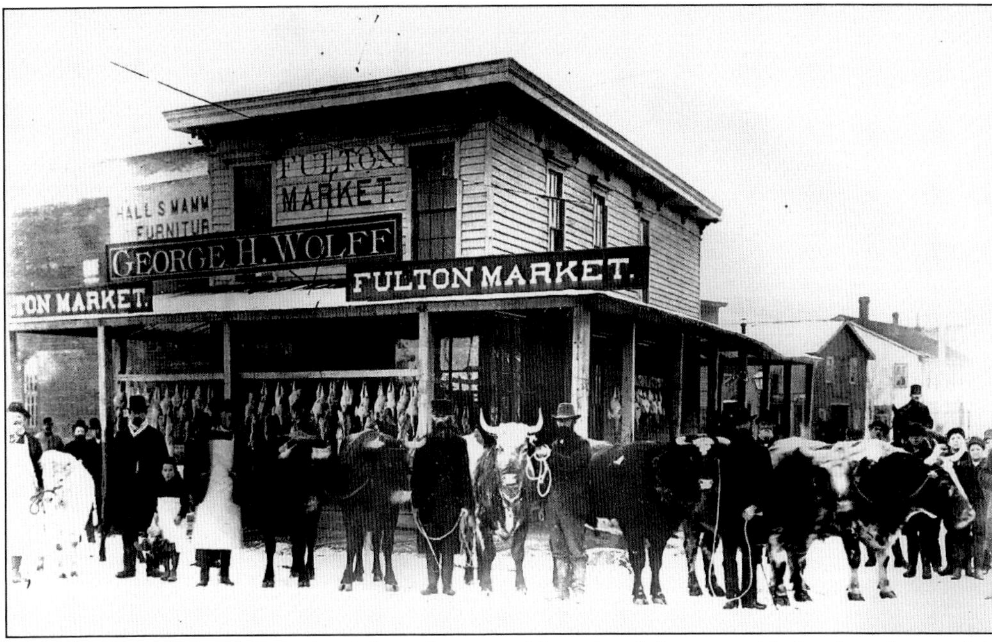

Titusville-area farms fed much of the oil region. Here, local farmers with beef cattle stand in front of George Wolff's Fulton Market, at Diamond and Martin Streets, c. 1880. Note the chickens hanging in front of store. (Courtesy of the Drake Well Museum.)

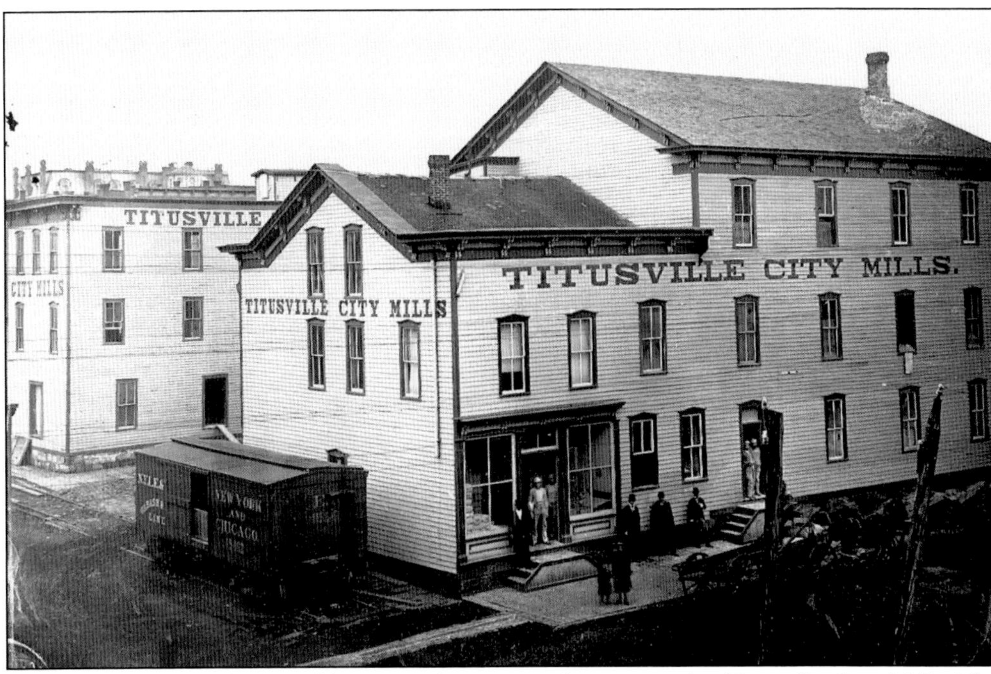

For many years, Titusville's oldest manufacturing industry was the Titusville City Mills. The water-powered gristmill remained in business on South Franklin Street from 1849 to 1934. A railroad boxcar and horse-drawn wagon can be seen in this *c.* 1880 view. Flooding from the millrace caused problems for many downtown merchants. (Courtesy of the Drake Well Museum.)

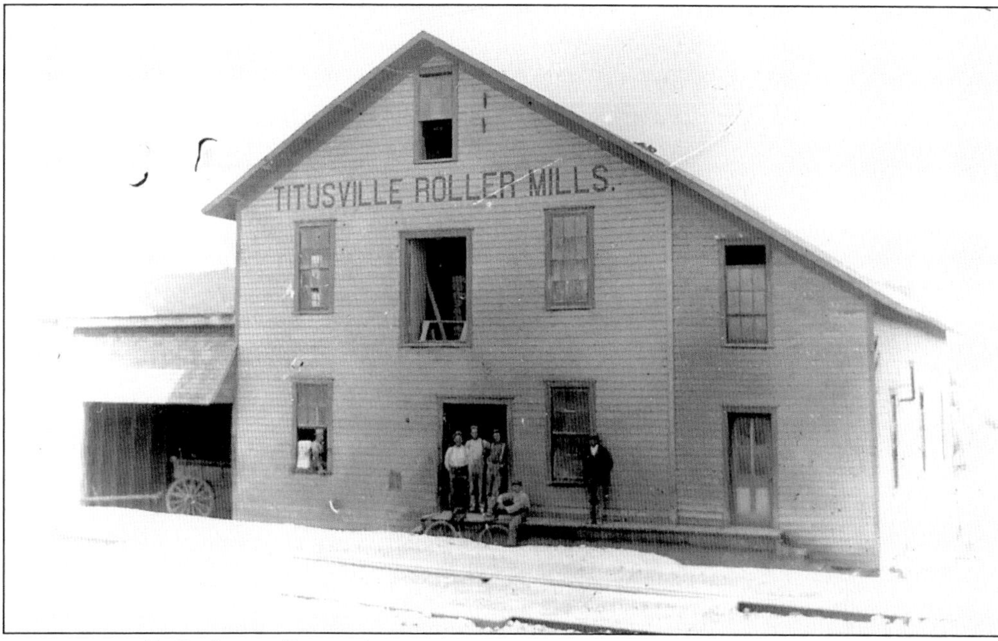

Kerr's Titusville Roller Mills stood on West Spring Street at the city limits. Fire destroyed the original wooden building in 1917. It was replaced by a five-story brick building later converted to a cold-storage unit. (Courtesy of the Drake Well Museum.)

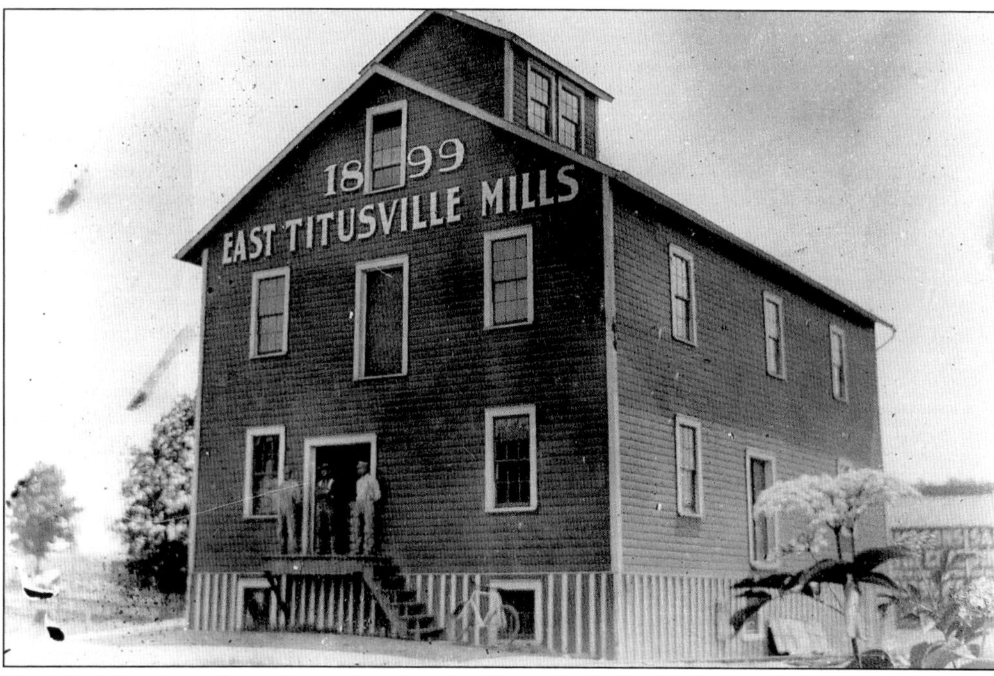

The Mack brothers, formerly employed at the Titusville Roller Mills, founded the East Titusville Mills in 1899. This business manufactured flour from locally grown buckwheat. Aunt Jemima Mills, of St. Joseph, Missouri, was a major customer of the East Titusville Mills. (Courtesy of the Drake Well Museum.)

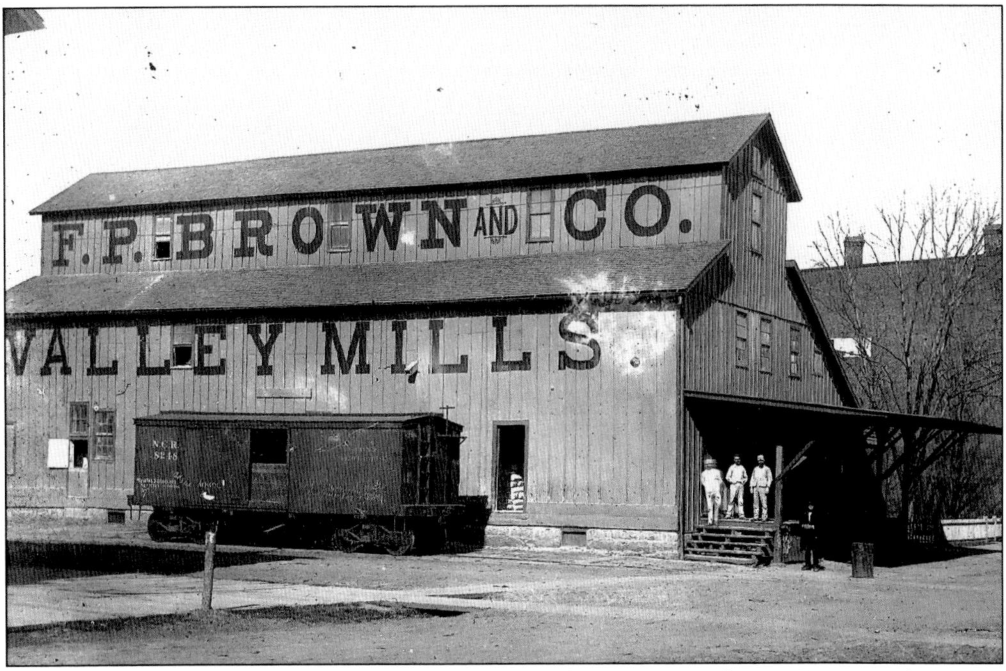

Brown and Company's Valley Mills stood at the northeast corner of West Spring and Monroe Streets in 1885. Next door stood the W. P. Cornell wholesale grocery. (Courtesy of the Drake Well Museum.)

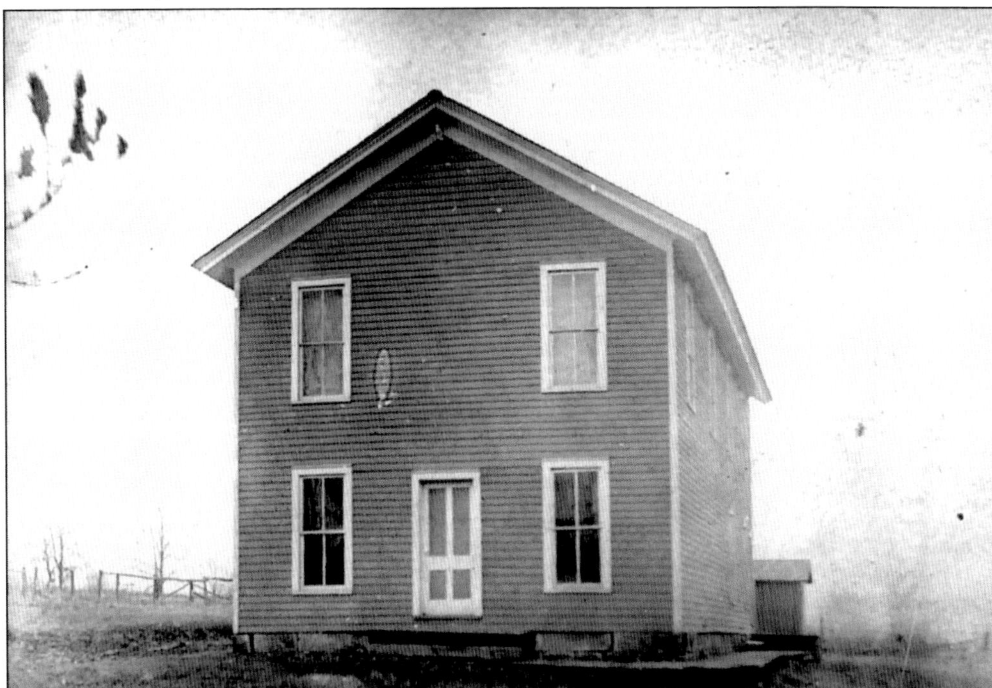

The Breedtown Grange was a community center for Cherrytree Township farmers. The Grange occupied this simple wooden structure for 100 years. (Courtesy of Kathryn Newson.)

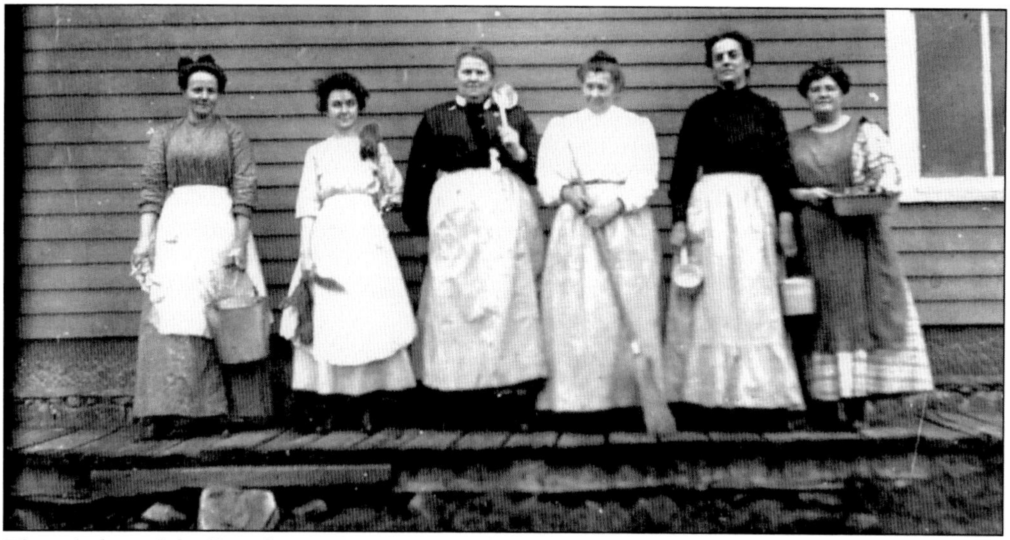

These ladies of the Breedtown Grange were photographed while cleaning the kitchen *c.* 1895. From left to right are Wealtha Alcom Warner, Eva O'Brien, Callie Peebles Thomas, Jennie Fulmer, Clair Whiting, and Merle Warner. (Courtesy of Kathryn Newson.)

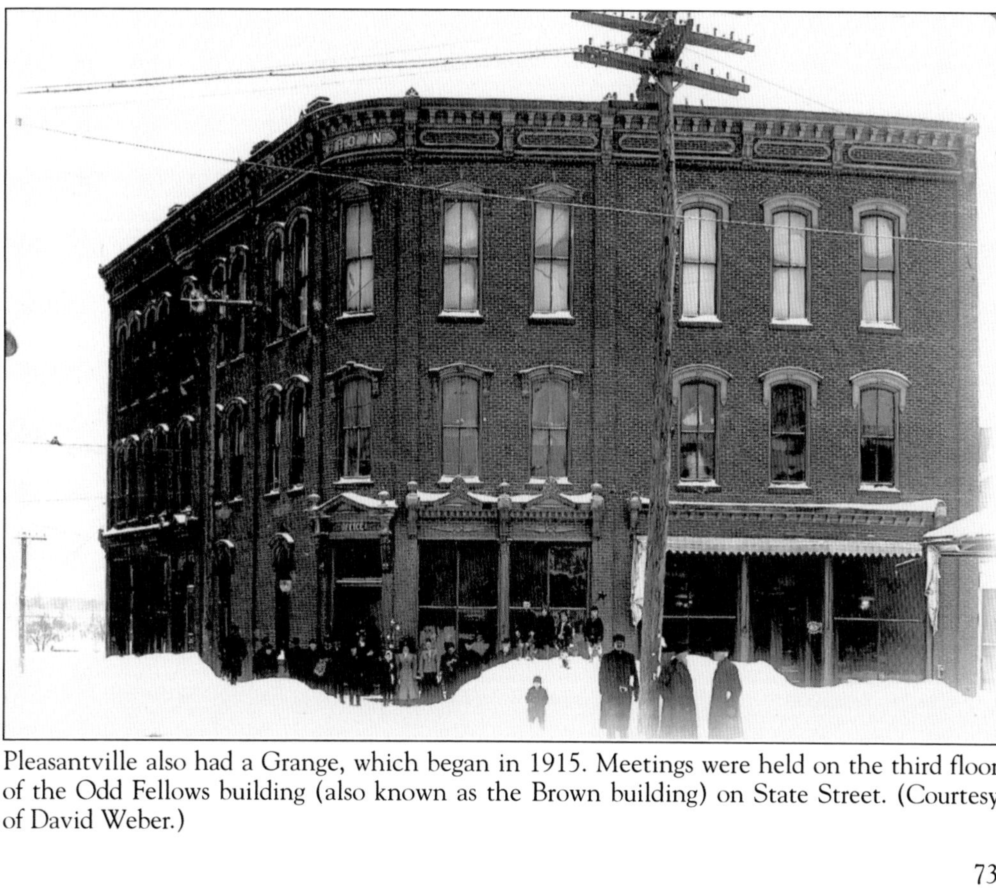

Pleasantville also had a Grange, which began in 1915. Meetings were held on the third floor of the Odd Fellows building (also known as the Brown building) on State Street. (Courtesy of David Weber.)

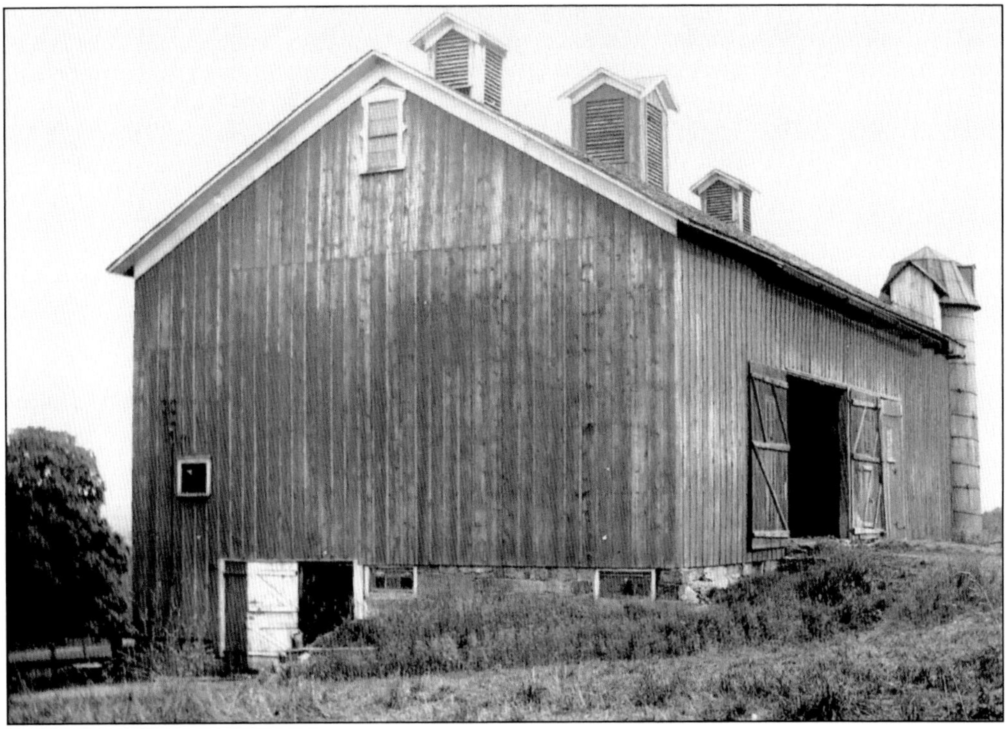

The Alcorn farm barn in Cherrytree Township was 100 years old by the 1930s. The silo on the right was a more recent addition. (Courtesy of the Drake Well Museum.)

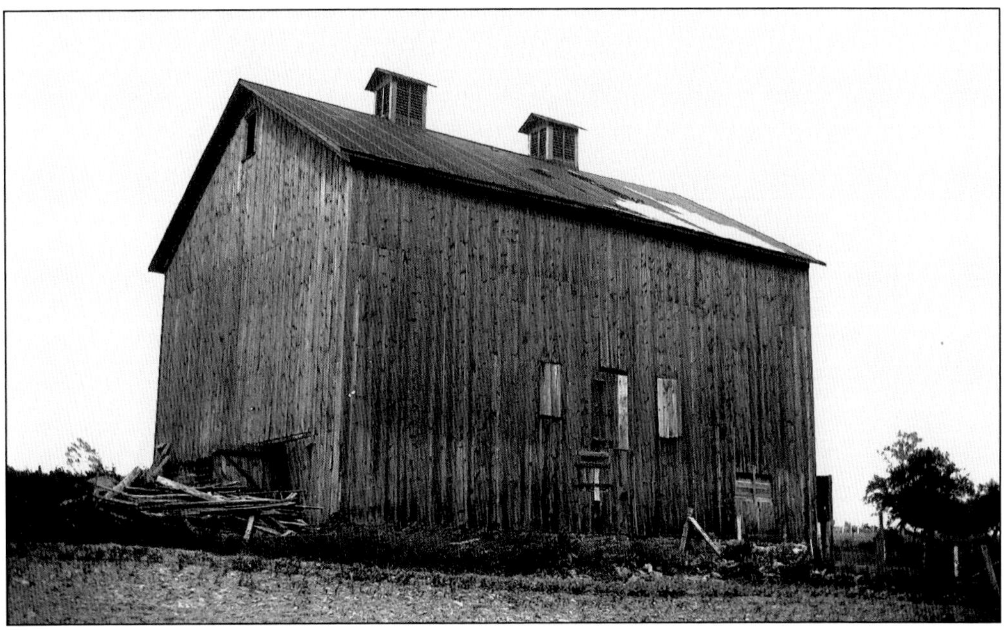

A Cherrytree Township bar had seen much use by the time this *c.* 1930 photograph was taken. The farm is unidentified. (Courtesy of the Drake Well Museum.)

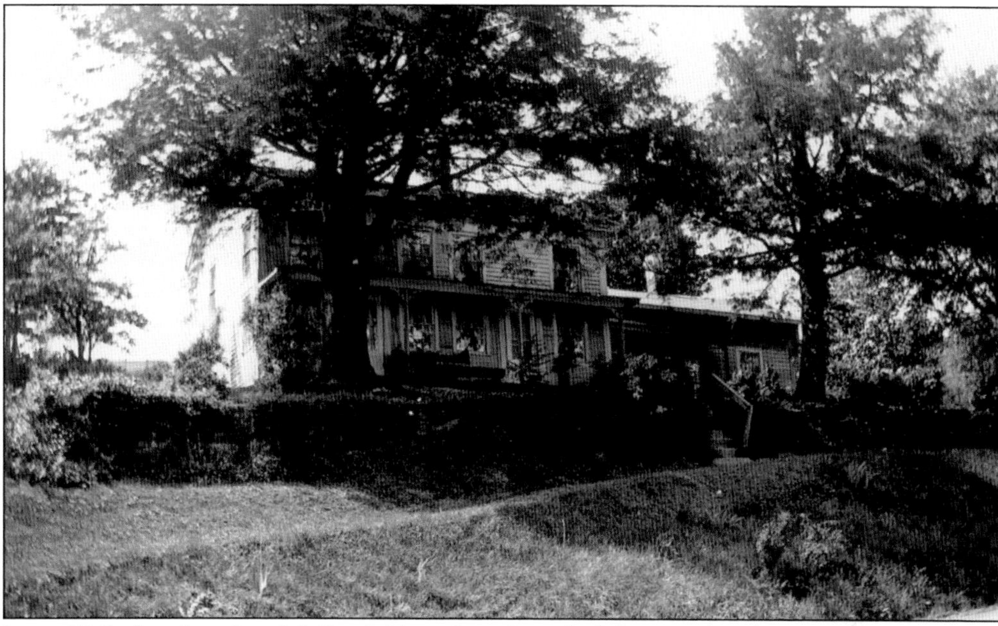

James Kelly lived in this Oil Creek Township, Crawford County, farmhouse. Kelly was also in the feed and builders' supply businesses. His family had occupied the North Perry Street farm for generations. (Courtesy of the Drake Well Museum.)

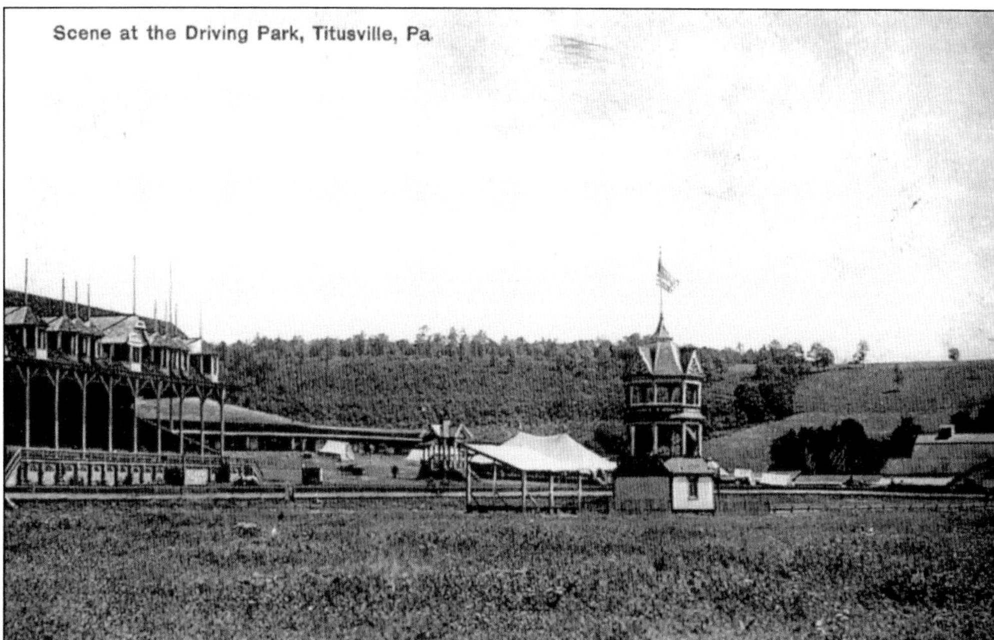

Wealthy oil barons founded the Titusville Driving Park Association in 1870. The Oil Creek Township, Crawford County, horse track evolved into fairgrounds where annual events were held. This 1909 view shows the track and grandstand. (Courtesy of Kathryn Newson.)

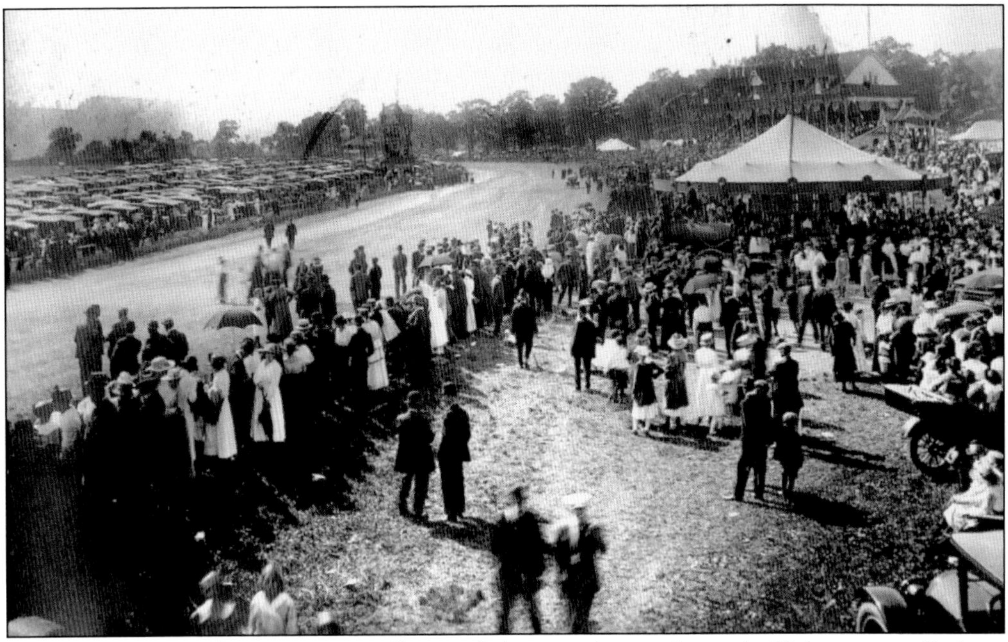

The annual Titusville Fair was a well-attended event during the early 20th century. Parking spaces for automobiles (completely filled), busy amusement rides, and throngs of people are seen in this undated photograph. A water wagon is beside the carousel. (Courtesy of the Titusville Herald.)

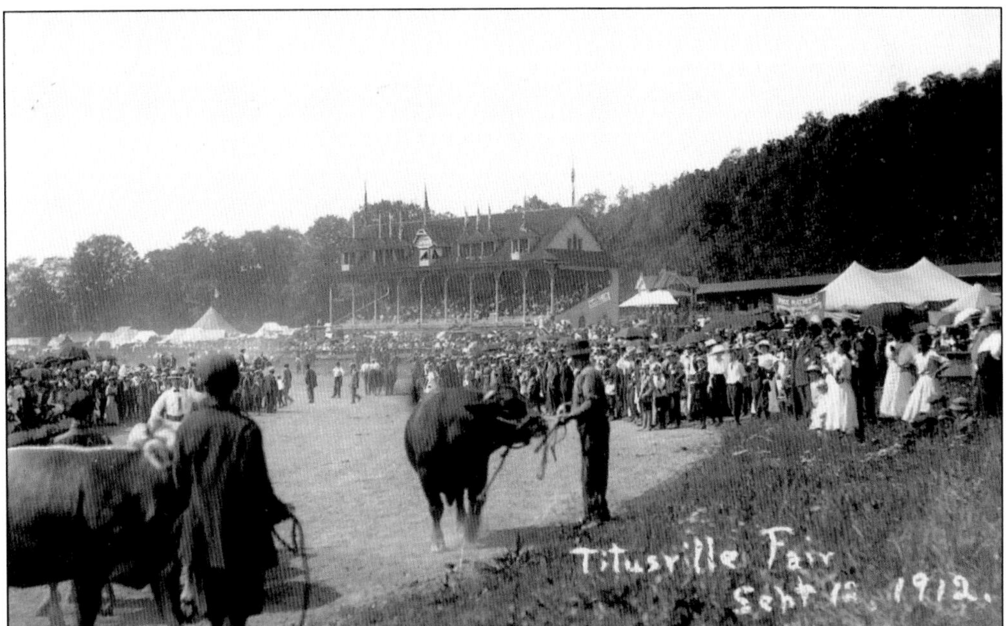

Cattle judging was taking place at the Titusville Fair in this September 12, 1912, view. Notice the tents for the carnival midway and Professor Mather's Circus. The last Titusville Fair was held in 1931. An industrial park occupies the former fairgrounds today. (Courtesy of the Drake Well Museum.)

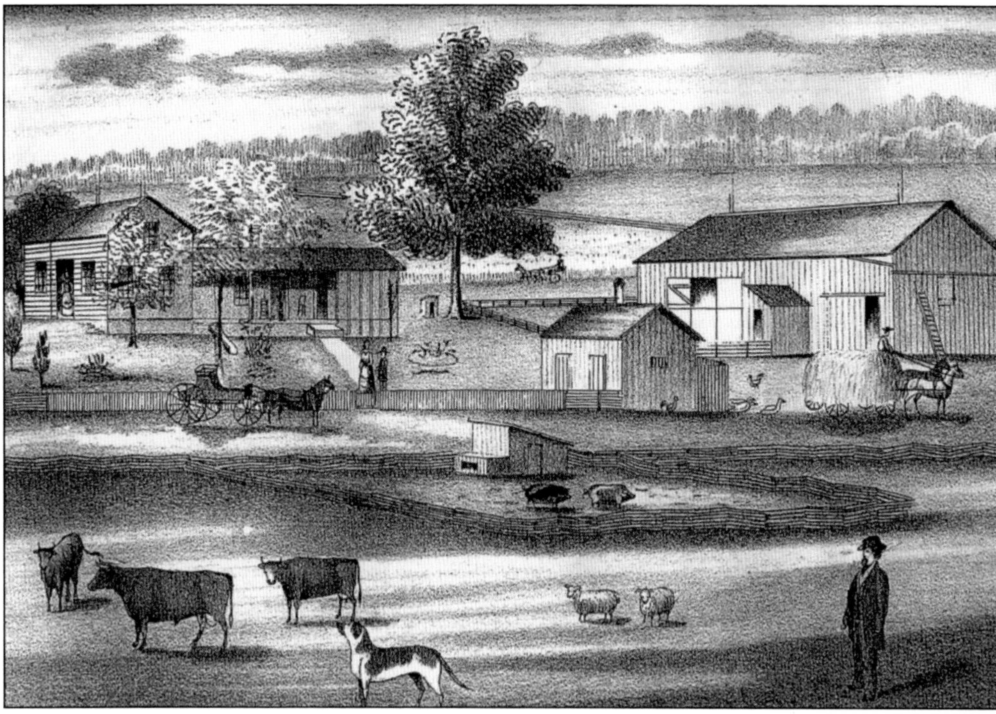

T. L. Cheney's farm was near Enterprise in Southwest Township, Warren County, in 1878. (From *Atlas of Warren County.*)

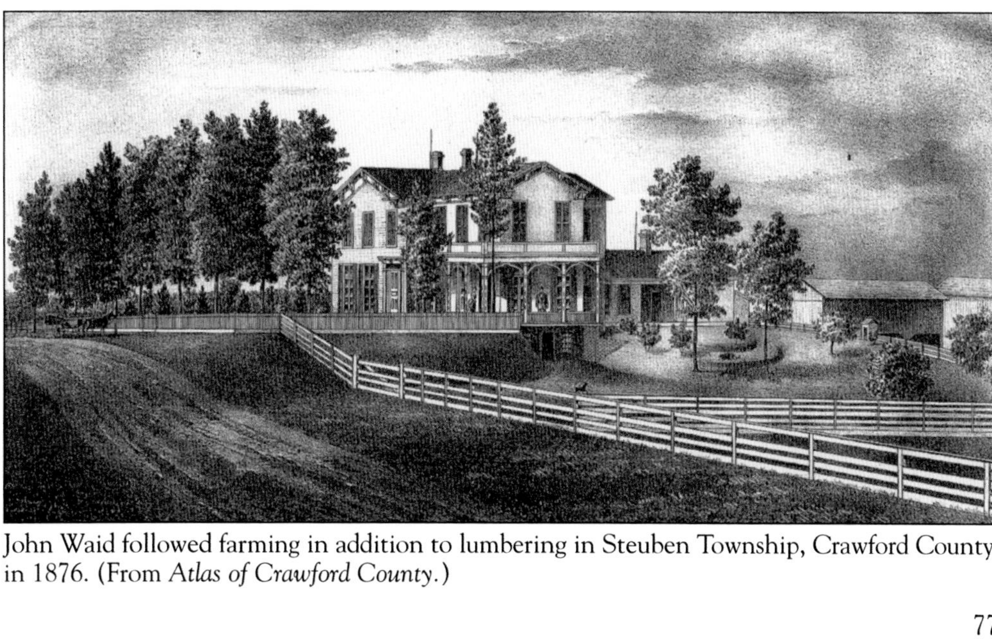

John Waid followed farming in addition to lumbering in Steuben Township, Crawford County, in 1876. (From *Atlas of Crawford County.*)

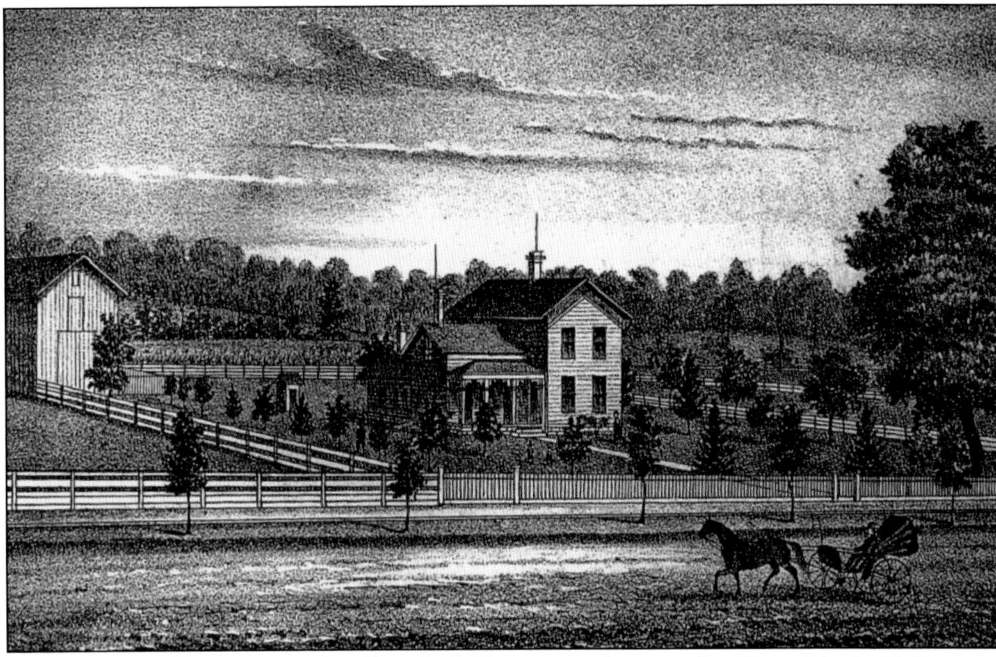

D. W. Tryon's farm was in the Crawford County settlement that bore his family's name, Tryonville. (From *Atlas of Crawford County.*)

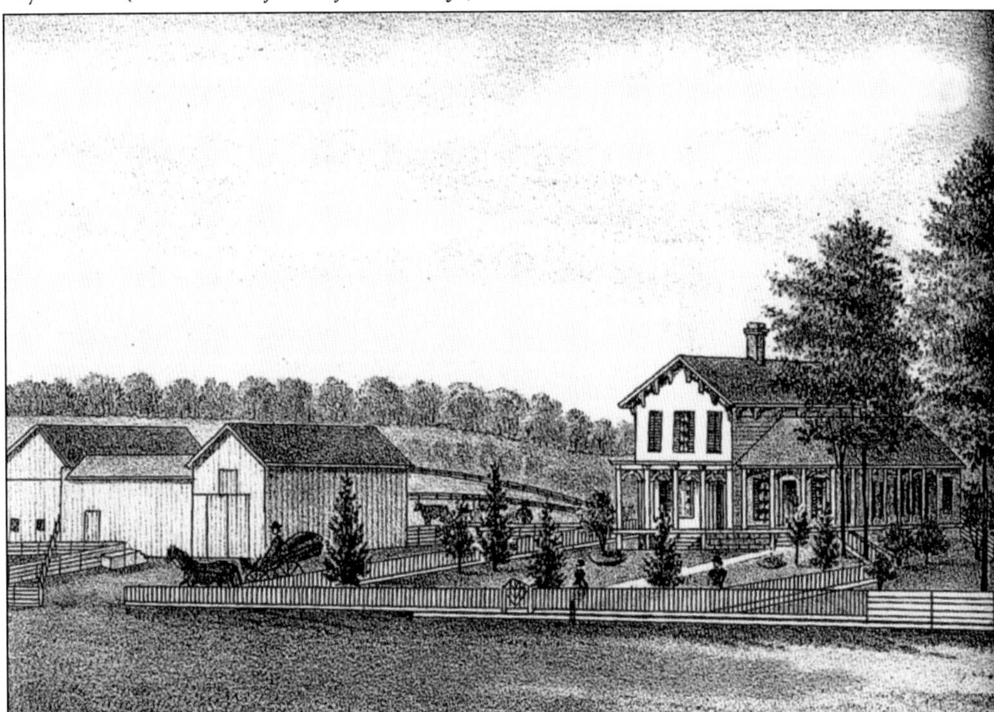

Harriet Hoyt (widow of G. R. Hoyt) farmed at Townville, Crawford County, in 1876. Large numbers of women have been involved with agriculture to the present times. (From *Atlas of Crawford County.*)

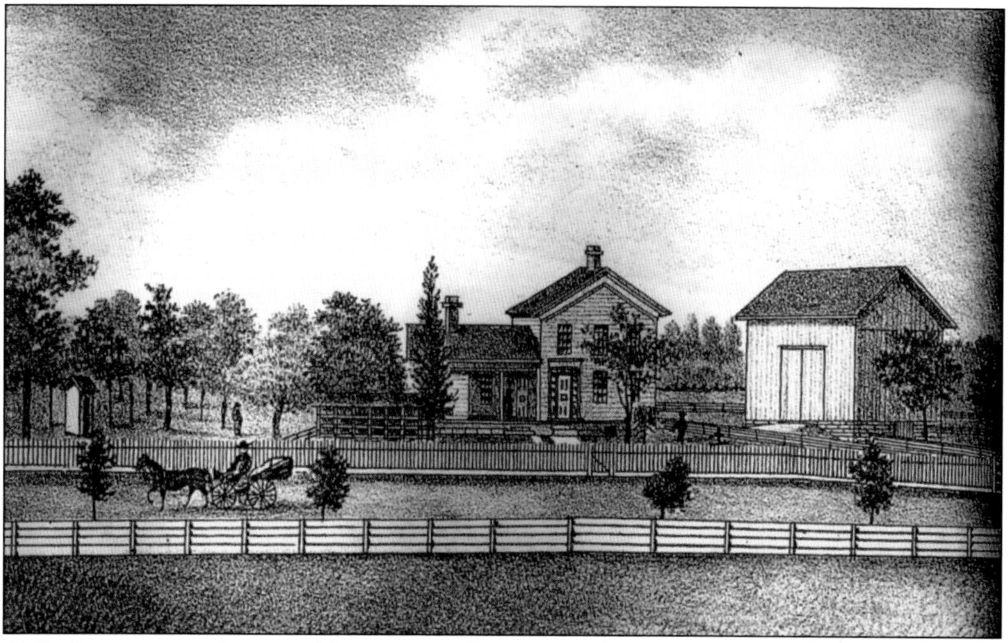

G. B. Conover's residence and farm were in Rome Township, Crawford County, in 1876. Rome Township has long been a center of agriculture, as well as lumber manufacturing. (From *Atlas of Crawford County*.)

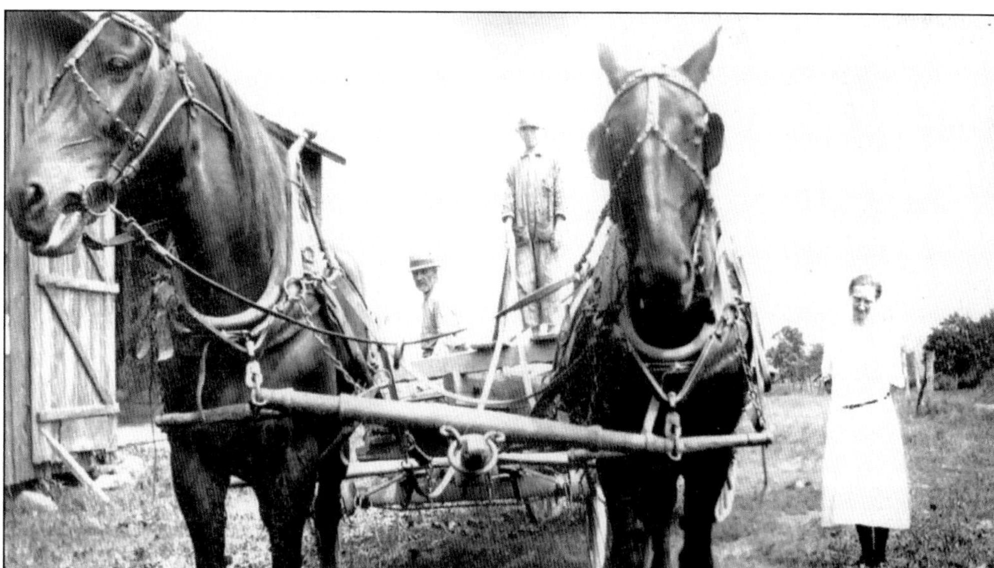

An unidentified family can be seen with a team of horses on a Titusville-area farm. Hay inside the barn is clearly visible. (Courtesy of Myrna Wescoat.)

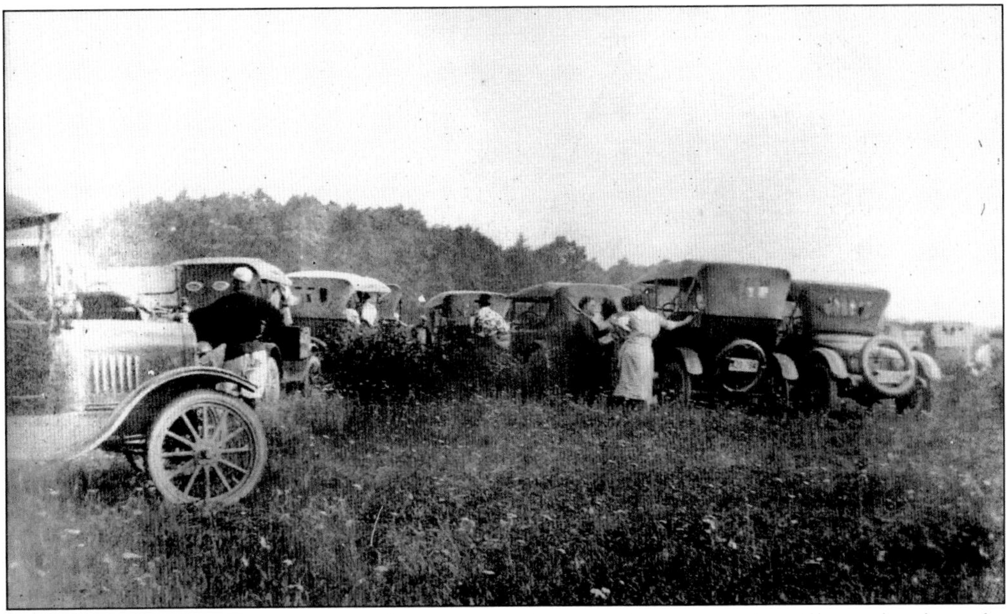

One of the last photographs taken of the annual Titusville Fair shows the villains that brought about its demise. Automobiles, which gave people freedom to travel (along with the Great Depression), brought down the curtain on the Titusville Fair Association. (Courtesy of Myrna Wescoat.)

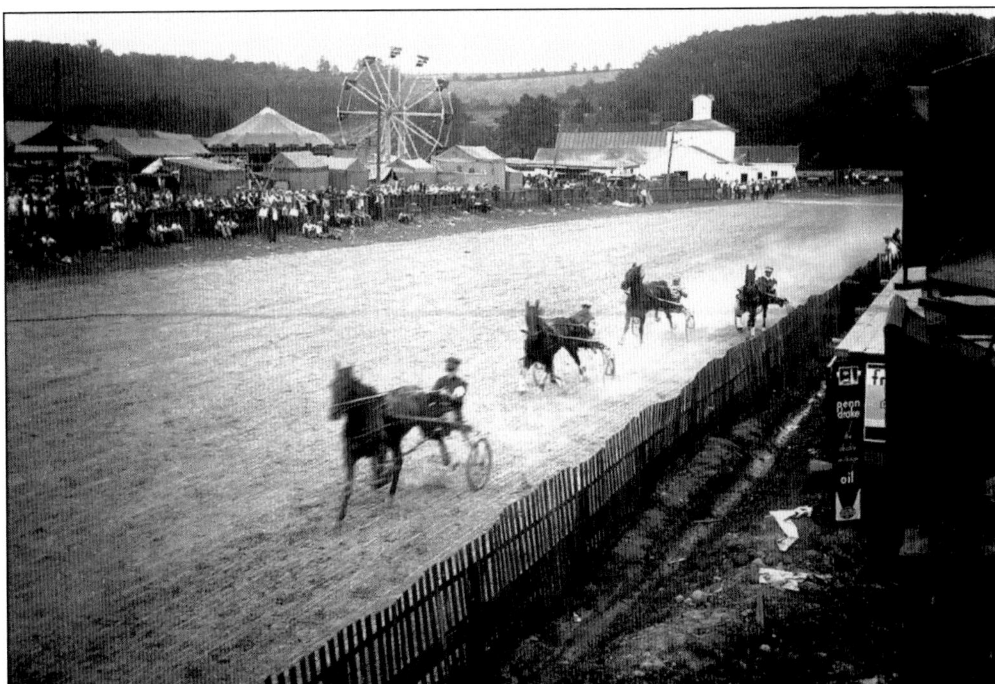

Many farmers considered horse and harness racing necessary evils because they led to improved breeds of livestock and better roads. Harness racing was a feature of the final Titusville Fair, in September 1931.

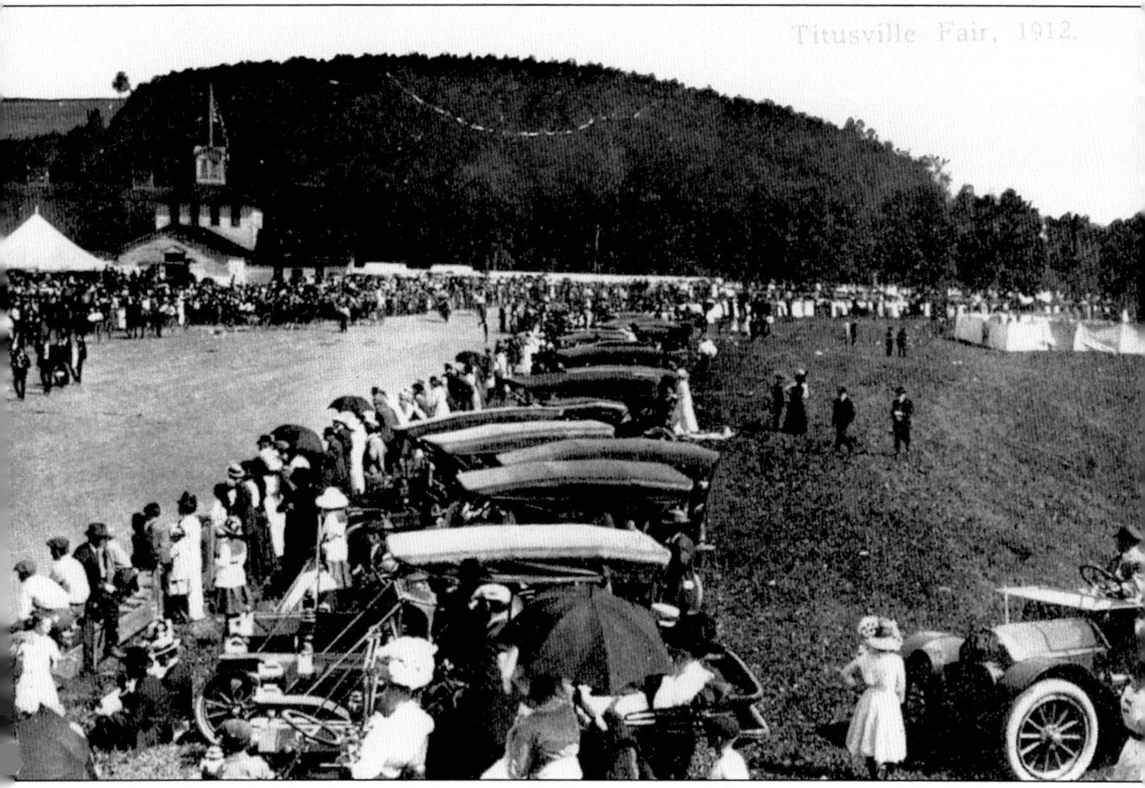

A second 1912 view of the Titusville fairgrounds shows automobiles, spectators, and exhibition areas. (Courtesy of Kathryn Newson.)

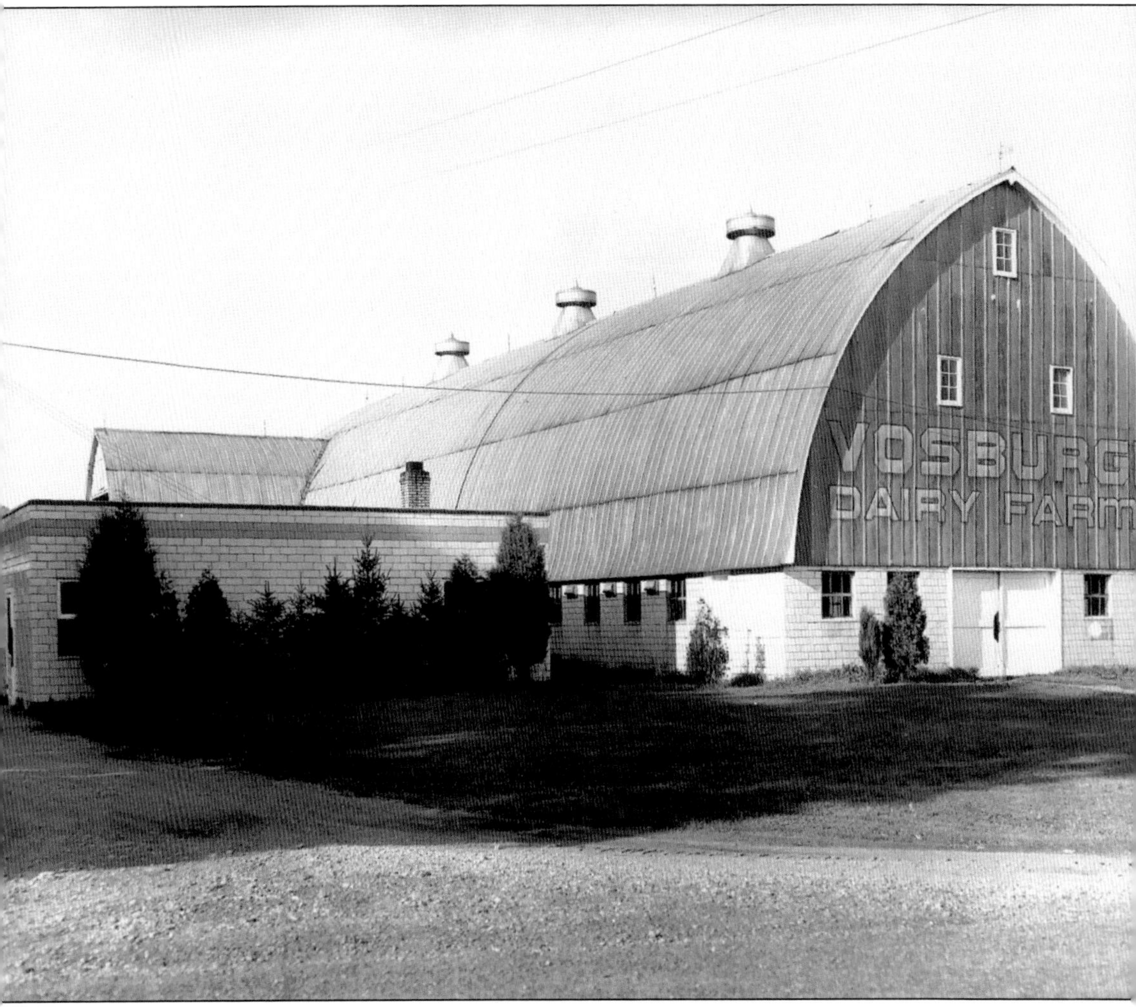

Nearly 30 Titusville dairy farms bottled and sold milk during the 1920s. The Vosburgh dairy farm was bottling pasteurized milk as late as the 1960s. This 1958 view of Vosburgh's Oil Creek Township, Crawford County, dairy barn shows the milk-bottling plant on the left. The Vosburghs also homogenized milk for other local dairies. Beef cattle have been raised on this site recently. (Courtesy of the Drake Well Museum.)

Six

Transportation and Communication

Early transportation in the Titusville area consisted of wagons, stagecoaches, and lumber rafts. The rafting method was later modified into the pond freshet system for moving oil barges downstream.

Oil boom activities of the 1860s brought rail transportation into the area. The Oil Creek Railroad (later the Pennsylvania Railroad) was constructed from Corry to Titusville in 1862. This line was gradually extended to Oil City (1866). In 1872, the New York Central's Dunkirk, Allegheny Valley, and Pittsburgh line linked Titusville to Warren. The Union and Titusville Railroad briefly extended from Titusville through the Canadohta Lake area to Union City.

Telephone service was brought into the Titusville area in 1878–1879. Thomas Watson, Alexander Graham Bell's assistant, came here to inspect the first phone installations.

Trolley cars came and went between 1898 and 1925. An electric streetcar line connected Titusville to Hydetown, Tryonville, and Pleasantville.

The invention of the automobile favorably impacted the local oil industry. Livery stables, blacksmith shops, and wagon shops were converted into repair garages and automobile dealerships. Aviation has also made a direct impact on Titusville.

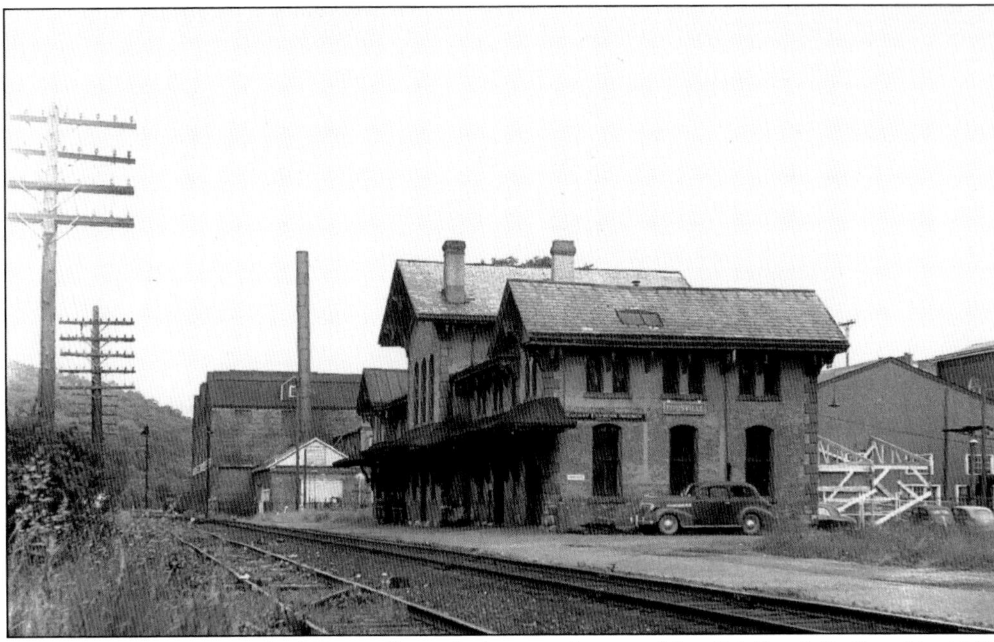

Railroad service first reached Titusville with the completion of the Oil Creek Railroad in 1862. The Pennsylvania Railroad passenger depot was constructed in 1870. This South Franklin Street landmark stood for nearly 100 years. Titusville Iron Works facilities can be seen in background. (Courtesy of the Drake Well Museum.)

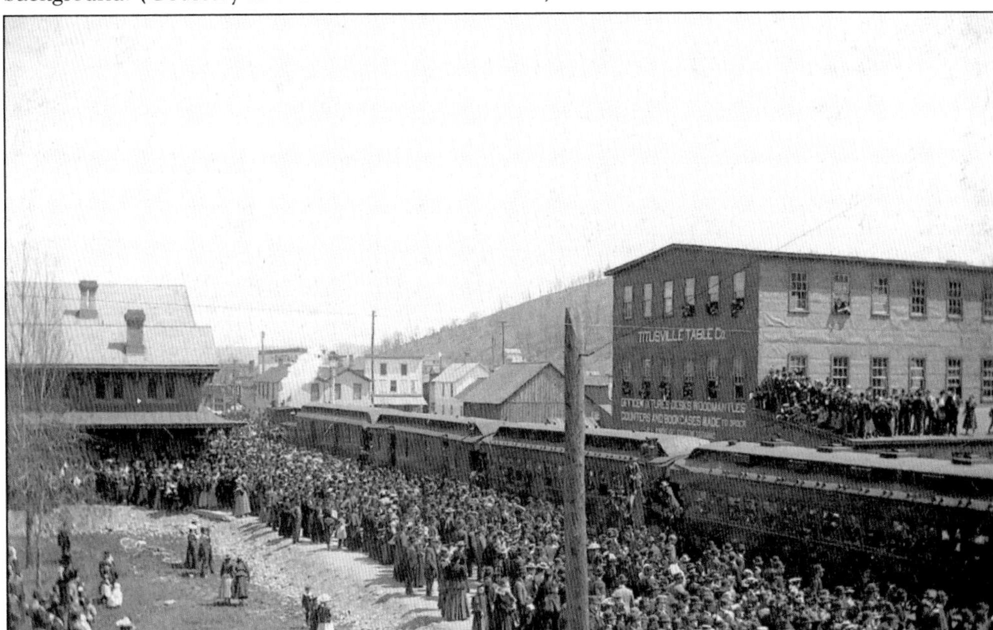

National Guard Company K is shown leaving the Pennsylvania Railroad passenger depot for Spanish-American War duty on April 27, 1898. This photograph shows the extent of local support for the troops; the steam locomotive can barely be seen due to the crowd's size. People can be seen on roof of the Titusville Table Company on the right. This woodworking establishment also manufactured office fixtures, desks, wood mantles, counters, and bookcases.

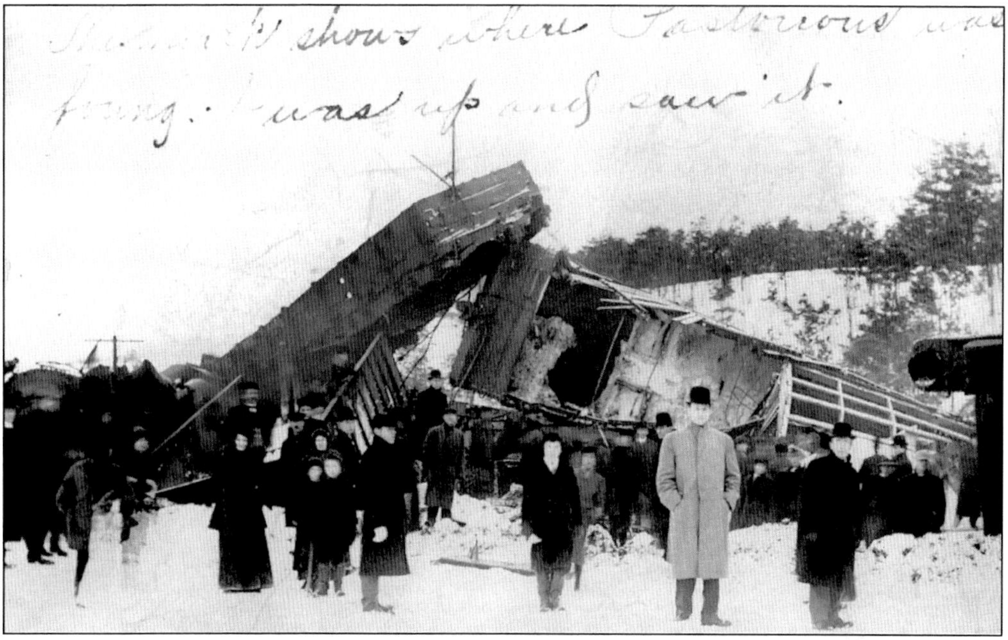

Train wrecks were once frequent occurrences. This particularly bad one took place on the Pennsylvania Railroad between Titusville and Hydetown. (Courtesy of Kathryn Newson.)

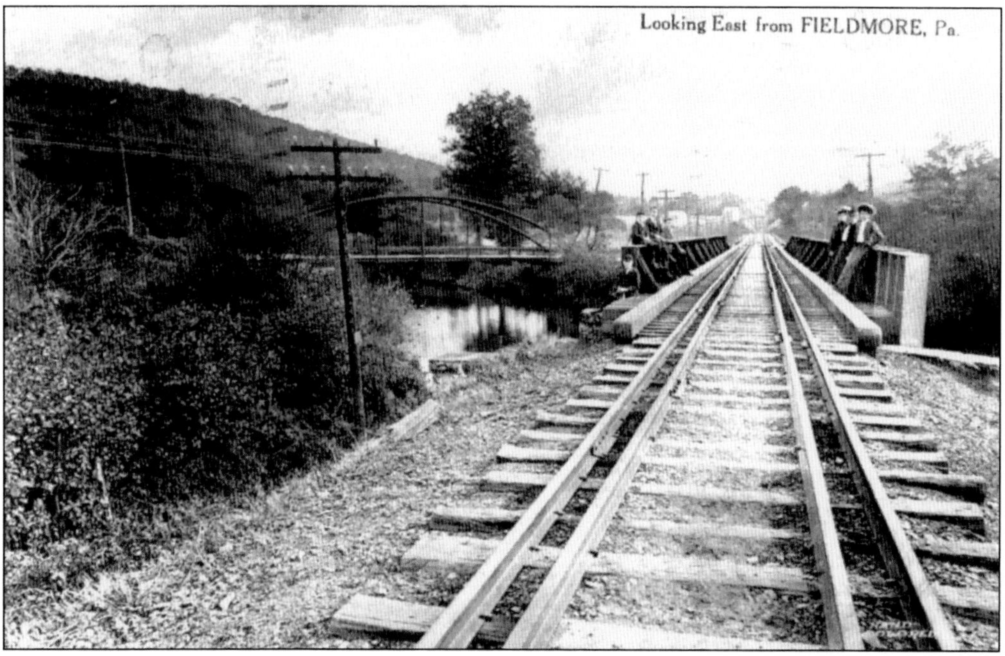

The New York Central Railroad (Dunkirk, Allegheny Valley, and Pittsburgh branch) first reached Titusville in 1872. This 1903 view, which looks east, shows the railroad bridge at East Titusville (also known as Fieldmore Station). (Courtesy of Kathryn Newson.)

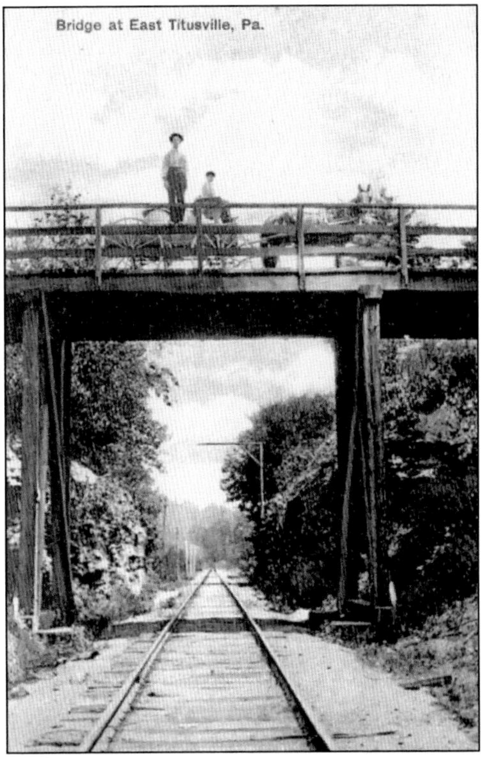

A wagon bridge crossed the New York Central tracks northeast of East Titusville. (Courtesy of Kathryn Newson.)

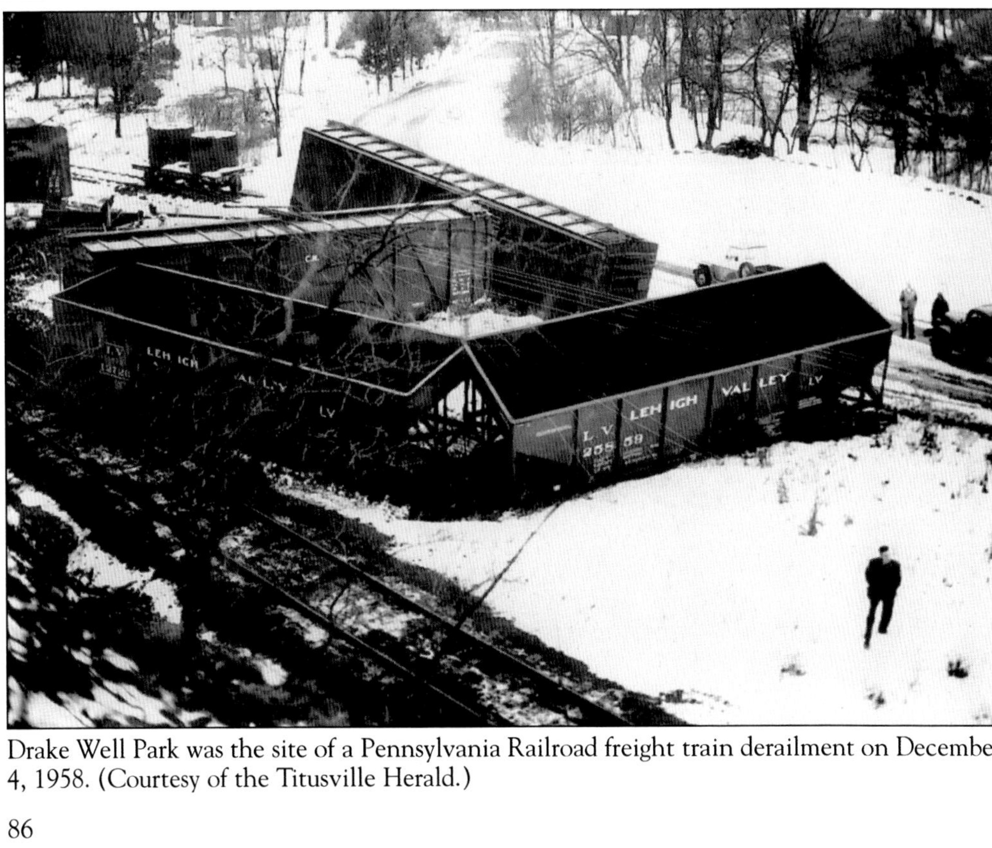

Drake Well Park was the site of a Pennsylvania Railroad freight train derailment on December 4, 1958. (Courtesy of the Titusville Herald.)

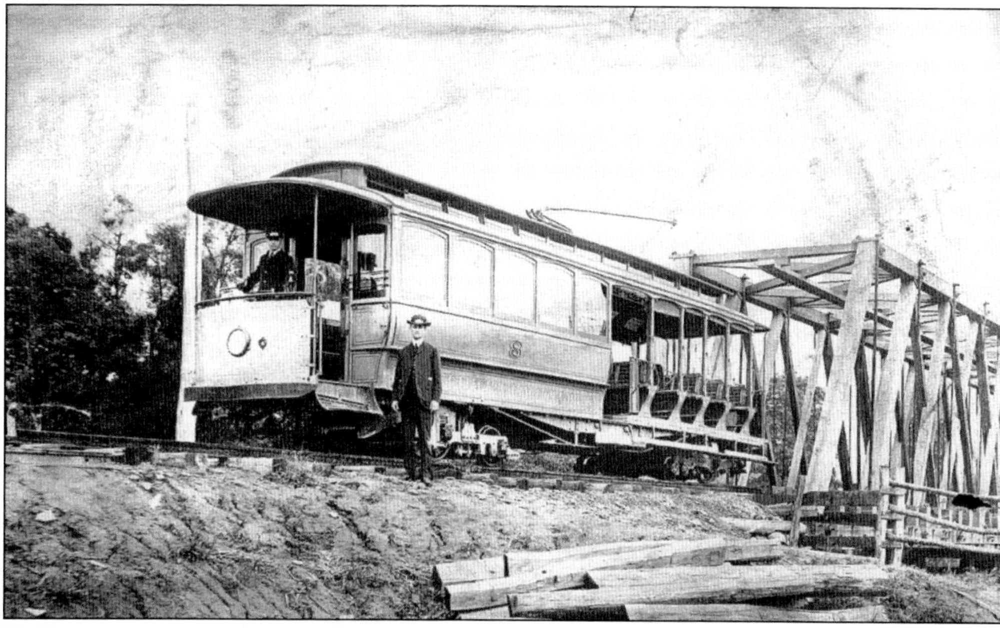

Trolley cars connected Titusville with Hydetown, Tryonville, and Pleasantville for 26 years. Titusville Electric Traction Company began operation in May 1898. This trolley car was photographed on a bridge near Hydetown sometime after 1901.

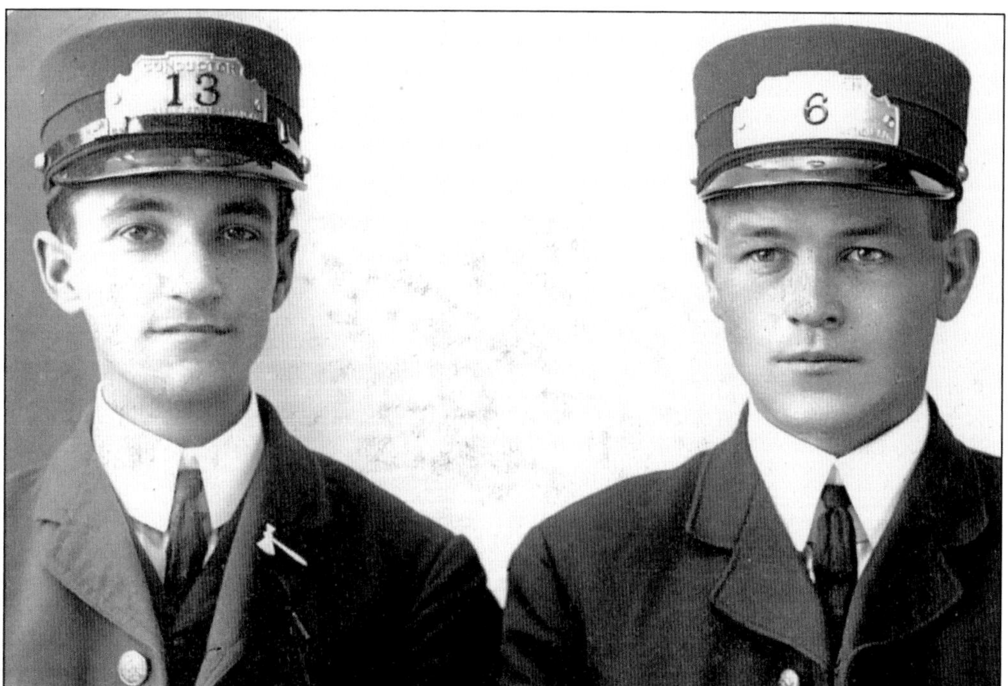

Clifford Jennings (left, a conductor) and John Mitcham (right, a motorman) were two Titusville Electric Traction Company employees. Jennings later worked for United Natural Gas Company. (Courtesy of Kathryn Newson.)

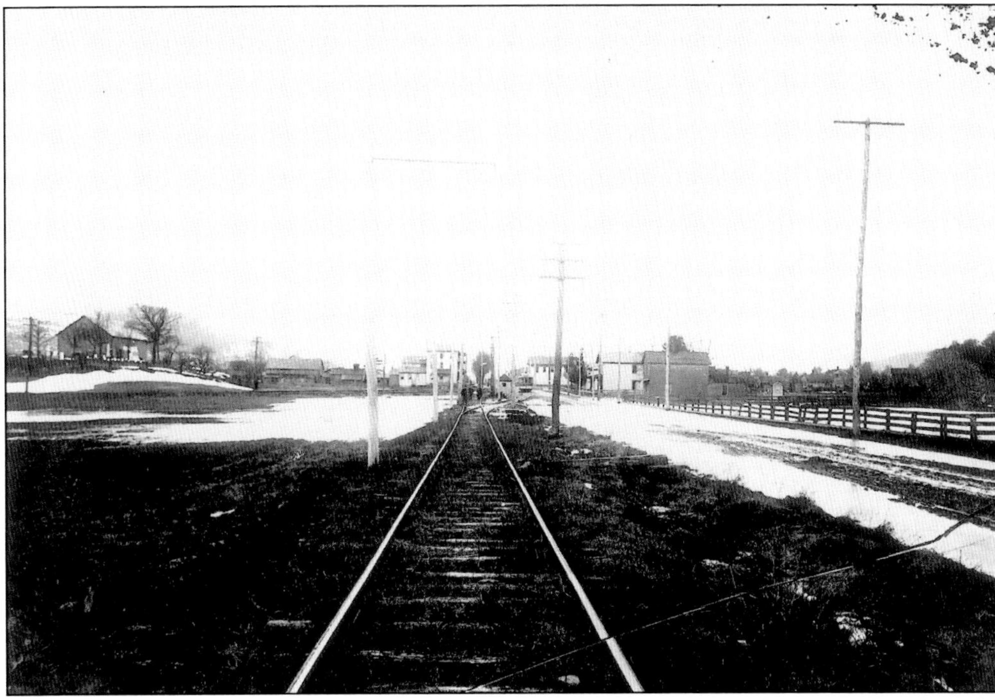

This Hydetown view shows where the trolley line crossed the Pennsylvania Railroad tracks. Passengers had to change the trolleys at this site because the railroad denied the streetcar line crossing rights. (Courtesy of the Drake Well Museum.)

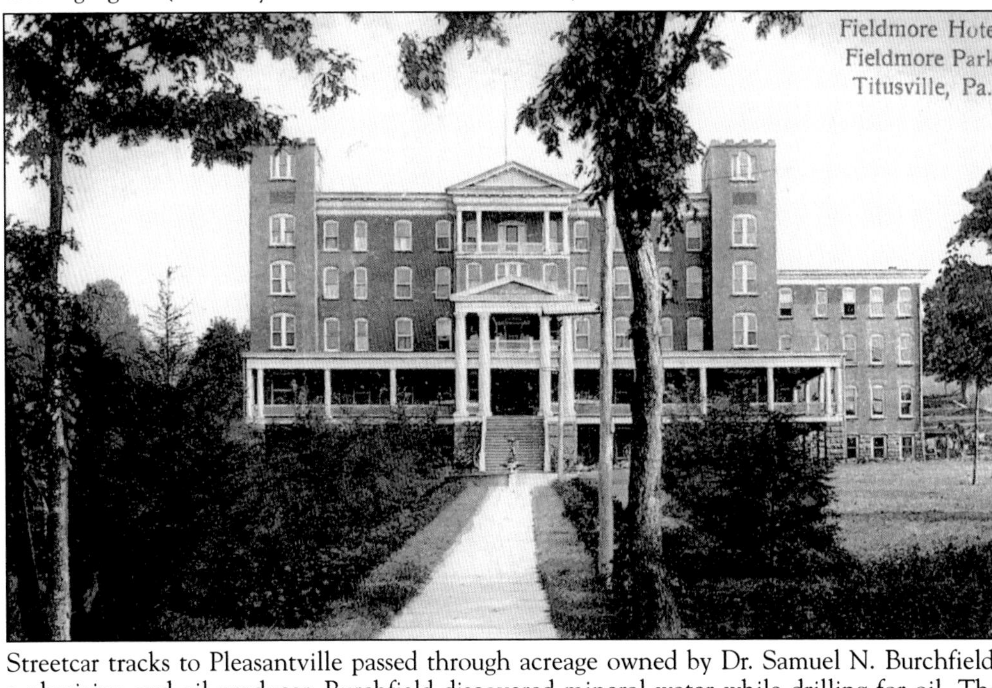

Streetcar tracks to Pleasantville passed through acreage owned by Dr. Samuel N. Burchfield, a physician and oil producer. Burchfield discovered mineral water while drilling for oil. The combination of mineral water and trolley service led to the construction of a hotel and resort, Fieldmore Springs Hotel and Fieldmore Park, in 1905–1907. (Courtesy of Kathryn Newson.)

Attractions on the grounds, in addition to the mineral springs, included picnic facilities, a refreshment stand, and a dance hall. Prohibition and the end of trolley car service doomed the hotel and resort. Dr. David Bashline purchased the five-story hotel and converted it into an osteopathic hospital and clinic in 1941. The 40-year-old landmark was destroyed by fire in January 1947. (Courtesy of Myrna Wescoat.)

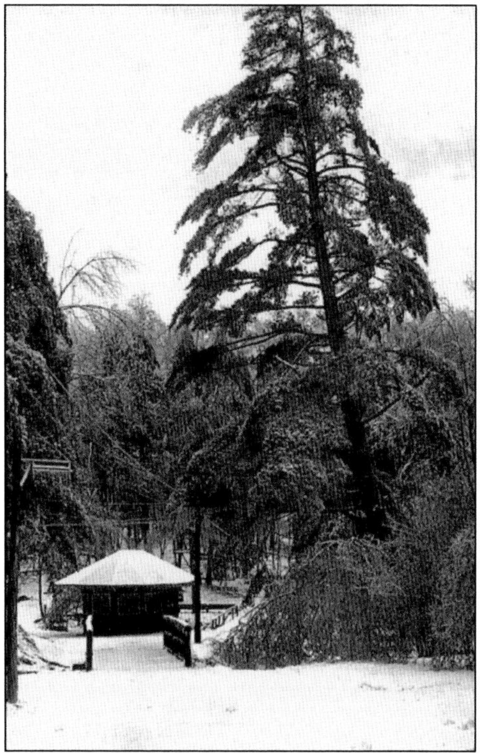

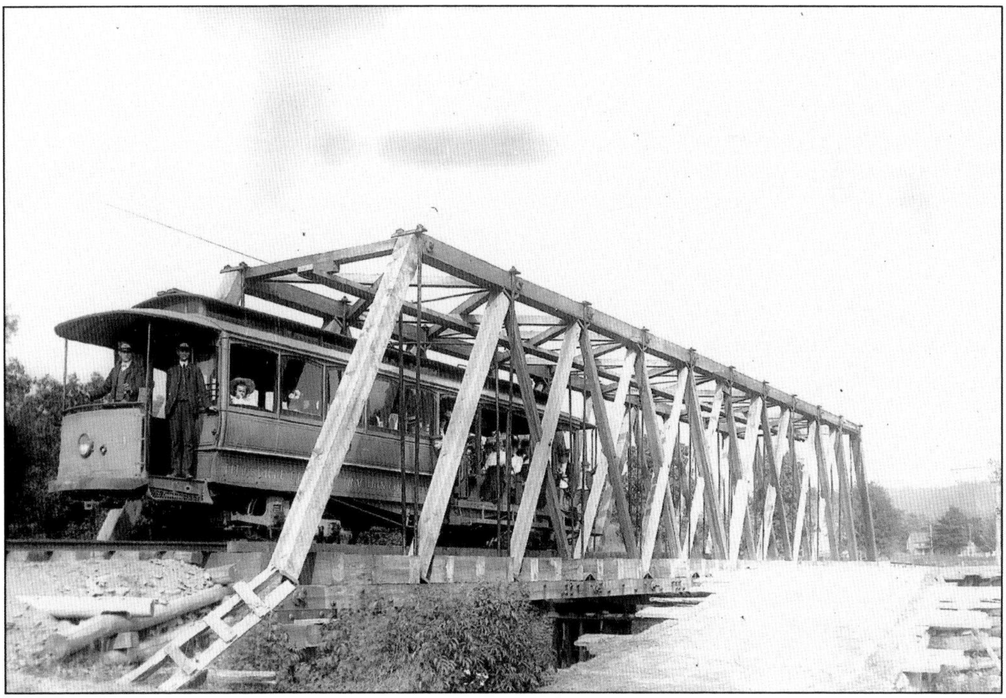

John Mitcham and Clifford Jennings are at the controls of streetcar No. 9 on the Hydetown Bridge. Passengers were returning from an outing at Mystic Park. (Courtesy of the Drake Well Museum.)

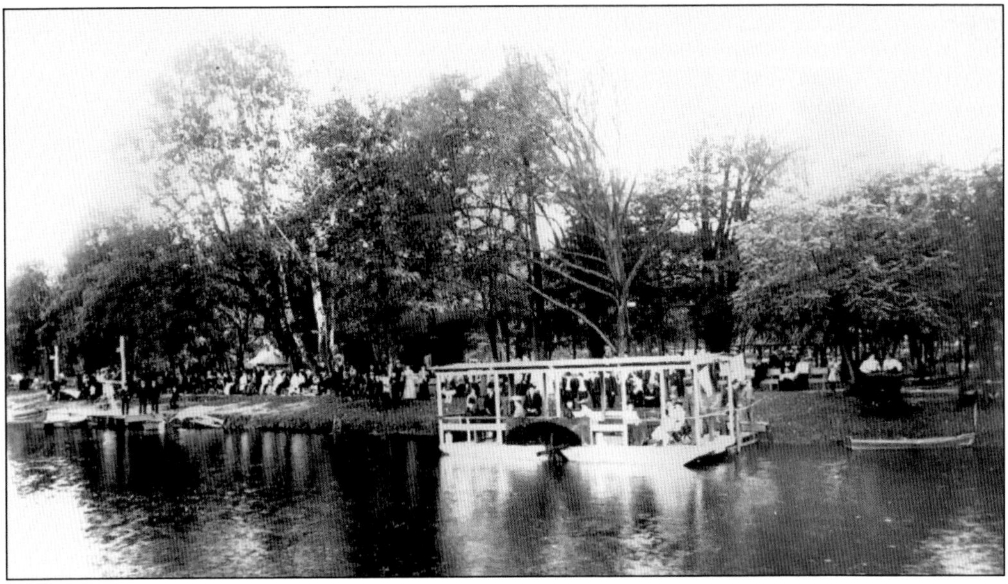

Mystic Park was opened by the Titusville Electric Traction Company nearly four miles above Hydetown in 1905. Facilities included a dance hall, refreshment stands, pleasure boats, and picnic tables. Several wealthy Titusville families owned summer cottages near the resort. Mystic Park remained in operation until 1920. (Courtesy of the Drake Well Museum.)

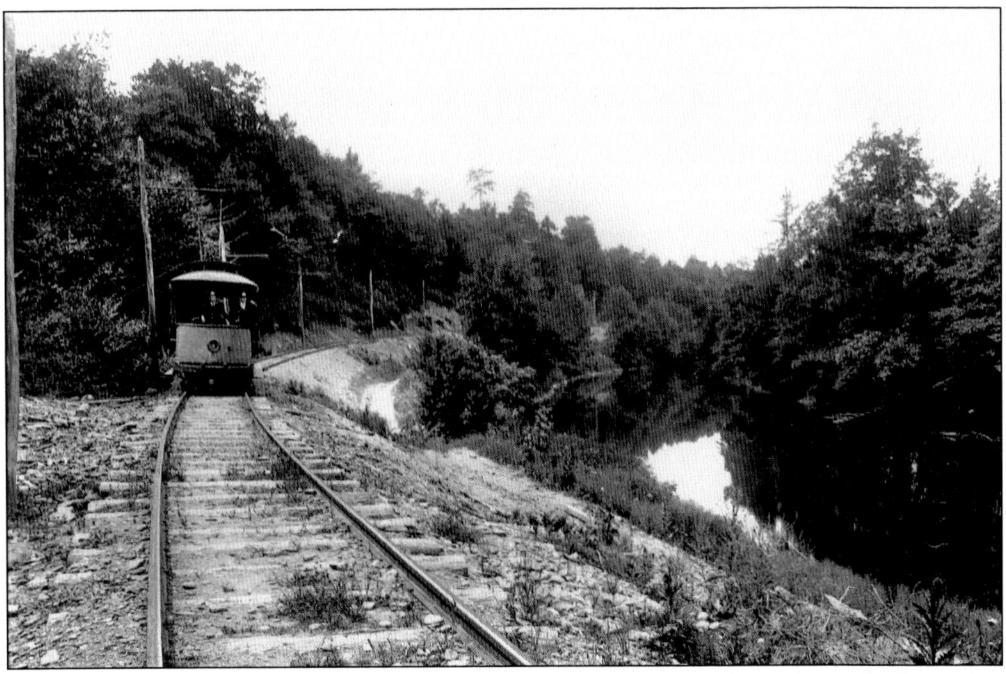

Seen is trolley No. 9 on the Hydetown, Mystic Park, and Tryonville line. The Caflisch Lumber Company used this section of trolley track for transporting logs to its Newtontown mill. This was the only location in Pennsylvania where a steam-powered logging railroad shared tracks with an electric trolley line. (Courtesy of the Drake Well Museum.)

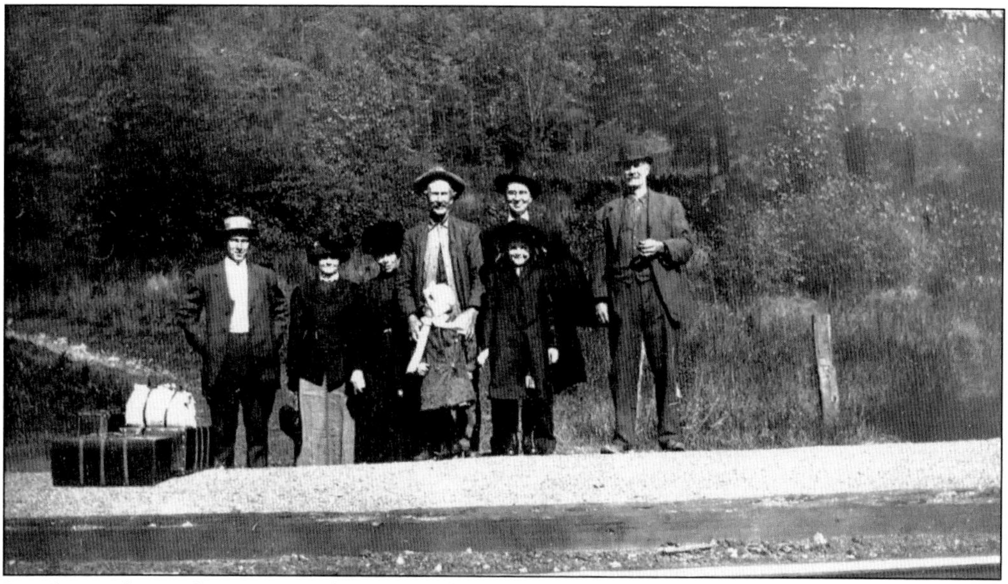

Residents of townships surrounding Titusville also used railroad flag stops. This 1910 group at the Miller Farm station of the Pennsylvania Railroad consists of, from left to right, Clyde Waddell, Jennie Hamilton, Margaret Gilson, William Hamilton, Ruth Gilson, Joe Hamilton, Florence Hamilton, and George Waddell. George Waddell (Clyde's father) was an uncle of Baseball Hall of Famer George "Rube" Waddell, who spent two of his childhood years in Titusville.

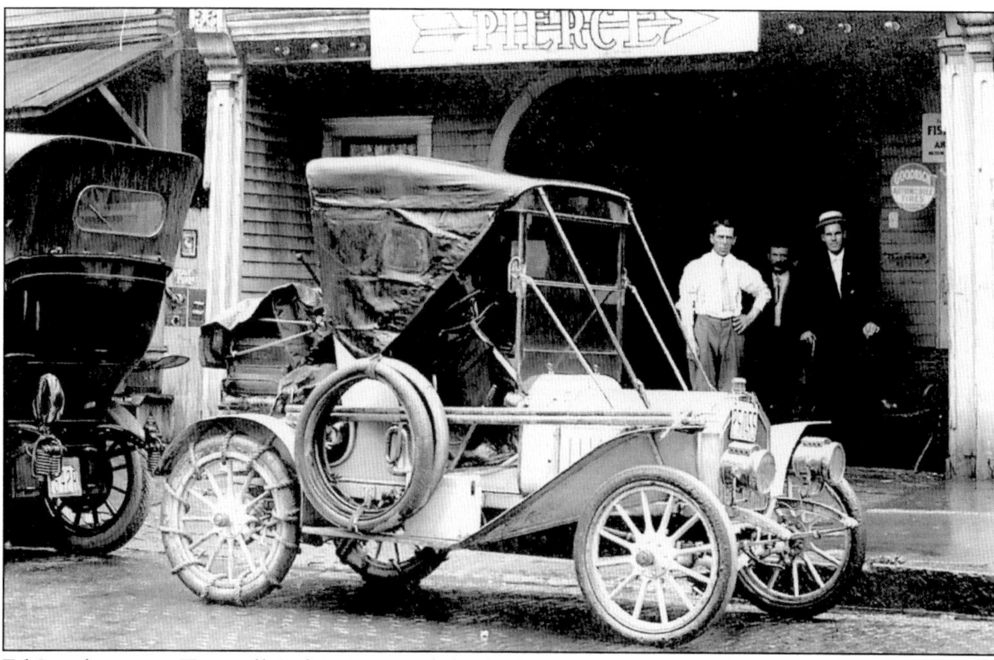

Ed Lambert was Titusville's first automobile dealer. This pre-1910 photograph shows a Pierce Arrow car in front of Lambert's North Franklin Street garage. He replaced the original structure with a two-story building that also contained lodge rooms used by the Elks and Moose clubs. (Courtesy of the Titusville Herald.)

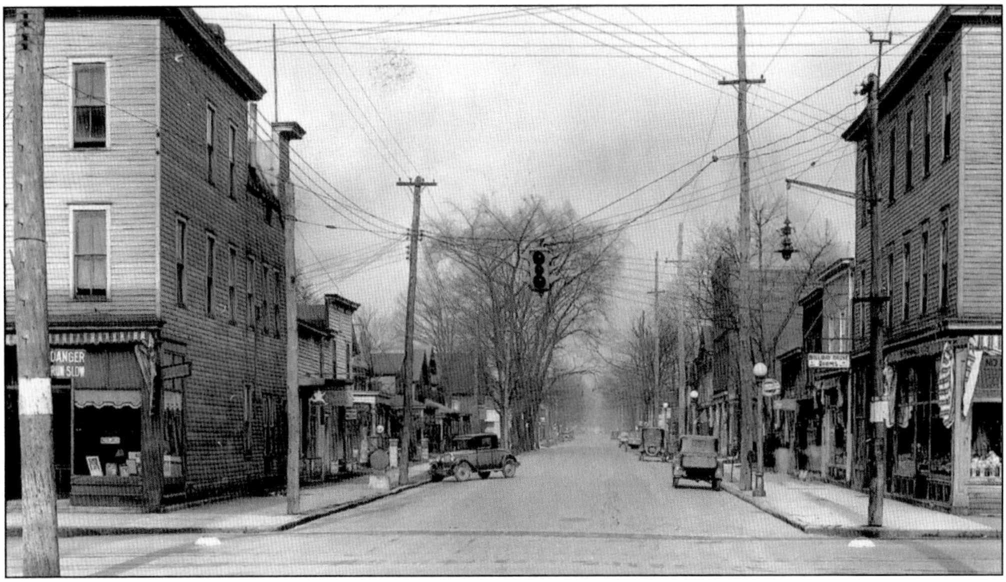

John Kurach's 1929 photograph of Washington Street and West Central Avenue is full of automotive-related businesses. On the left side of West Central Avenue is the Reliable Vulcanizing Shop. An automobile repair garage is on the opposite side of street. Note the traffic signal, Ford and Chevrolet cars, and street signs. Kurach's photography studio was in the building in front of the tire shop. All of the structures on the left were razed one year later. (Courtesy of the Titusville Herald.)

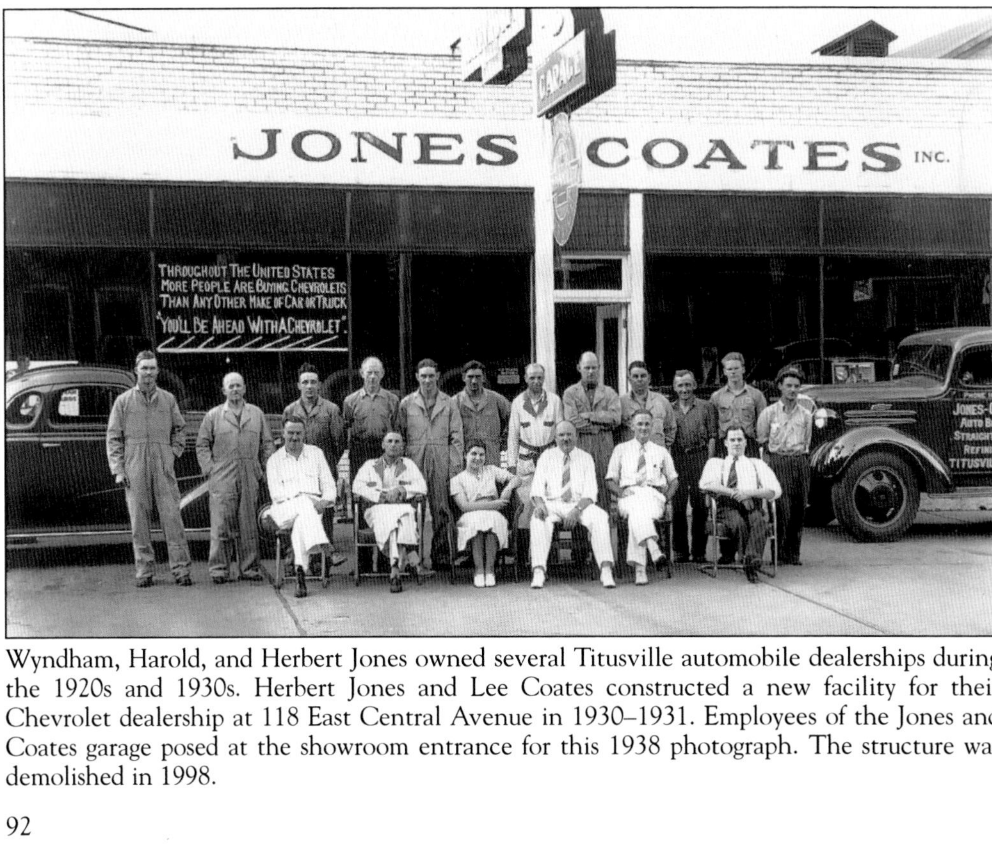

Wyndham, Harold, and Herbert Jones owned several Titusville automobile dealerships during the 1920s and 1930s. Herbert Jones and Lee Coates constructed a new facility for their Chevrolet dealership at 118 East Central Avenue in 1930–1931. Employees of the Jones and Coates garage posed at the showroom entrance for this 1938 photograph. The structure was demolished in 1998.

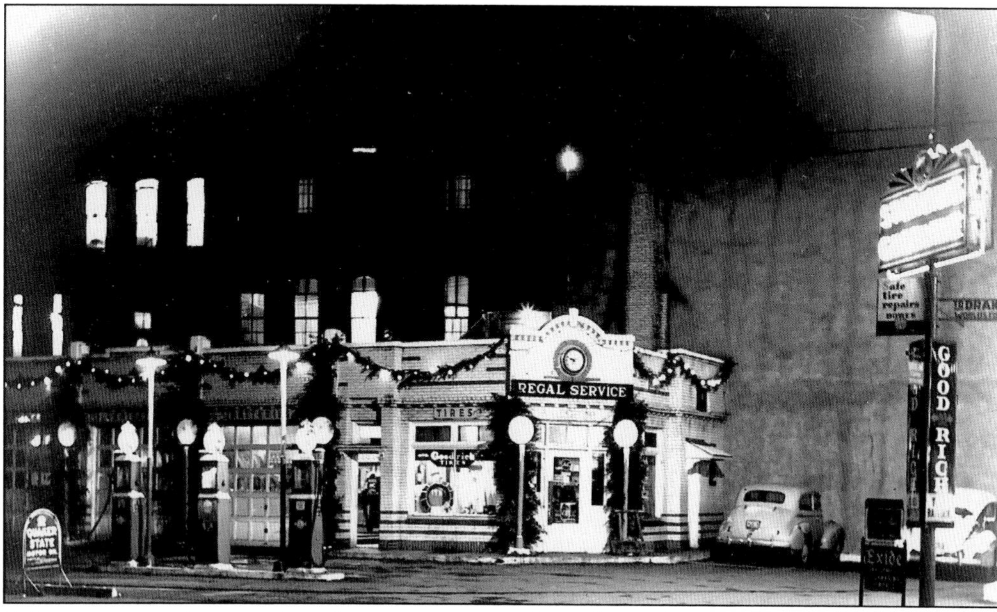

Full-service gasoline stations became popular throughout America after the 1920s. One example in Titusville was the Sterling and Quaker State gasoline station at the southeast corner of Franklin Street and East Central Avenue. Regal Service, owned by Arthur and Albert Reagle, is shown decorated for Christmas in this 1940 photograph. Lights can be seen in rooms occupied by clubs in background buildings. (Courtesy of the Drake Well Museum.)

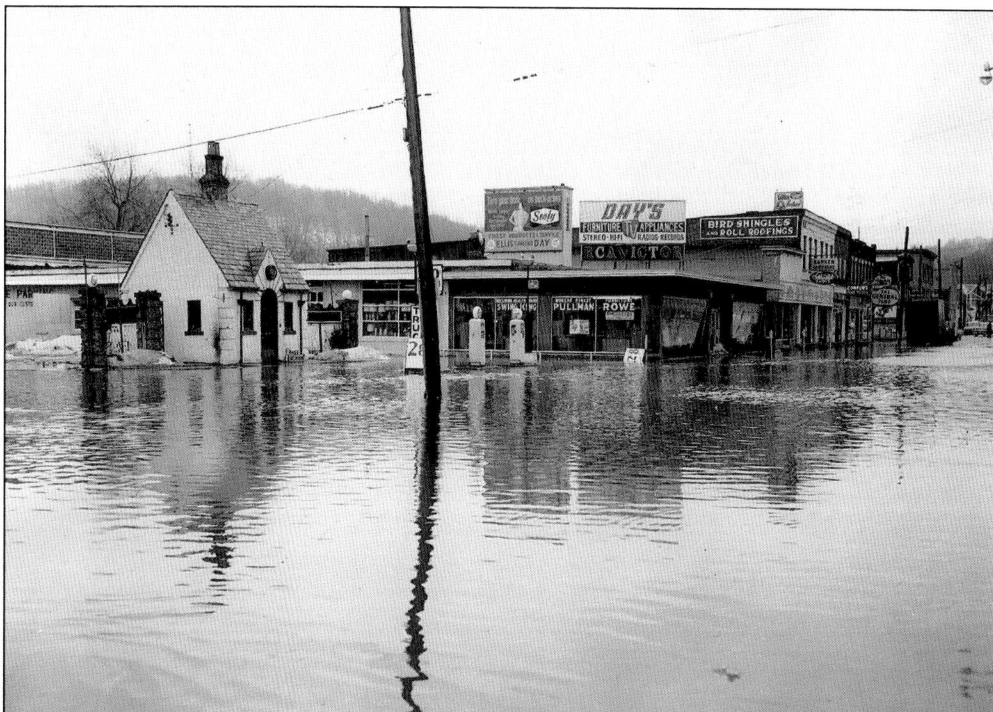

Floodwaters submerged the former Pennsylvania Refining Company gasoline station entrance on South Franklin Street on March 5, 1964. (Courtesy of the Titusville Herald.)

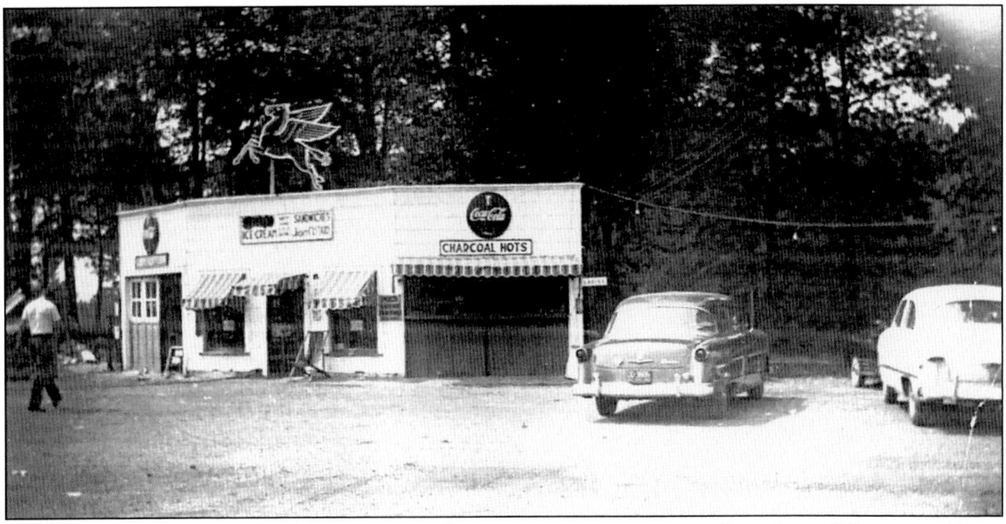

Vern Redfield opened a combination gasoline station–restaurant at the edge of Pleasantville in Oil Creek Township, Venango County, in 1937–1938. Bruce Meabon operated the landmark business, which dispensed Mobil gasoline, sandwiches, ice cream, and more during the 1950s and 1960s. It was destroyed by fire in 1979. (Courtesy of Colleen Weekley.)

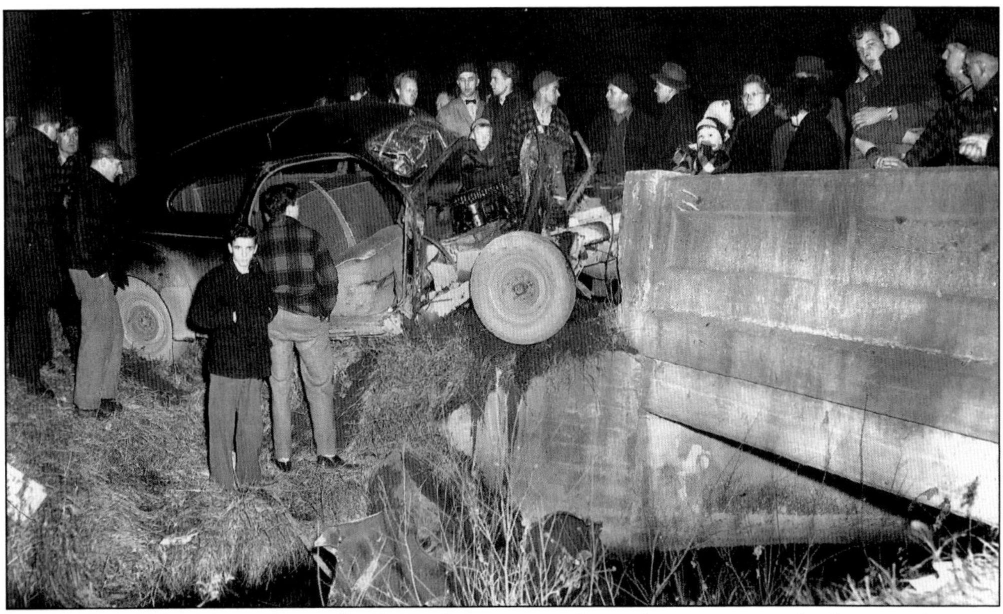

Highways leading into Titusville have been twisted winding routes, which caused many automobile accidents. Death Curve, at the Bates Run culvert in East Titusville, was one of the most dangerous stretches of highway. During the 1930s and 1940s, fatal accidents took place when speeding cars struck the culvert headwall. Serious wrecks have been nearly eliminated at Death Curve because the road has been widened and the structures blocking visibility have been razed.

Titusville's Oil Exchange building housed the post office from 1900 to 1917. The building appeared like this prior to 1908, when it was remodeled. Demolition of the 128 West Spring Street landmark occurred in 1956. (Courtesy of Kathryn Newson.)

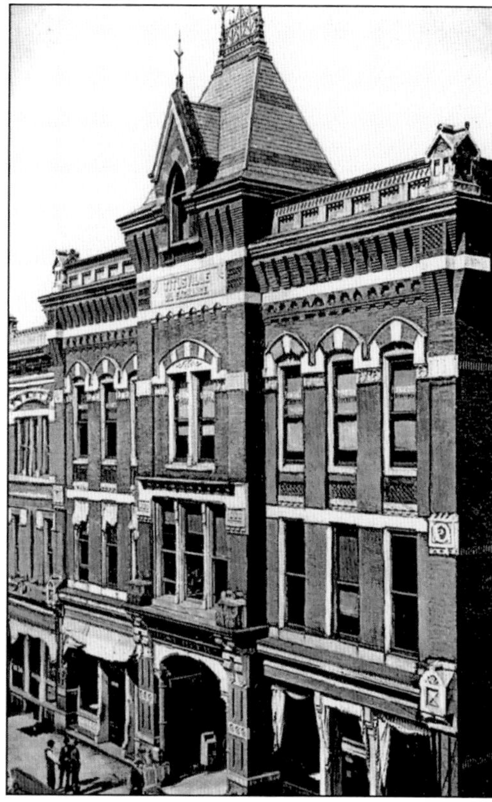

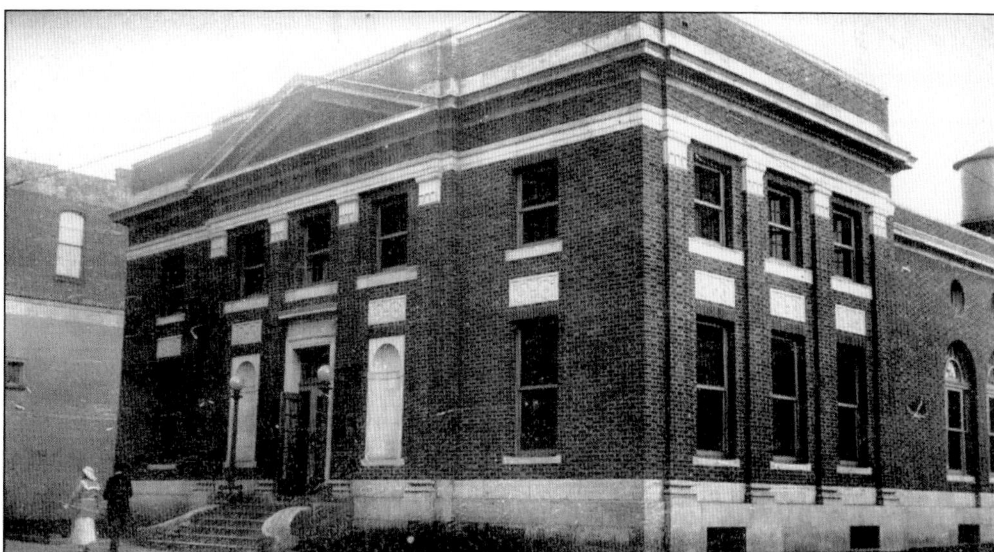

A new structure was erected at West Spring and South Washington Streets to house the Titusville post office in 1917. It remains in use today.

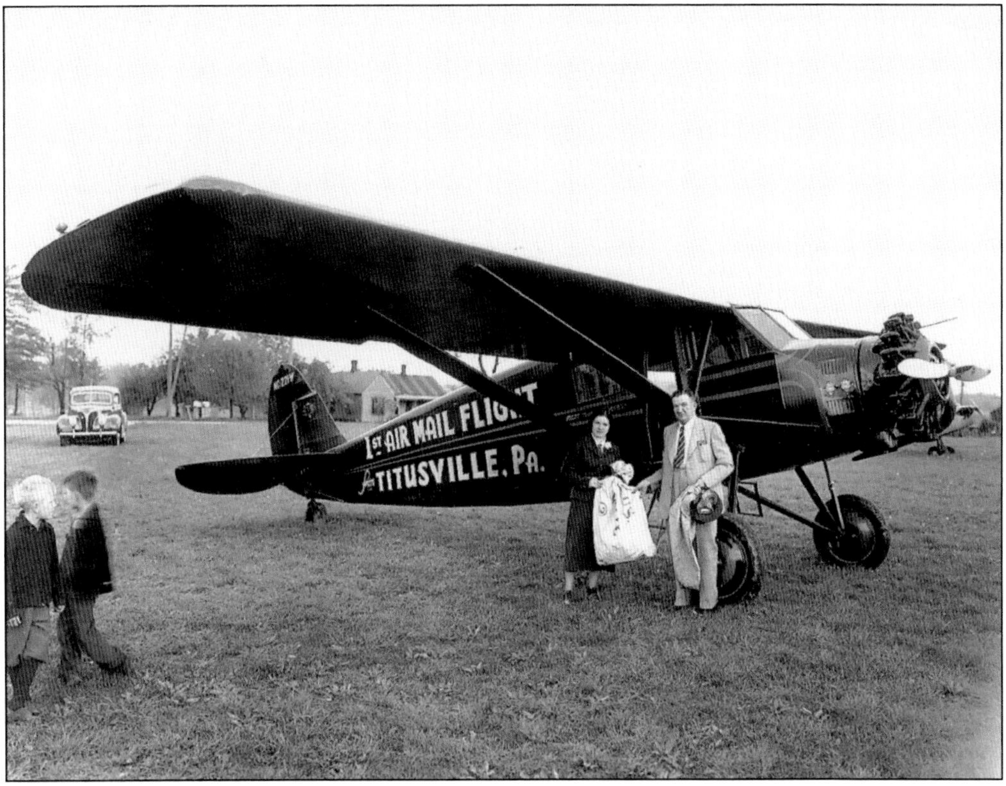

A special airmail flight was made from Titusville to Pittsburgh on May 20, 1938. Pilot Phyllis Burchfield (the daughter of Fieldmore Hotel owner Dr. S. N. Burchfield) received the mailbag from Ralph Seep, the Titusville postmaster. The Stinson airplane took off from Colonel Drake Airport in Cherrytree Township and landed in Pittsburgh 40 minutes later.

Covers were issued to commemorate Titusville's first airmail flight.

Throughout much of the *Titusville Herald*'s existence, only two families—the Bloss and Stevenson families—published the paper. Joseph M. Bloss (right), who published the *Titusville Herald* until 1922, is shown with his successor, Edgar T. Stevenson, at the entrance to the newspaper's South Franklin Street offices in June 1955. Both men died the following year. (Courtesy of the Titusville Herald.)

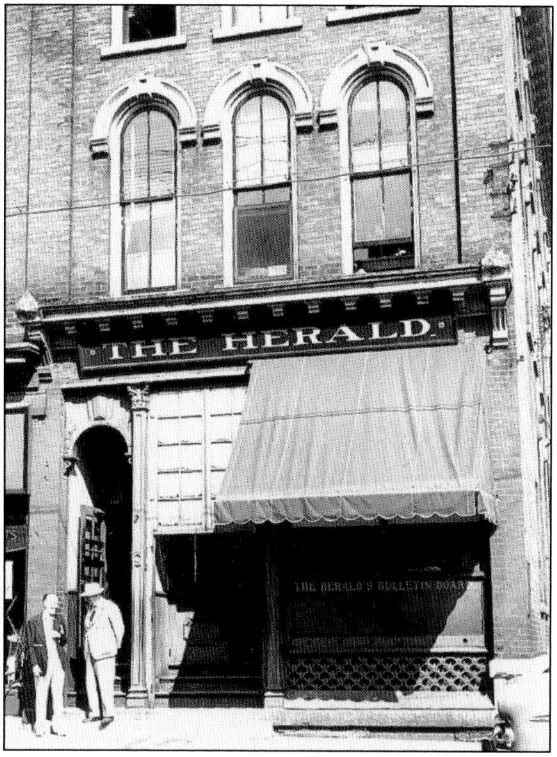

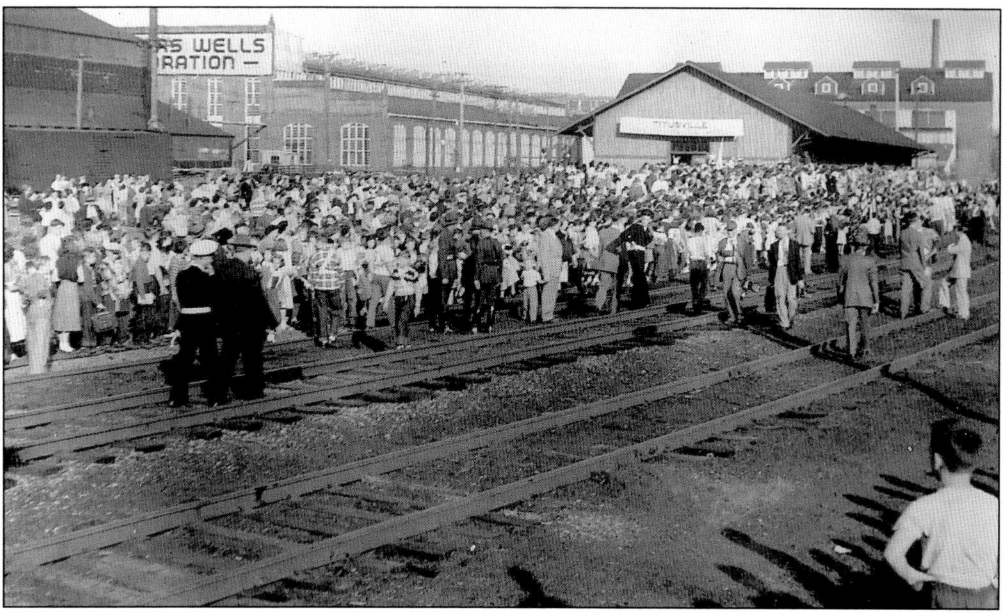

Titusville's business community annually observed Pennsylvania Week during the 1940s and 1950s. The 1950 Pennsylvania Week celebration included the arrival of a special train via the Pennsylvania Railroad. A large crowd of area residents can be seen gathered at the Pennsylvania Railroad freight station on South Perry Street. Notice state police troopers as well as military personnel in uniform. The Titusville Iron Works boiler shop building dominates the background. (Courtesy of the Titusville Herald.)

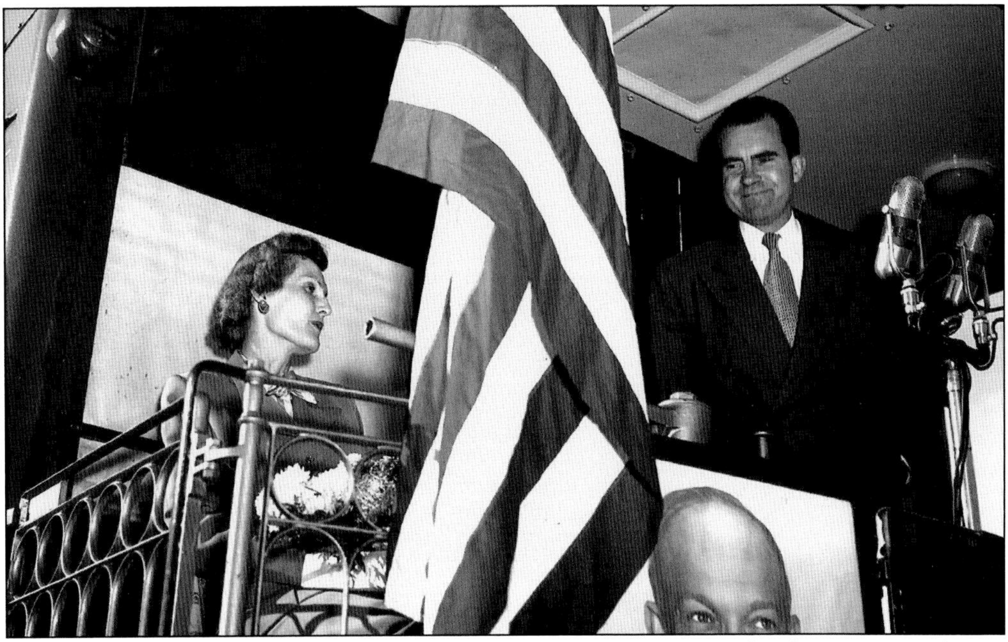

Whistle-stop political campaigns have become virtually extinct. Richard M. Nixon, then a U.S. senator, visited Titusville via the Pennsylvania Railroad while campaigning for the vice presidency in October 1952. His wife, Pat, is on the left. Less than one year later, passenger train service to Titusville faded into history. (Courtesy of the Titusville Herald.)

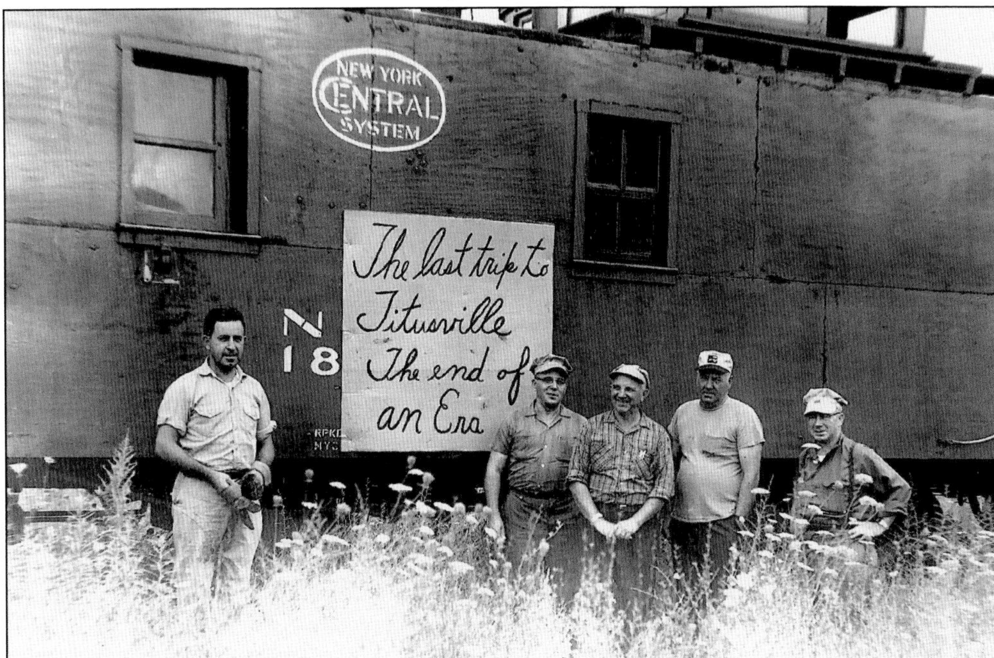

On August 19, 1967, the New York Central Railroad made its last freight run to Titusville. The train crew consisted of, from left to right, L. Muscarella, Howard Shope, C. W. Holcomb, Leonard Dugan, and O. M. Mear. (Courtesy of the Titusville Herald.)

Seven

SURROUNDING COMMUNITIES

Titusville's history has always been intertwined with that of its suburbs. Hydetown was founded by Peter Titus, the father of Titusville's progenitor, Jonathan Titus. Both settlements were originally centered around the lumber industry, as were the nearby hamlets of Enterprise (Warren County), Centerville (Crawford County), and Cherrytree.

Pleasantville, Titusville's largest suburb, was first settled between 1796 and 1821. Commercial development took place when land agent Aaron Benedict opened a blacksmith shop and the first of several stoneware potteries. Oil production commenced between 1865 and 1868. This northern Venango County borough once had the highest percentages of residents employed in the petroleum industry of any of the Titusville area settlements. It remains a thriving active town today.

Boughton, Meredith, Miller Farm, Shaffer, Shamburg, Atkinson (East Shamburg), Backus City, Tip Top (Wageforth City), and Red Hot were nearby oil boom communities that disappeared long ago. Grand Valley, a Warren County settlement founded around lumbering, agriculture, and oil production that was a borough until 1940, has largely met the same fate.

Other neighboring hamlets and boroughs—Townville, Diamond, Chapmanville, Tryonville, and Spartansburg—have owed their long existence to agriculture and lumber production.

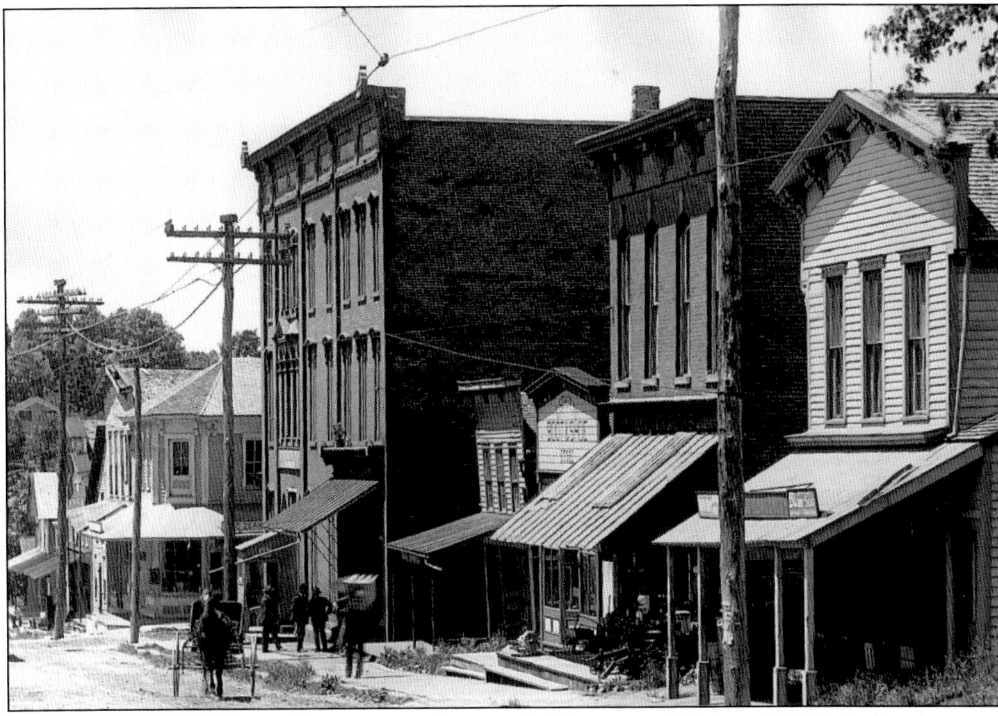

Pleasantville, in Venango County, was first settled between 1796 and 1821. It has been an incorporated borough since the 1840s. Pictured in this *c.* 1900 view is the State Street business district. The buildings seen here housed, from left to right, the Stoeltzing furniture store and funeral home, the H. C. Zeamer drugstore, the Eagle Hotel, the Corwin tin shop, the Schott boot and shoe store, the Corwin brothers' hardware store, and the George Bugbee grocery. (Courtesy of the Titusville Herald.)

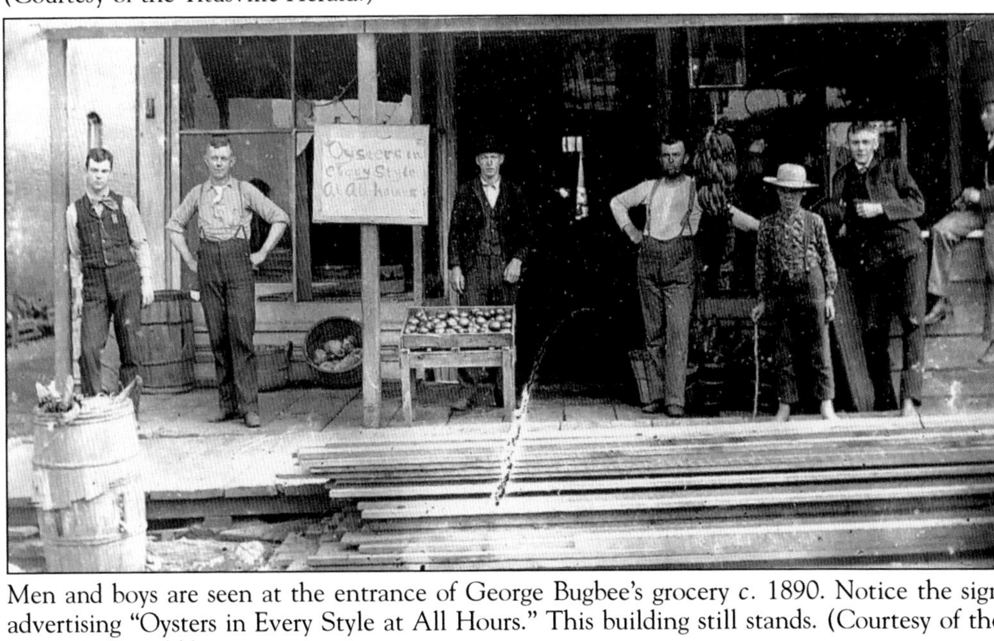

Men and boys are seen at the entrance of George Bugbee's grocery *c.* 1890. Notice the sign advertising "Oysters in Every Style at All Hours." This building still stands. (Courtesy of the Titusville Herald.)

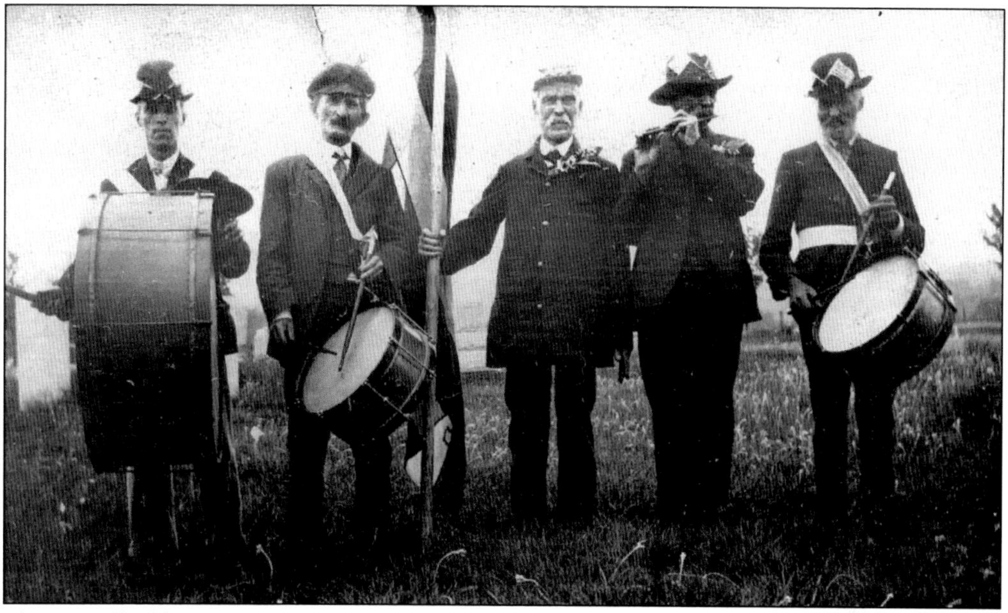

Pleasantville, like many other communities, had a Grand Army of the Republic post. Civil War veterans with fife and drums were photographed standing in Fairview Cemetery.

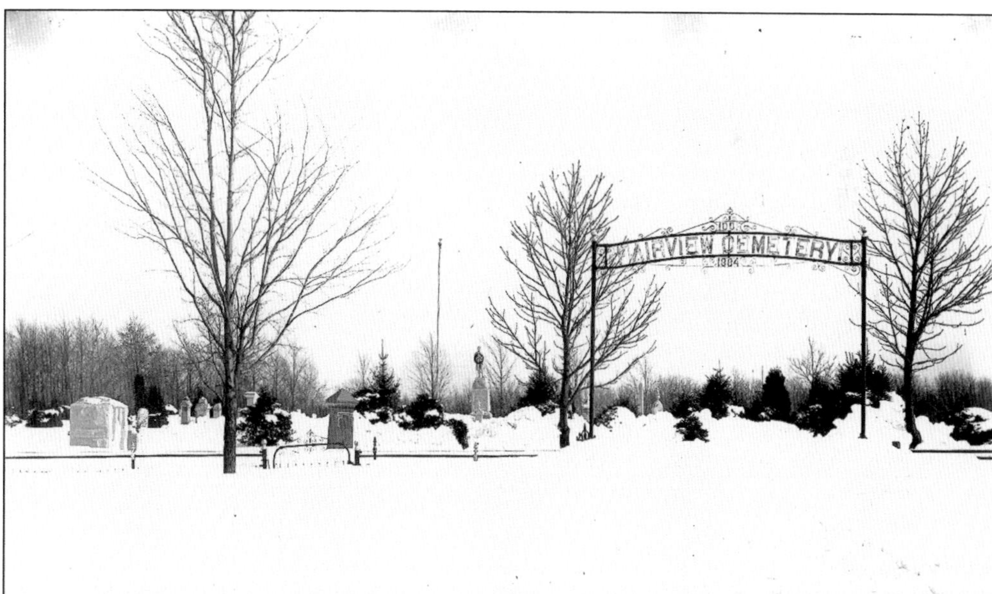

This is a winter photograph of Fairview Cemetery. The Pleasantville Independent Order of Odd Fellows lodge laid out the burial grounds in 1884. Burials have continued to the present day. The fence and gateway were removed many years ago. (Courtesy of the Titusville Herald.)

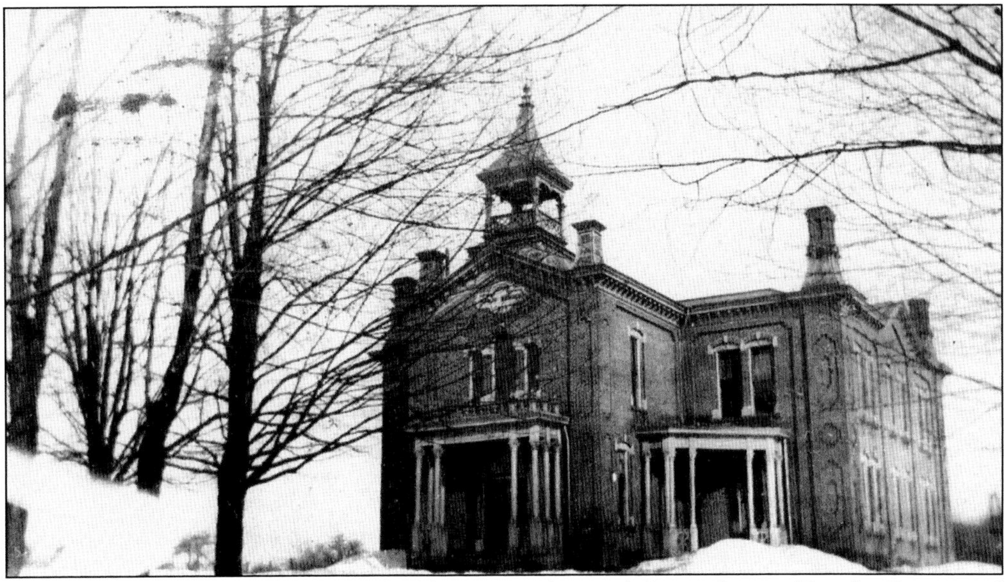

This Pleasantville public school building was designed by architect Enoch Curtis and constructed from locally made brick in 1873. The school bell was removed from the roof in 1955. High school classes were held in Pleasantville until 1969, when Pleasantville schools merged with Titusville Area Schools District. The badly deteriorated school building was demolished in 1977. (Courtesy of Kathryn Newson.)

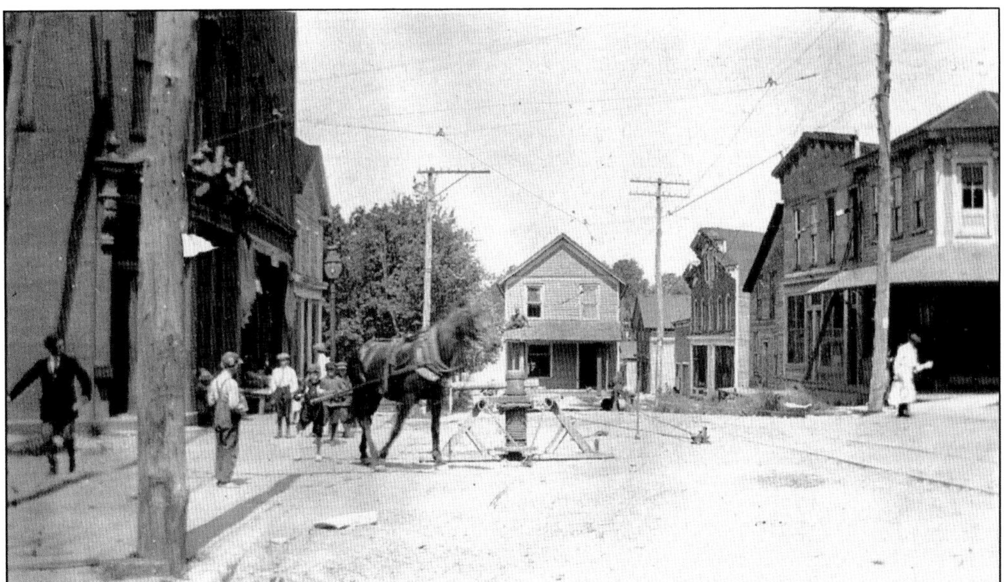

Seen is moving day on State Street in Pleasantville. Numerous homes have been moved from one location to another within the borough limits. Horses and a capstan-type device were used to change this structure's location. The date of this unusual photograph is unknown, but it was probably between 1900 and 1910. (Courtesy of Kathryn Newson.)

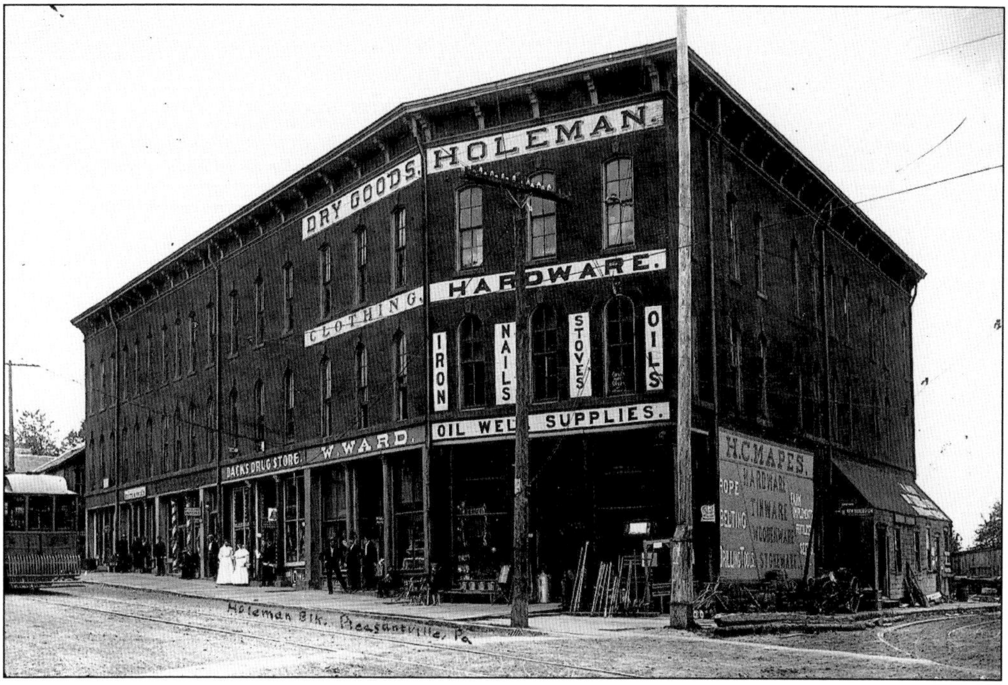

Ashbel Holeman constructed a three-story brick block at the southeast corner of Main and State Streets to replace structures destroyed in a December 1871 fire. The Holeman Block contained an opera house, offices, and several storefronts. Occupants of the building when this 1906 photograph was taken included the H. C. Mapes hardware store, Wiley Ward dry goods, Dack's drugstore, and Samuel Chestnut boots and shoes. A streetcar can be seen on the tracks at the far left. The Harrison C. Mapes lumberyard and planing mill is at the far right. This venerable landmark was destroyed by fire on December 24, 1992.

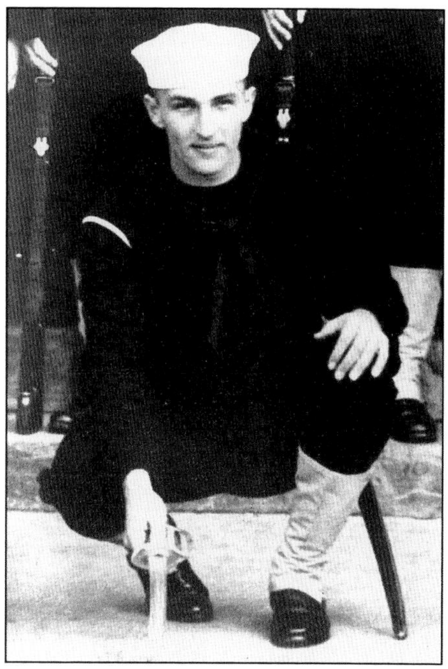

Robert W. Clark Jr. was a resident of Oil Creek Township, Venango County, and a Pleasantville High School graduate. He joined the U.S. Navy in 1940. Clark was killed on board the battleship USS *Arizona* at Pearl Harbor on December 7, 1941, at age 24. He was the first vicinity World War II casualty.

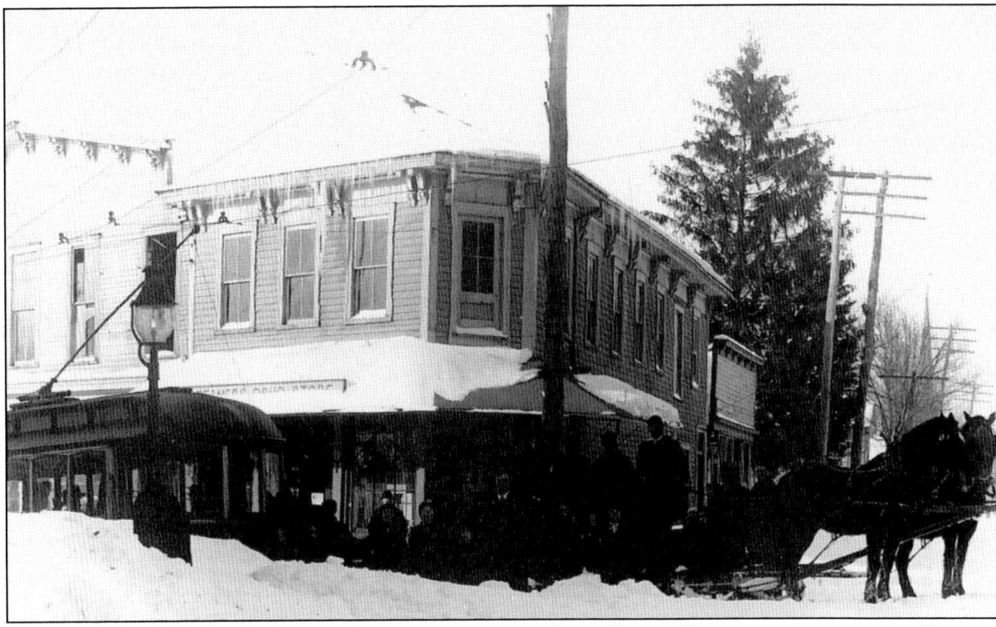

Two modes of transportation, a horse-drawn sleigh and a trolley car, are seen in front of Zeamer's drugstore in Pleasantville. Rooker's Restaurant occupied this landmark structure during the 1930s and 1940s. It was torn down in 1954.

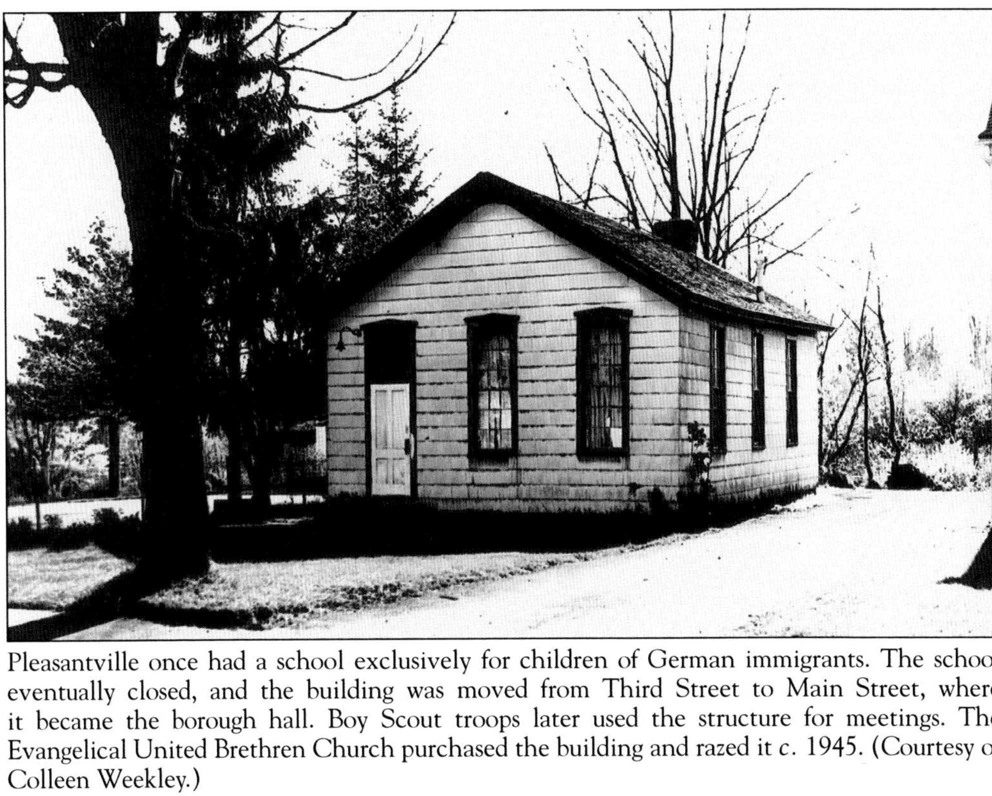

Pleasantville once had a school exclusively for children of German immigrants. The school eventually closed, and the building was moved from Third Street to Main Street, where it became the borough hall. Boy Scout troops later used the structure for meetings. The Evangelical United Brethren Church purchased the building and razed it *c.* 1945. (Courtesy of Colleen Weekley.)

The Methodist church in this photograph was erected in 1870. It replaced an earlier 1846 house of worship. Demolition of this second wooden church took place in 1923. A brick building that is still used by the congregation was subsequently erected on the same site, at the intersection of Main and Merrick Streets.

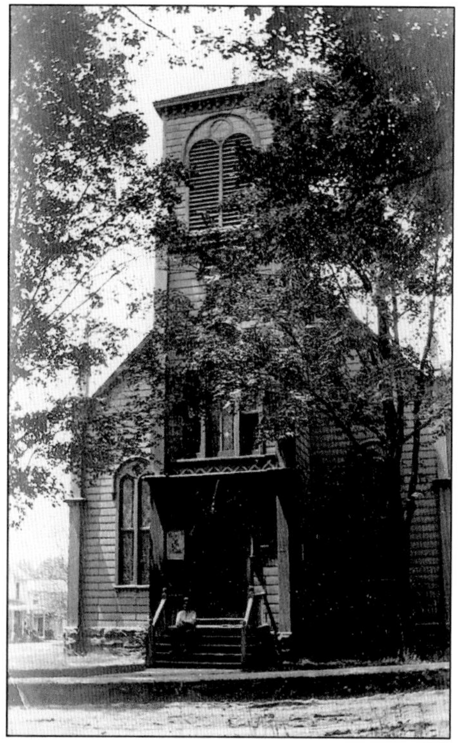

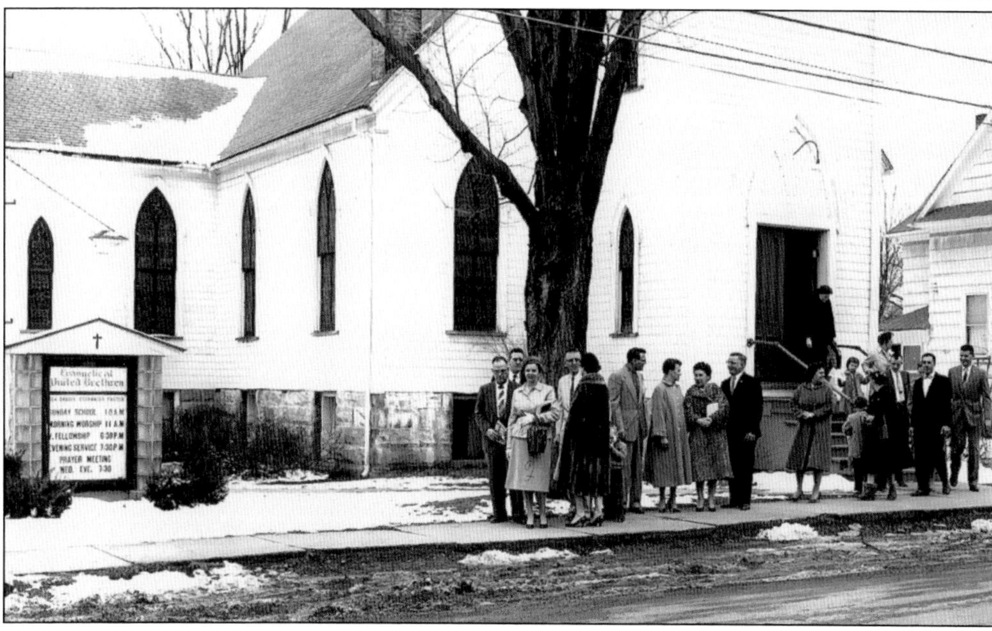

The Evangelical United Brethren Church occupied this North Main Street building from 1885 until 1973. Some of the people leaving the church building in this *c.* 1960 photograph are Carl and Margaret Johnson, Frank and Geraldine Valone, Mildred Dean, Ardell Dean, Byron Carson, and Wayne Cubbon. The congregation eventually merged with the Methodists, and the building was sold. An independent Baptist group owns the church structure today. (Courtesy of Colleen Weekley.)

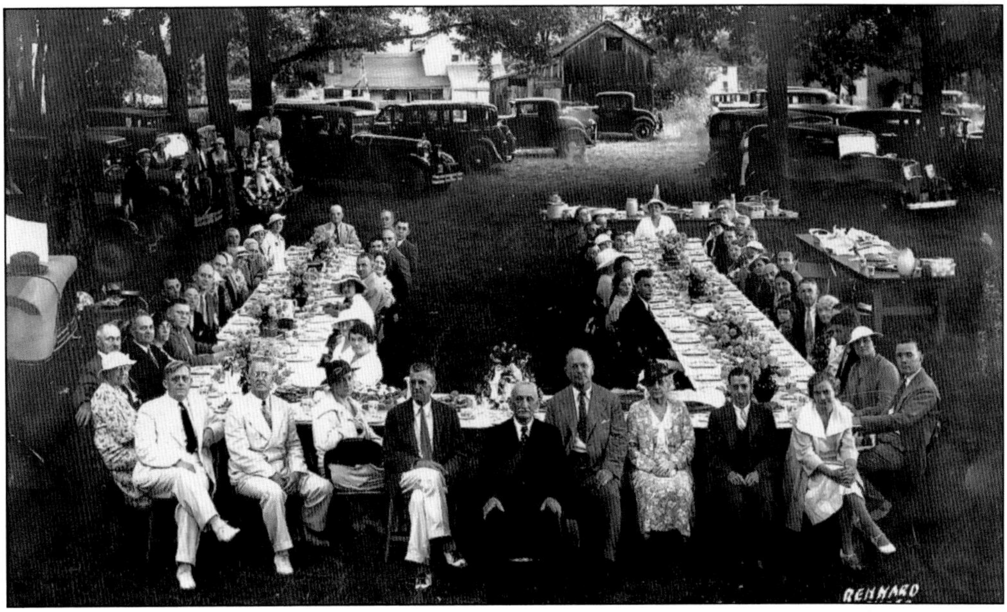

Town physicians were once revered father figures in many communities. Dr. Walter J. Proper practiced medicine in Pleasantville for half a century. He was honored at a Pleasantville merchants' picnic on August 31, 1935. Proper is seated in the center of the front row. Other area physicians seated near the front are Dr. Carl Hazen of Titusville and Dr. Ronald Redfield. (Courtesy of Thomas and Jean Beason.)

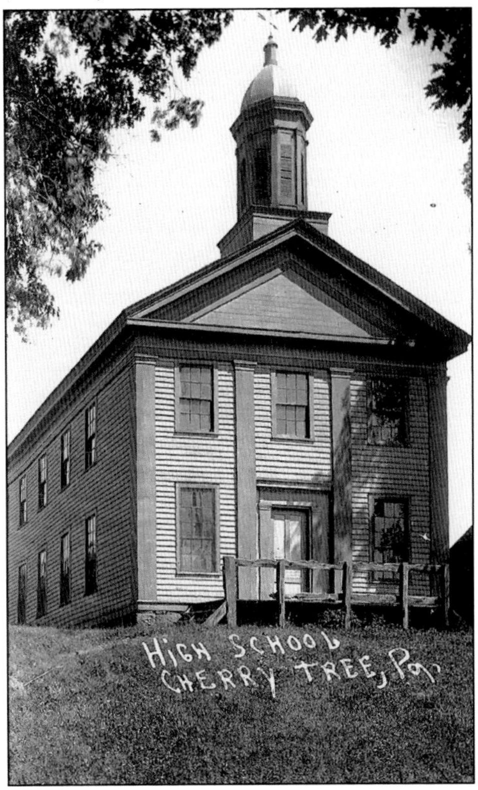

Cherrytree, Venango County, once had an academy. The four-room school building was constructed in 1854. High school classes were later discontinued, but elementary students used the landmark school building into the 1950s. (Courtesy of the Titusville Herald.)

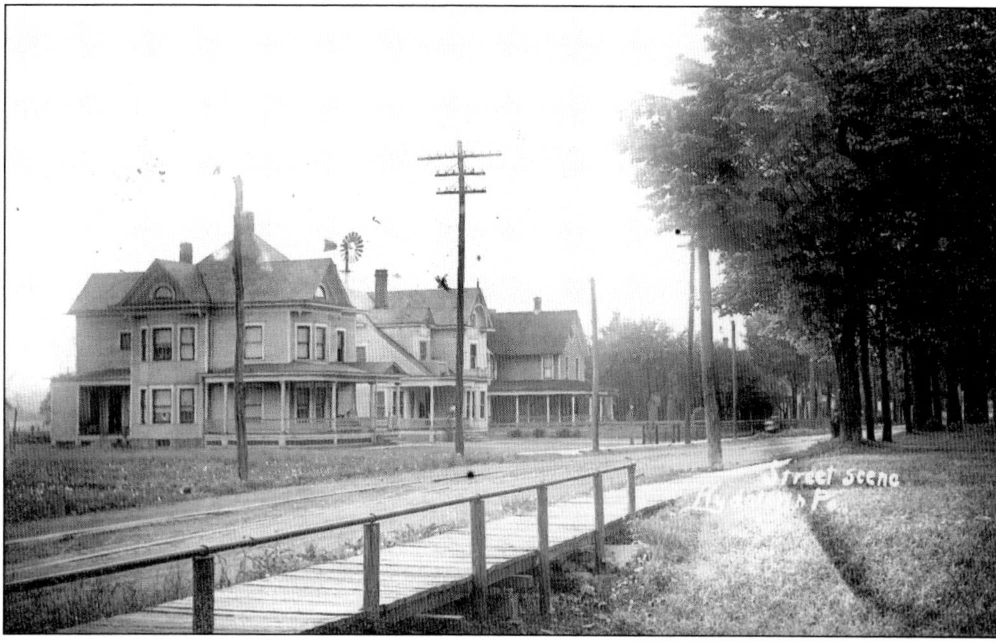

Hydetown, Crawford County, was originally named Oil Creek. This *c.* 1900 view shows Main Street with sidewalks and trolley tracks. A windmill can be seen behind the three homes on the left. (Courtesy of Kathryn Newson.)

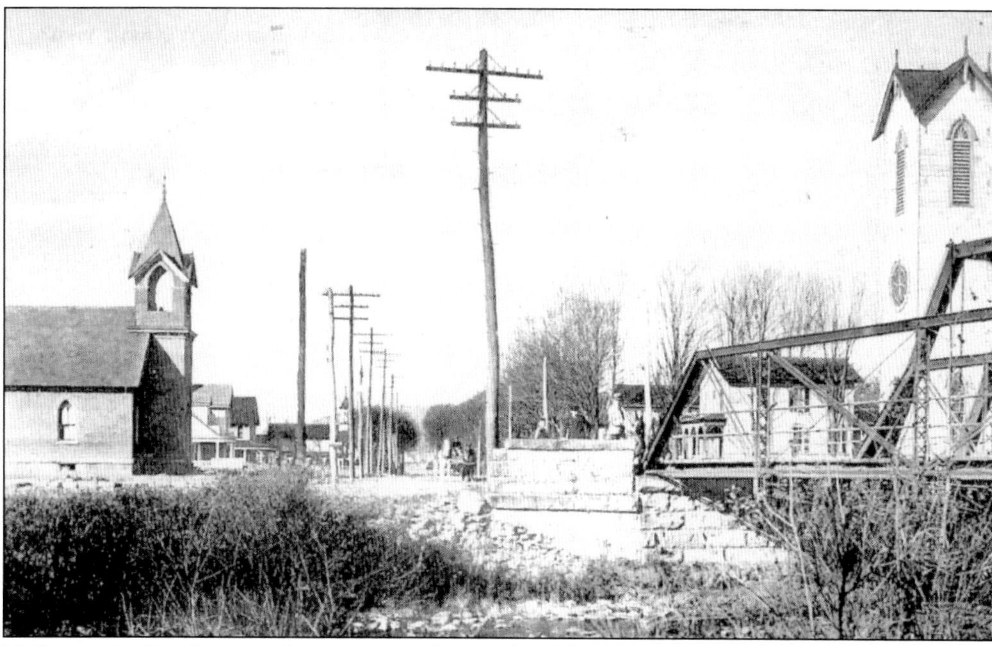

Hydetown's churches are shown in another early-20th-century scene. The brick structure on the left is the Baptist church that was completed in 1908. Near the center of the photograph is the Methodist church, erected in 1886. The building on the right was the Union Church, constructed by Samuel Ridgway in 1890. Methodist and Baptist buildings remain active as churches today. The Ridgway Union Church was torn down and rebuilt in Union City in 1945. (Courtesy of Kathryn Newson.)

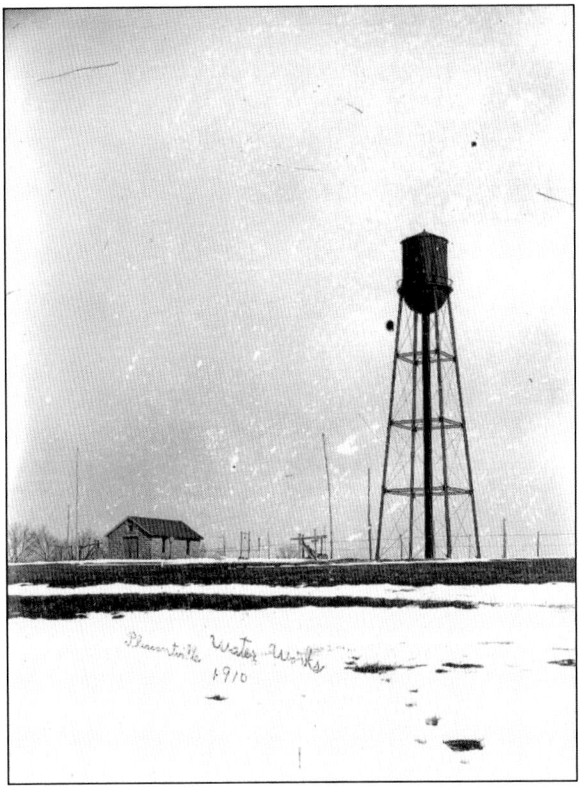

Pleasantville's waterworks was constructed in 1909–1910. This 1910 view shows the central powerhouse, which operated several water wells and the adjacent standpipe, or water tower. Wells were abandoned in the 1960s, but the water tower remains in use. (Courtesy of the Titusville Herald.)

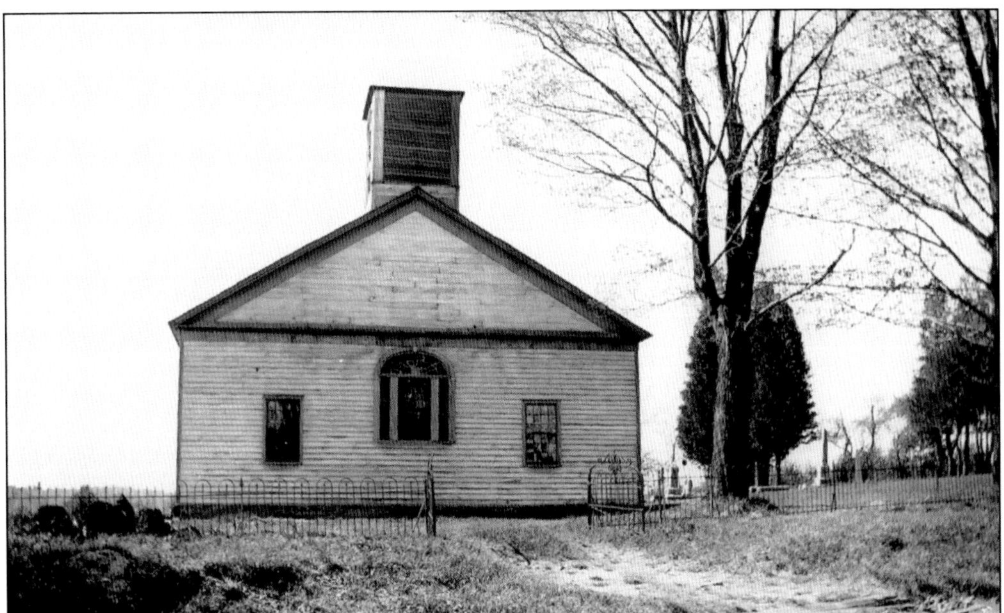

Cherrytree Presbyterian Church was constructed in 1837. The cemetery on the right contains graves that predate the church building. Although considered to be the oldest church building in Venango County, the structure is now vacant. (Courtesy of the Drake Well Museum.)

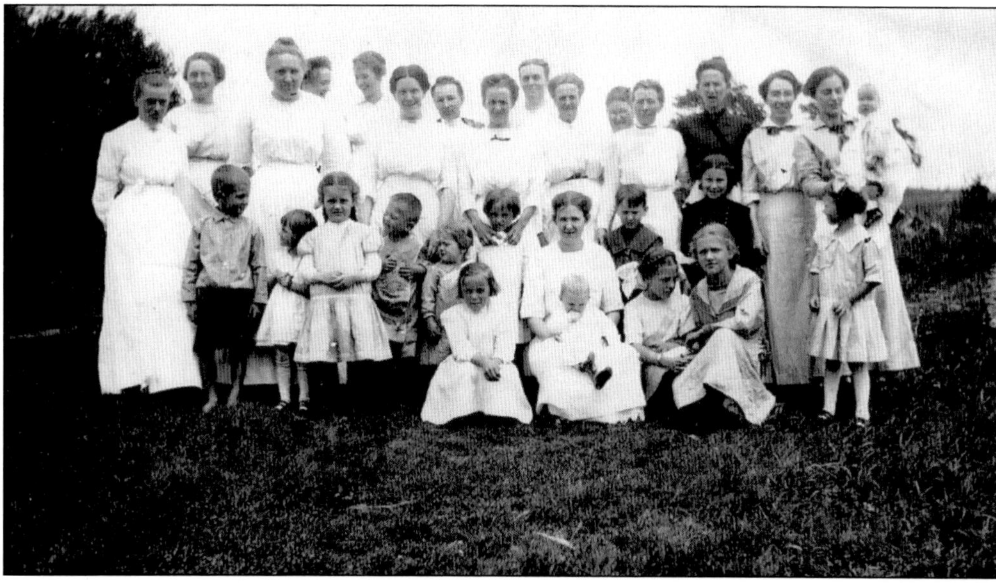

In Jamison Corners, Cherrytree Township, was a church with a ladies' aid society in 1912. Some of the women and children pictured here are Renna Sims, Mary Armagost, Edna Armagost Warner, Anna Kirkwood Owens, Roxie Seley, Julia Warner Strawbridge, Geneva Sheve, Addie Sheve Armagost, Margaret Murry Marsh, Lura Strawbridge Newson, Margaret Seley, Glenn Newson, Gladys Sheve, and Genevieve Armagost. (Courtesy of Kathryn Newson.)

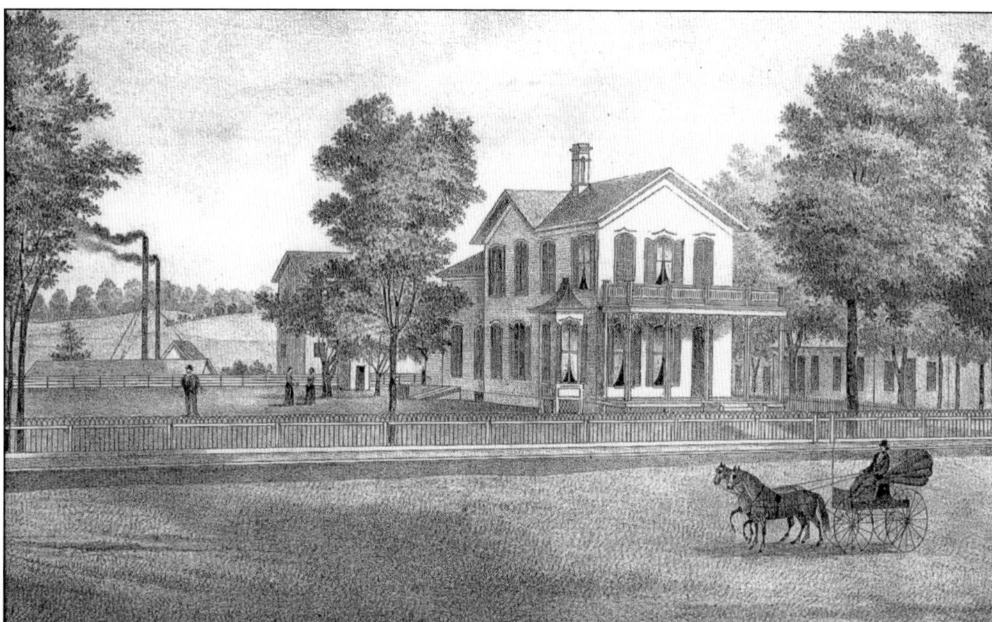

Townville, in the southwest corner of Steuben Township, Crawford County, was named for early lumberman Noah Town. Its incorporation as a borough took place in 1867. Pictured here is the home of carriage maker and merchant Charles Delamater. (From *Atlas of Crawford County*.)

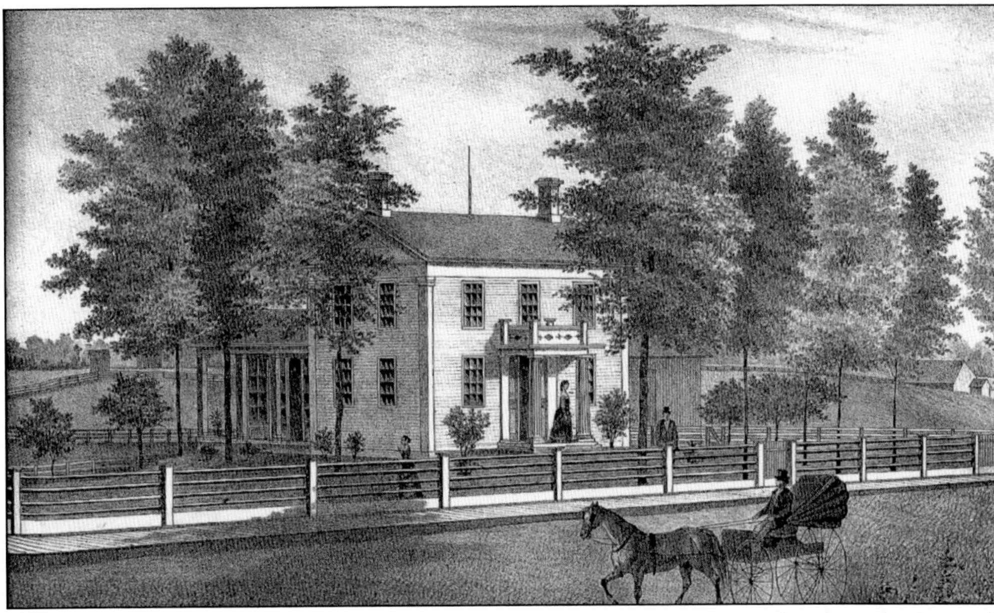

Almon Heath, who resided in this early-19th-century dwelling, farmed within the borough limits. (From *Atlas of Crawford County*.)

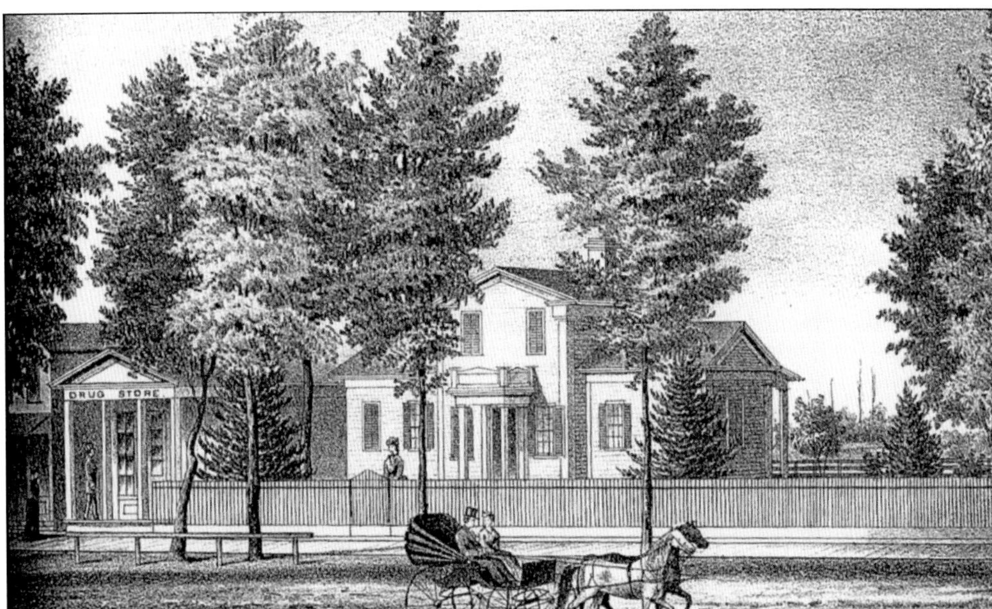

Dr. William Nason was Townville's physician and druggist in 1876. Many small-town doctors also operated drugstores during the 19th century. (From *Atlas of Crawford County*.)

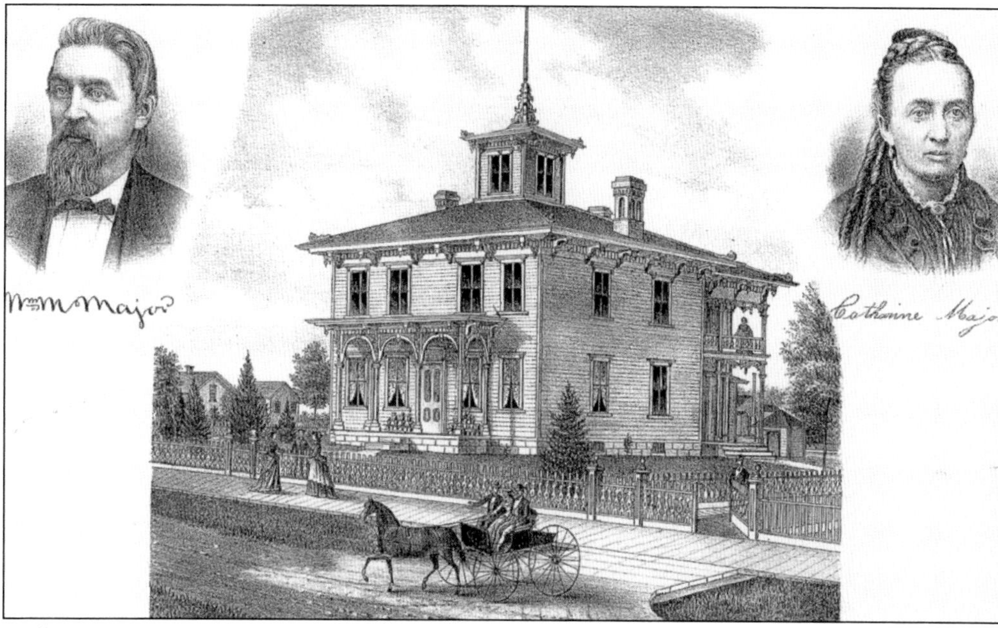

William Major's surname was an indication of his stature in Spartansburg, Crawford County. Major's sawmill and planing mill businesses enabled him to reside in this elaborate house. Italianate-style homes were often embellished with fancy woodwork, which made this a fitting residence for a successful lumberman. (From *Atlas of Crawford County*.)

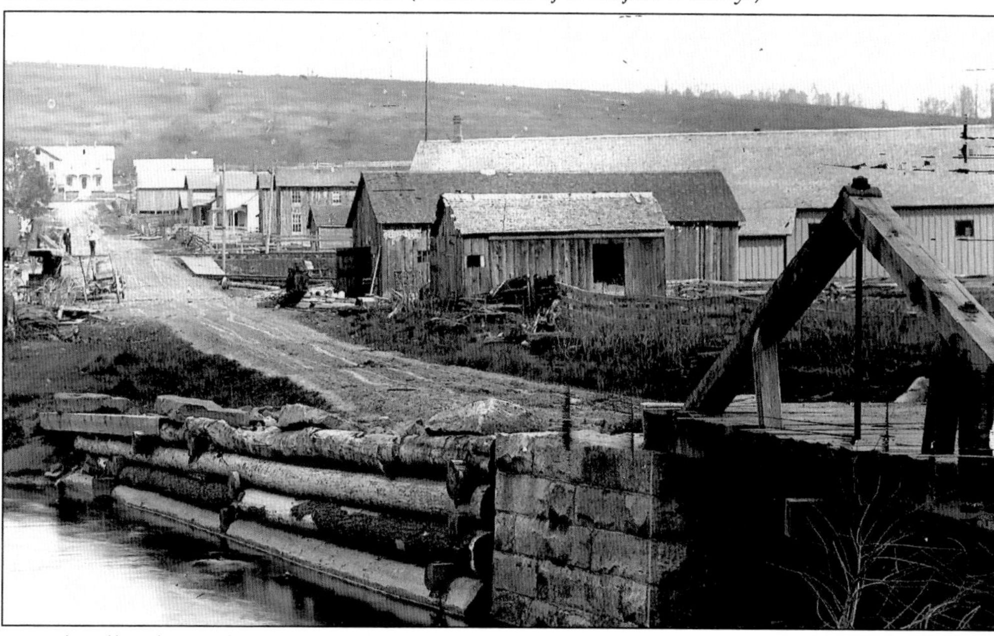

Grand Valley, located in Eldred Township, Warren County, was once a thriving borough with an economy centered around lumber, agriculture, and oil production. This 1880s view looking east shows the railroad depot on the far right and hotel on the left (at the head of the street). The building with a circus poster was probably a machine shop. A steam engine bed can be seen at the front entrance. Men, buggies, and wagons gathered near the railroad crossing. (Courtesy of the Drake Well Museum.)

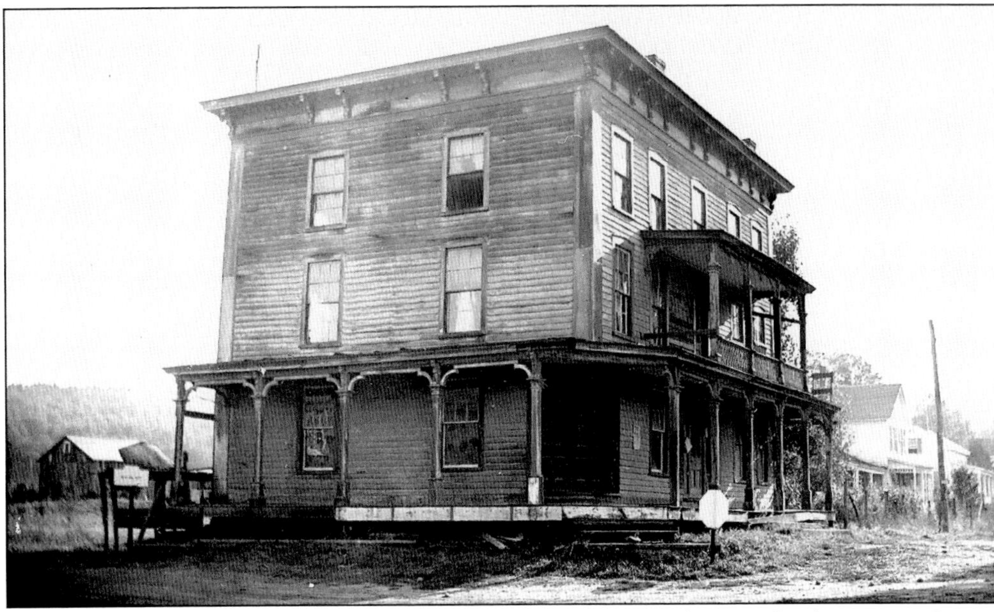

Enterprise, Southwest Township, Warren County, was once a thriving lumber town. Capital from sawmills enabled some of its residents to become successful oil producers. Selden Spencer's hotel, built in 1850, long catered to oil producers and lumbermen. It was still standing in 1930. (Courtesy of the Drake Well Museum.)

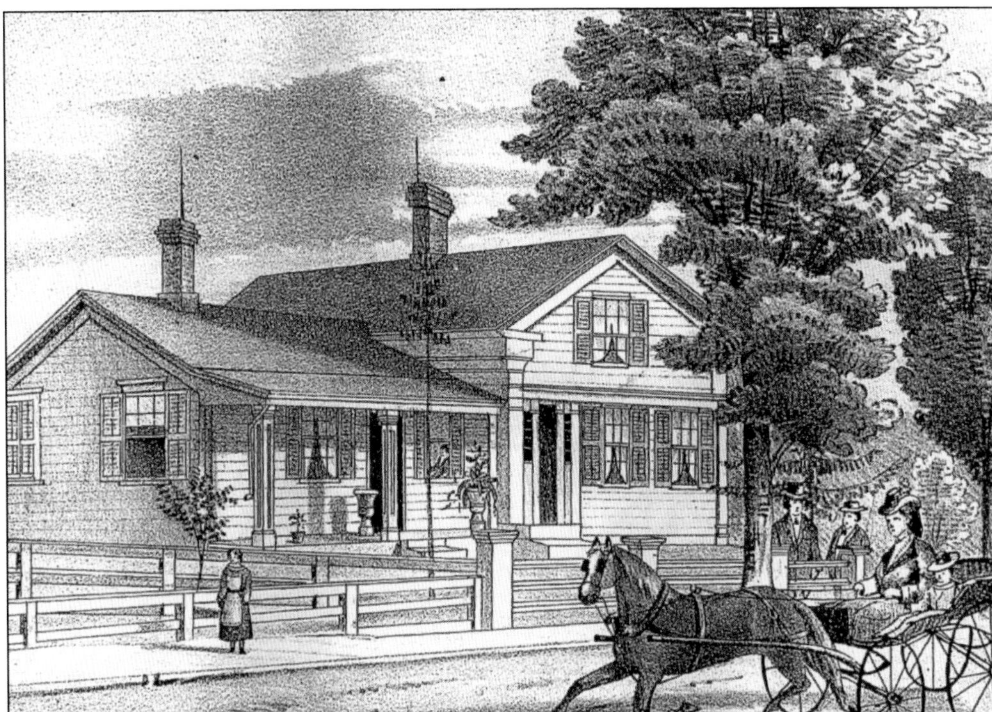

Myron Dunham, an Enterprise merchant, was also a Warren County commissioner who served two terms. The former Dunham residence still stands today. (From *Atlas of Warren County*.)

Eight

People, Institutions, Events, and Celebrations

Titusville and the surrounding region already had permanent institutions in place long before the 1859–1870 oil boom. Schools, churches, and fraternal organizations guaranteed the region's long-term survival.

The first oil rush (and, later, the 1890–1920 industrial boom) changed the community structure. The arrival of more people from other regions (and nations) led to the establishment of additional religious denominations and fraternal organizations. Titusville's transition into a third-class city in 1866 eventually ensured law and order through the organization of paid police and fire departments.

The Titusville Hospital was founded by subscription among leading community members in 1900–1901. Similar community involvement started the local YMCA and YWCA programs, parks, playgrounds, and numerous charities.

The establishment of Titusville High School in 1869 was followed in later decades by extracurricular activities that have lasted to the present day. Church services, fraternal lodges, service club activities, high school sports events, and celebrations of all types have helped create the Titusville community spirit.

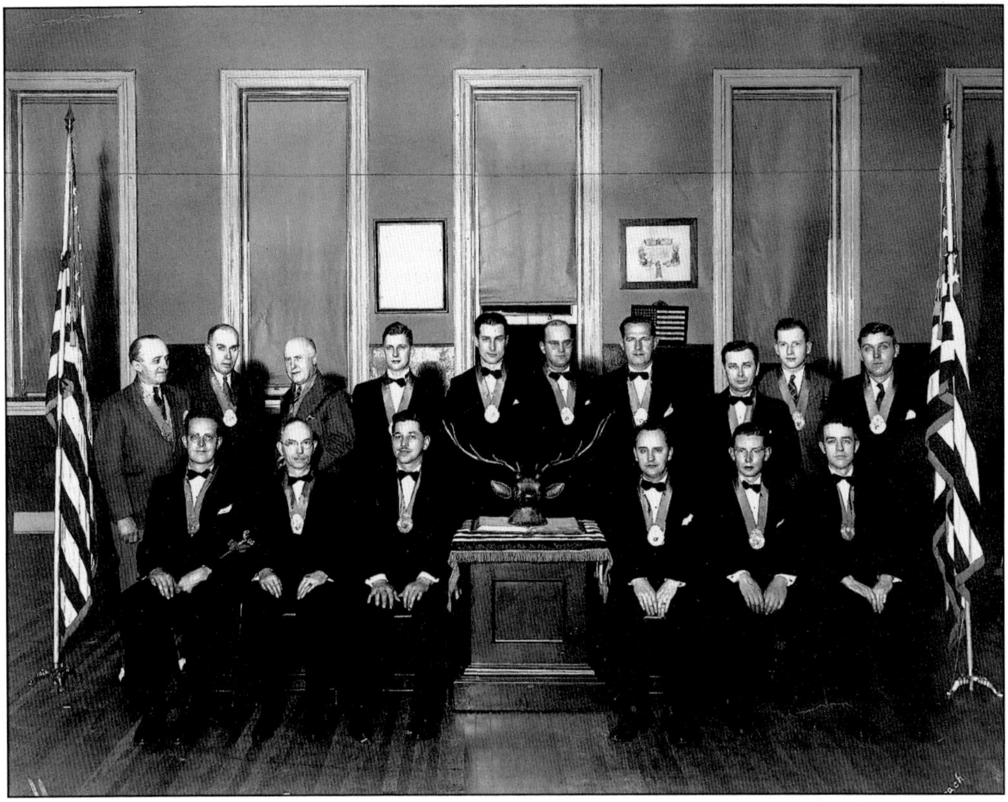

Titusville Benevolent and Protective Order of Elks Lodge No. 264 was organized on June 21, 1893. Since then, its members have included a cross section of the community. Some of the men seen here on May 13, 1942, are Chester Hampton, Edward Helfrich, John Harvey, Ralph Archer, John Johnston, William J. Fleming, Fred McLucas, Lessor Levy, and Willard Bengston.

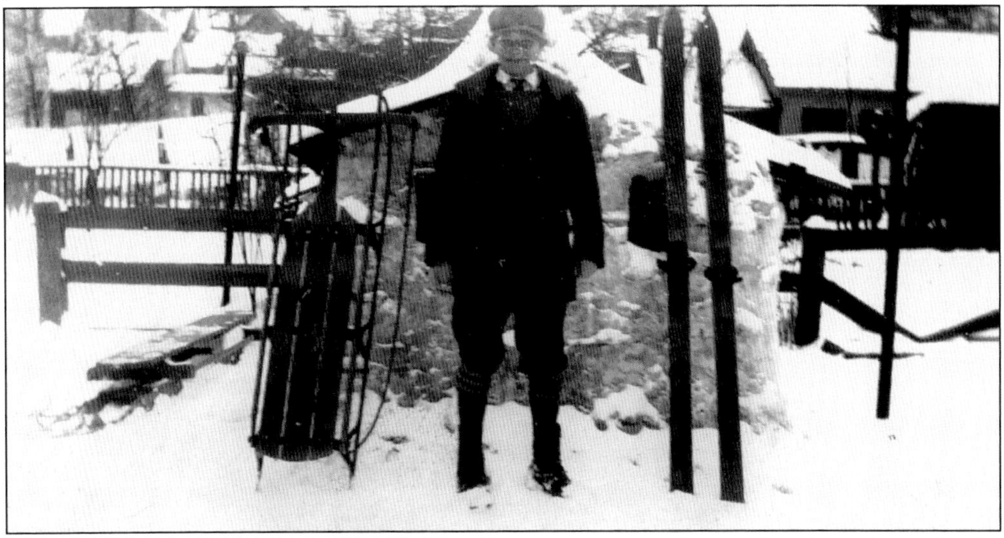

Frank Newson stands in front of a snow house he constructed in 1927–1928. This North Drake Street winter scene is complete with sleds and skis. It is a good reminder of the January days Titusvillians are accustomed to. (Courtesy of Howard Newson.)

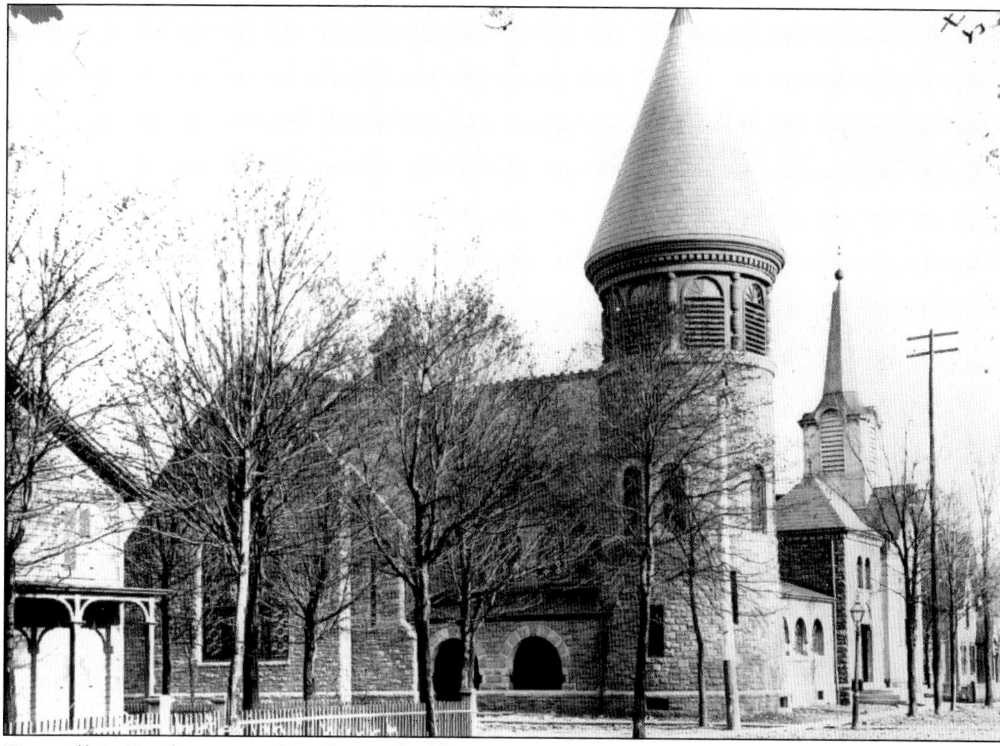

Titusville's Presbyterians first began holding services in 1802. The congregation since then has occupied five church buildings. The present edifice at Walnut and Franklin Streets was photographed shortly after it was constructed, in 1887–1888. (Courtesy of the Drake Well Museum.)

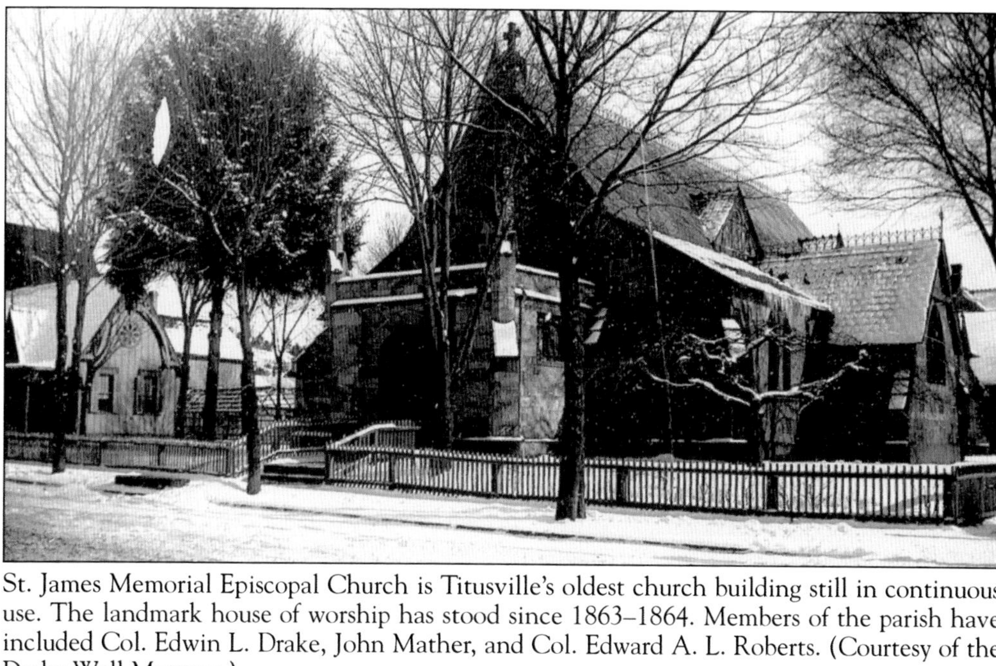

St. James Memorial Episcopal Church is Titusville's oldest church building still in continuous use. The landmark house of worship has stood since 1863–1864. Members of the parish have included Col. Edwin L. Drake, John Mather, and Col. Edward A. L. Roberts. (Courtesy of the Drake Well Museum.)

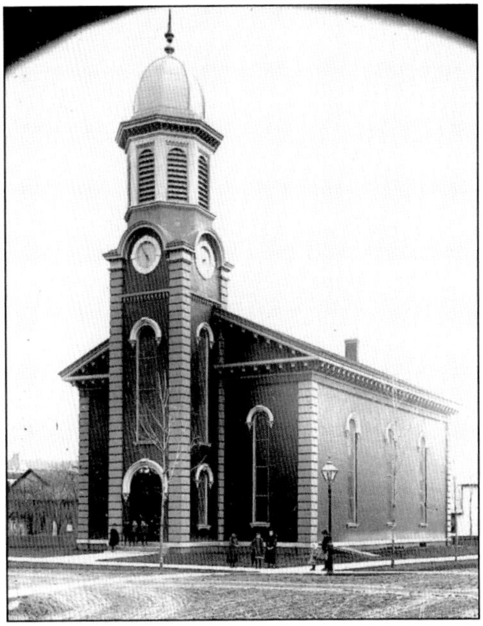

The chiming of the town clock at Main and Perry Streets has been a familiar Titusville sound since 1866. The landmark clock is housed in the tower of the former Universalist church. Since 1924, the Church of Christ has owned the structure and its quaint clock. The building looks much the same today as it does in the *c.* 1880 view, although the tower dome was removed by the present occupants. (Courtesy of the Drake Well Museum.)

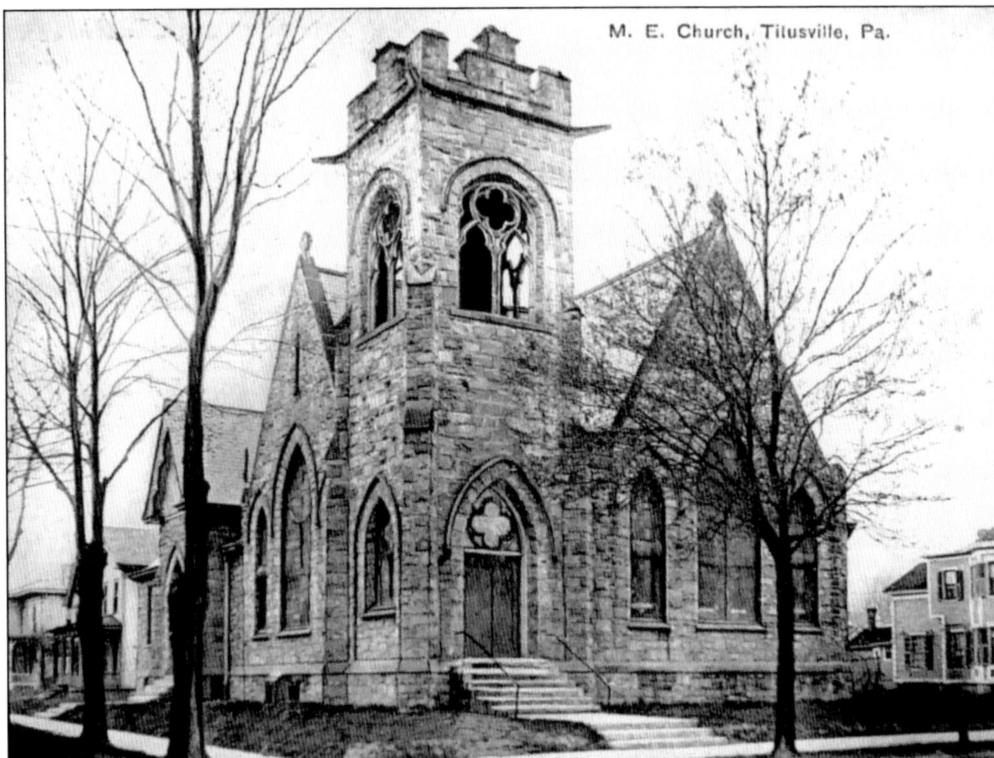

John D. Archbold, John D. Rockefeller's successor as head of the Standard Oil Company, gave Titusville's Methodist congregation $10,000 to erect a new house of worship in 1901. Located at the intersection of Walnut and Perry Streets, the church building was constructed from locally cut stone and contained a pipe organ donated by Andrew Carnegie. Fire destroyed the 50-year-old edifice on April 4, 1952. (Courtesy of David L. Weber.)

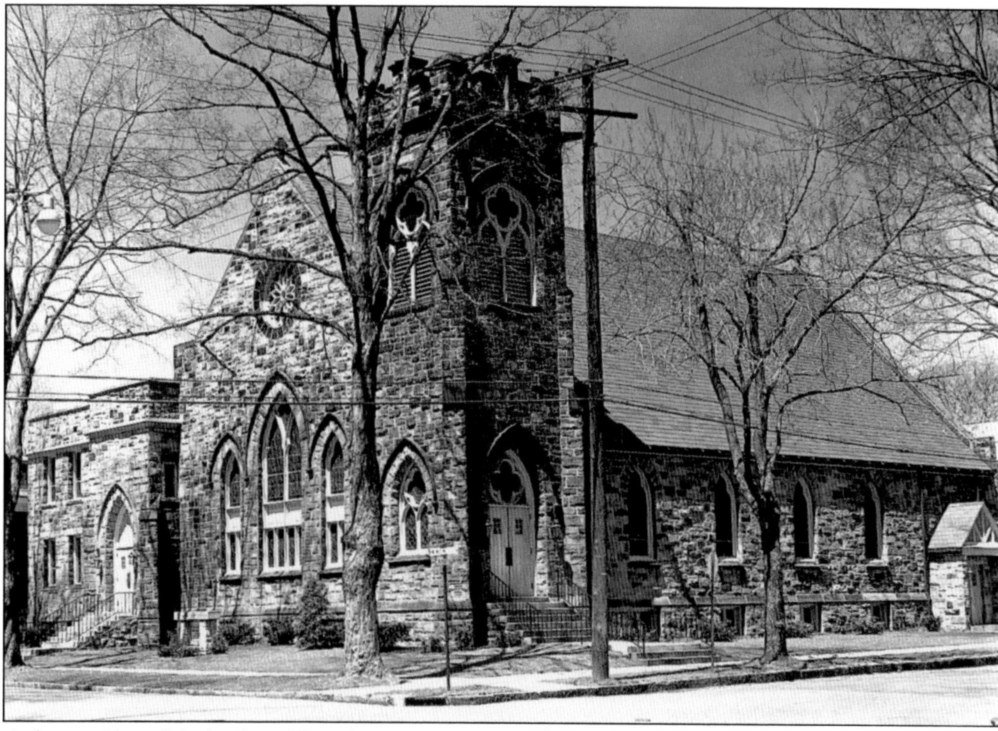

A larger First Methodist Church was constructed on the site devastated by fire. The new church, dedicated on July 25, 1954, contains the bell salvaged from the previous building. This bell has rung since 1864. (Courtesy of the Titusville Herald.)

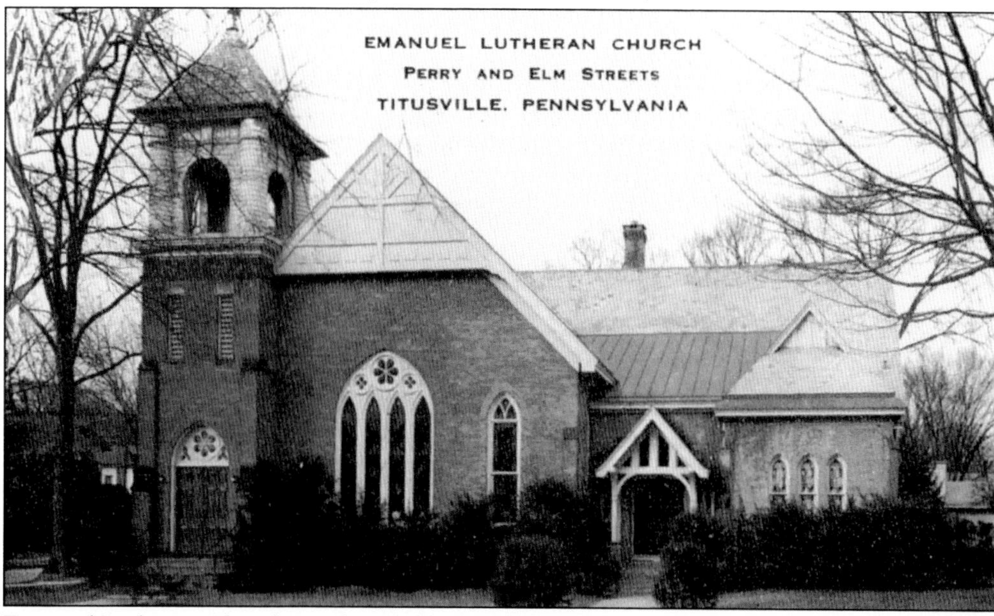

Emanuel Lutheran Church was founded by Swedish-speaking immigrants on October 10, 1871. The congregation's present edifice was constructed at Elm and Perry Streets between 1891 and 1893. Christmas Day worship was observed here at 5:30 a.m., as was the tradition in Sweden. (Courtesy of David L. Weber.)

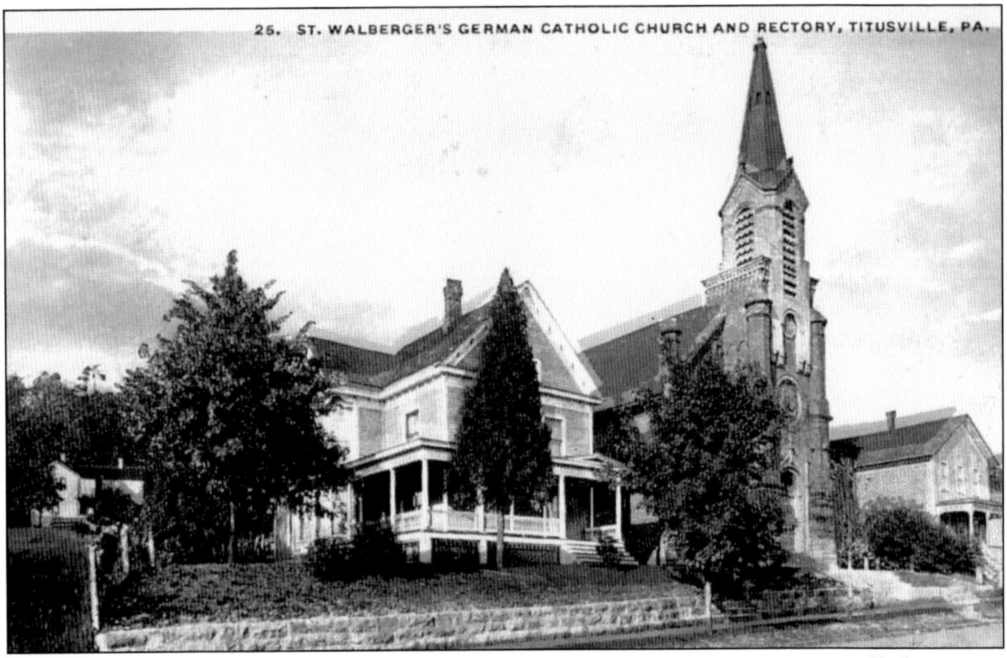

St. Walburga's Roman Catholic Church, located at 124 Brook Street, was originally known as St. Mary's Church. Immigrants from Germany and Austria founded the parish. Later, members of Titusville's Polish and Ukrainian communities attended St. Walburga's. Both the church and the adjacent rectory (on the left) were erected in 1893. (Courtesy of Kathryn Newson.)

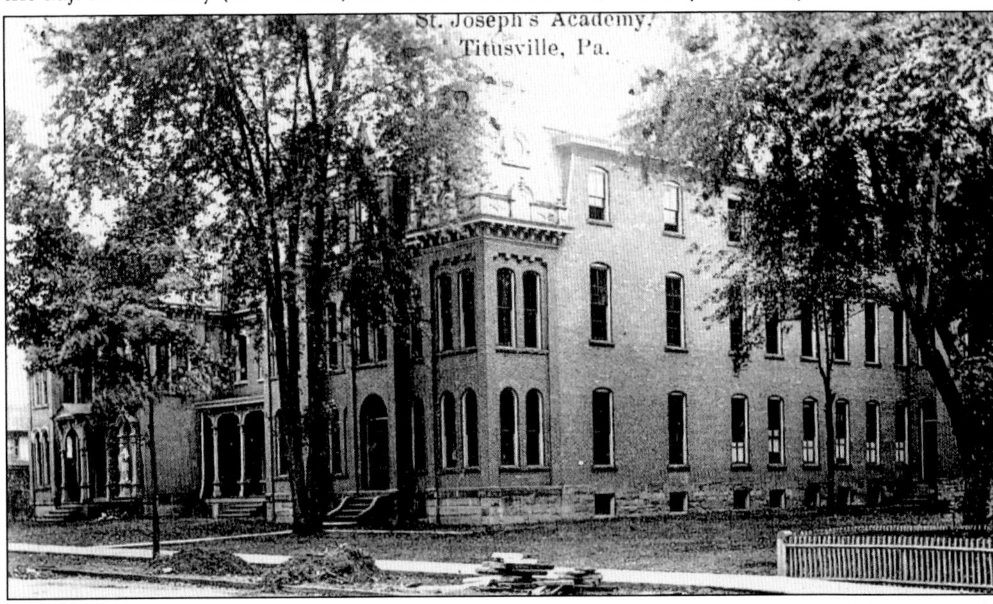

St. Joseph's Academy, operated by the Sisters of Mercy, was formerly a well-known girls' boarding and day school. The school, founded in 1871, also contained the Sisters of Mercy's motherhouse. Mercyhurst College and Mercyhurst Prep High School, of Erie, are outgrowths of the original St. Joseph's Academy. St. Joseph's Academy high school later occupied this massive West Main Street complex from 1932 until 1969. The convent, chapel, and school building have since been demolished. (Courtesy of Kathryn Newson.)

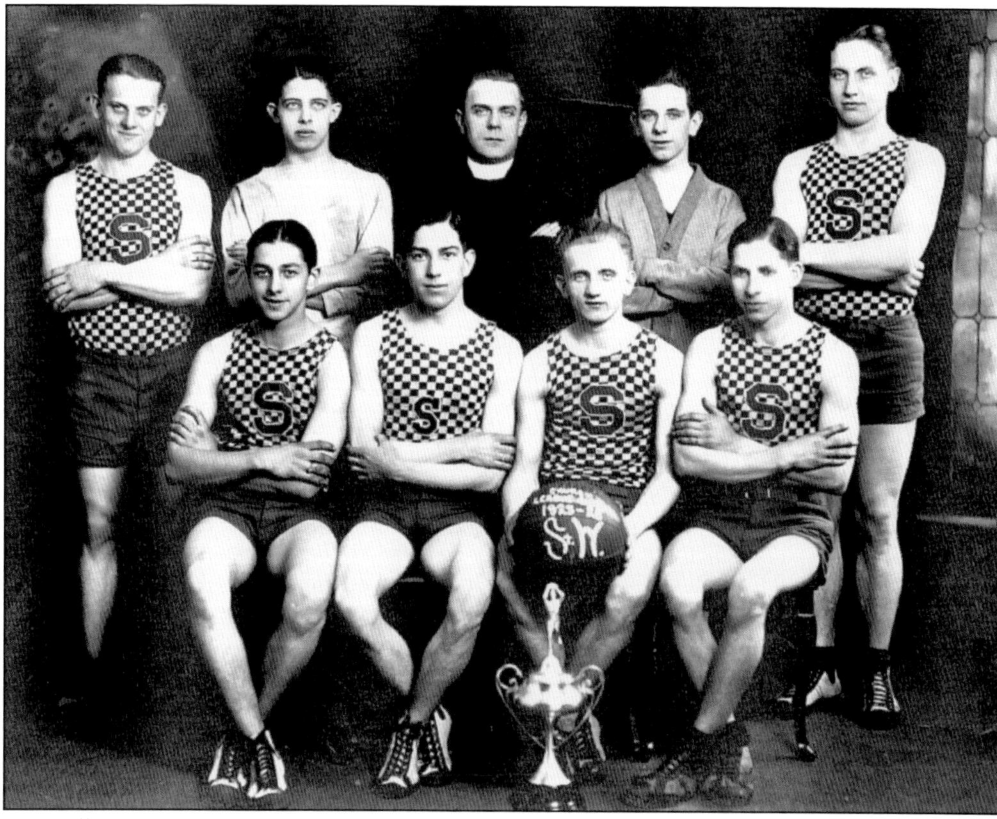

St. Walburga's Roman Catholic Church formerly had a parish school with a basketball team. The team is pictured with the 1925–1926 church league championship trophy. Seen here are, from left to right, the following: (front row) Ed Helfrich, Jim Sexton, Mike Kielp, and Bill Helfrich; (back row) "Timber" Burns, Fr. Carl Heidt, John Dunn, and Ed McDonald.

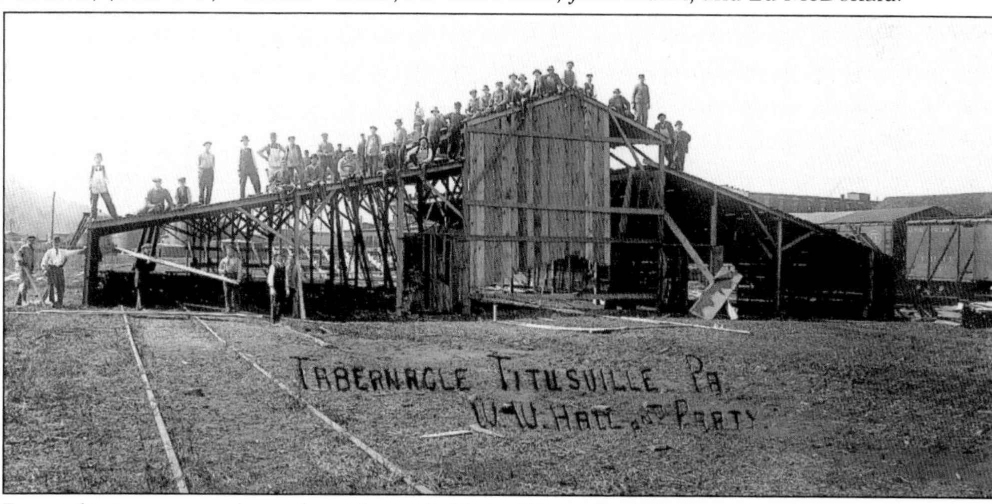

Evangelistic services have long been held in Titusville. Workers can be seen erecting a temporary South Monroe Street tabernacle for Rev. W. W. Hall. The Titusville Oil Works, Queen City Tannery, and Howard & Beaver grocery warehouse are in the background. Notice the freight car at the right for automobiles.

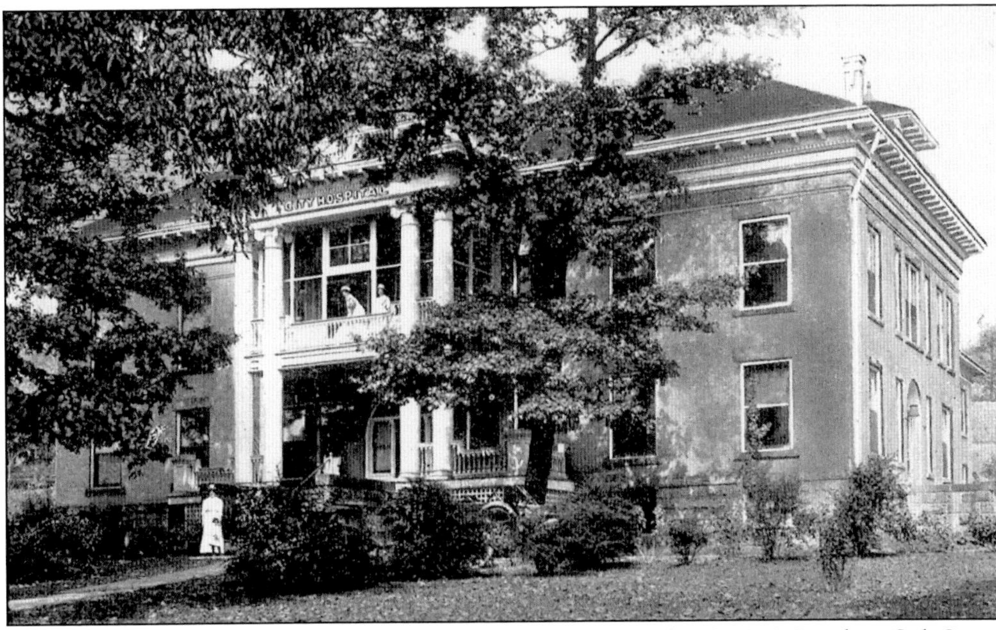

Leaders of the community founded Titusville Hospital on March 26, 1900. Land on Oak Street between First and Monroe Streets was acquired in June 1900. The building constructed on this site served the community until 1972. It was the beginning of the present medical facility, which remains on this site. (Courtesy of Kathryn Newson.)

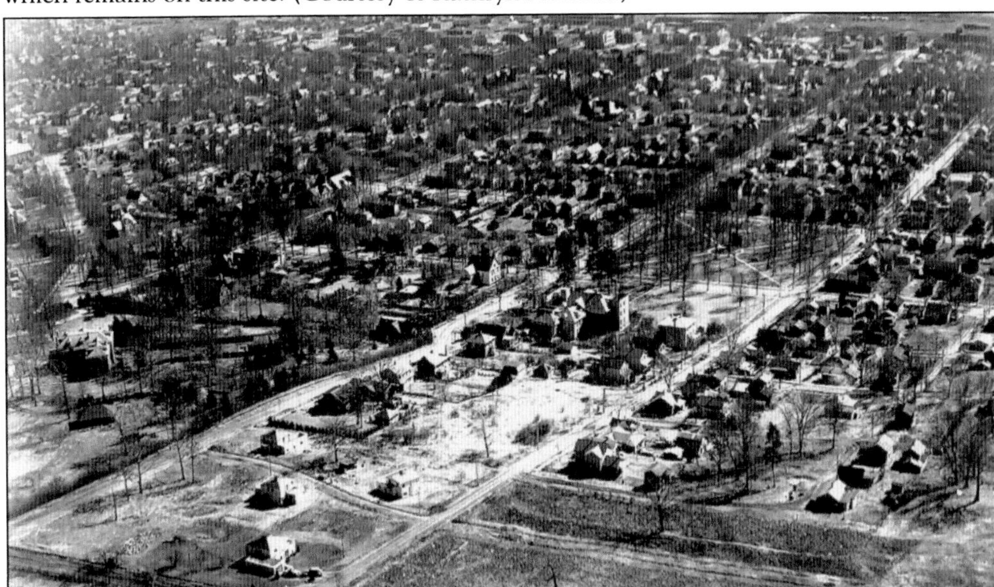

This 1938 photograph of Titusville (looking south) is a bird's-eye view of the hospital, including the 1903 Barnsdall annex and the 1924 nurses' home additions. At the rear of the hospital are the former John Emerson estate and Maxwell Chick's housing development. Two oil wells are in the lower foreground. In the distance are the Union Street School, St. Paul's German Reformed Church, the First Presbyterian Church, the Emanuel Lutheran Church, the old First Methodist Church, and the First Baptist Church, which can easily be recognized. In the upper center are the Titusville Iron Works building and adjacent railroad facilities.

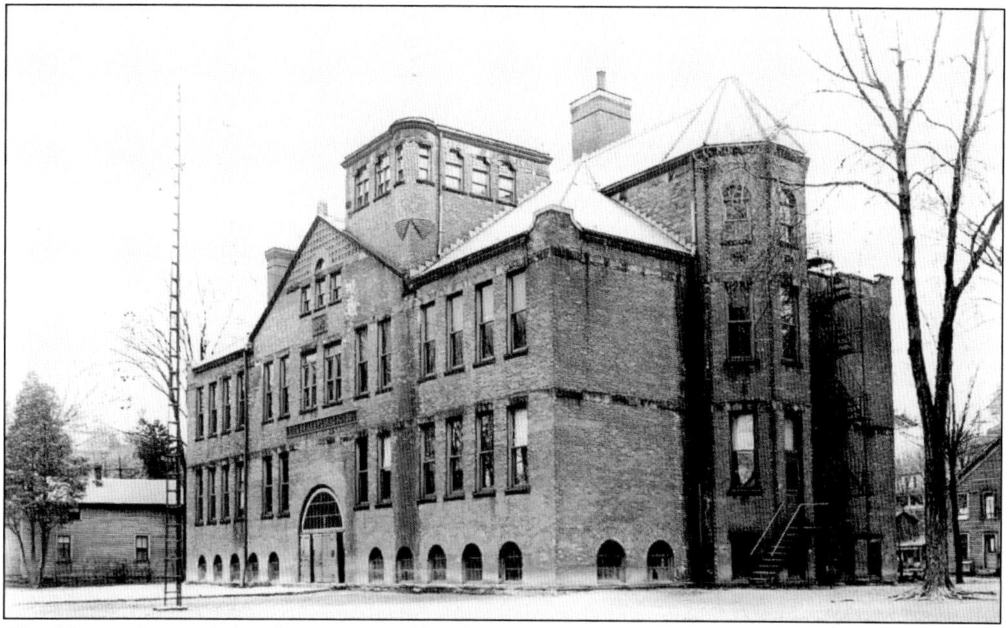

The Union Street School was Titusville's high school from 1893 to 1912. It was used as an elementary school until 1957. Demolition occurred in 1960.

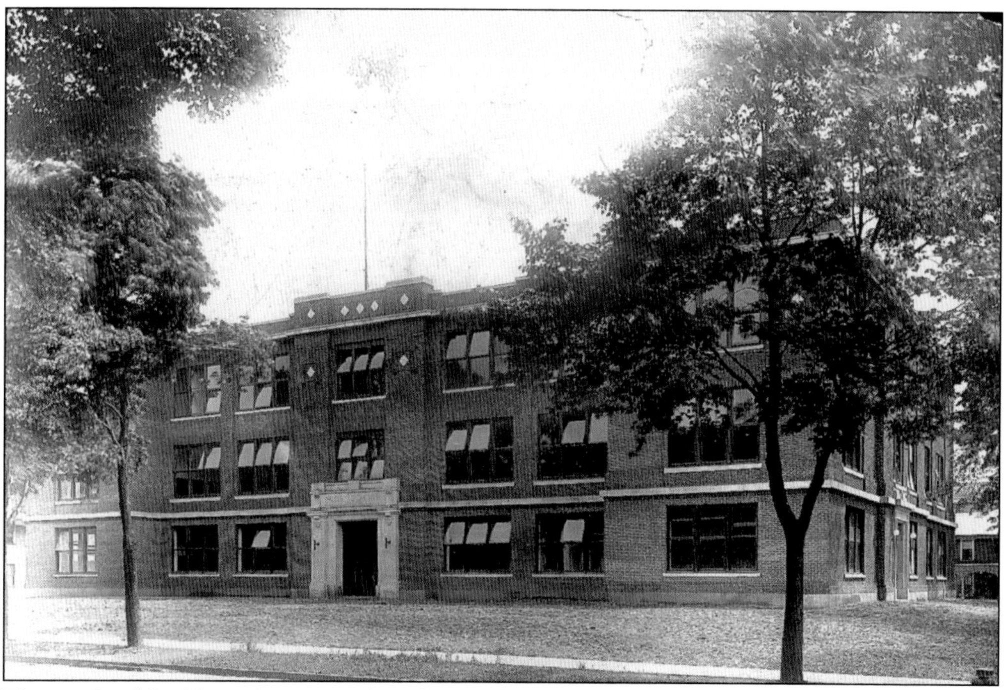

Three school buildings have stood at the southeast corner of Main and Washington Streets. The first one was destroyed by fire in 1866. A new schoolhouse was subsequently constructed, and it remained until 1910. Its replacement was a large, three-story high school building that was completed in 1912. A temporary pneumonia hospital was housed here from October to November during the 1918 Spanish flu epidemic. The Main Street school building was a junior high school from 1932 until 1957, and since then it has been used for elementary classes.

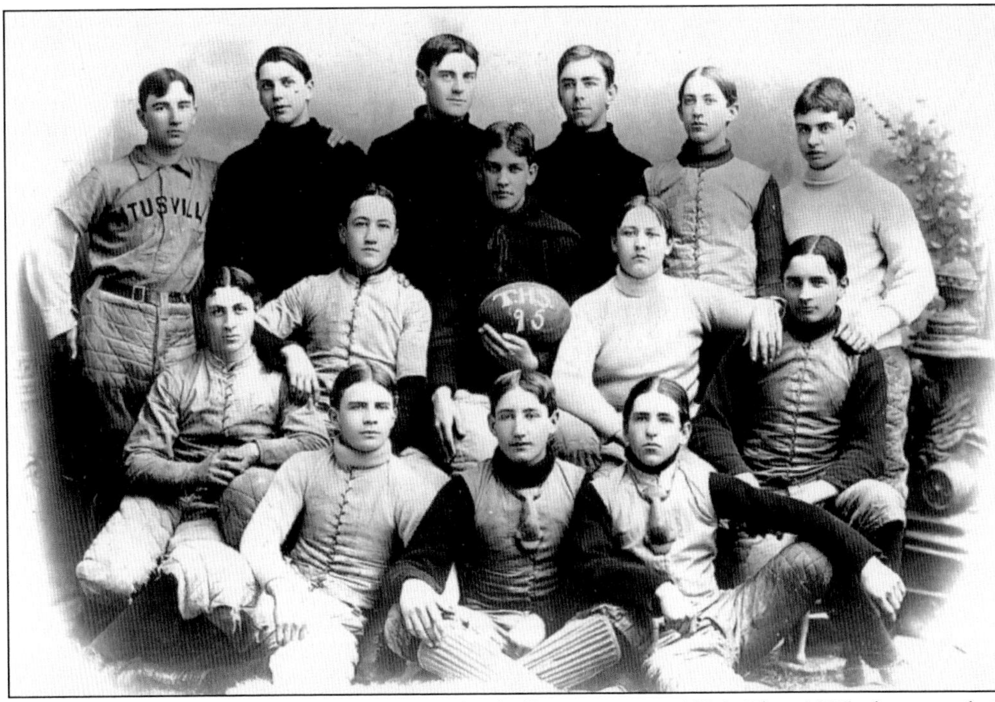

Titusville High School has fielded varsity football teams since 1884. This 1895 photograph is the oldest one known to exist of a Titusville High School football team. Second from the left in the back row is Joseph E. Fleming Sr., later a prominent Titusville oil producer and refiner. To the left of the football is Axtell Byles, later the president of Tidewater Oil Company and the American Petroleum Institute.

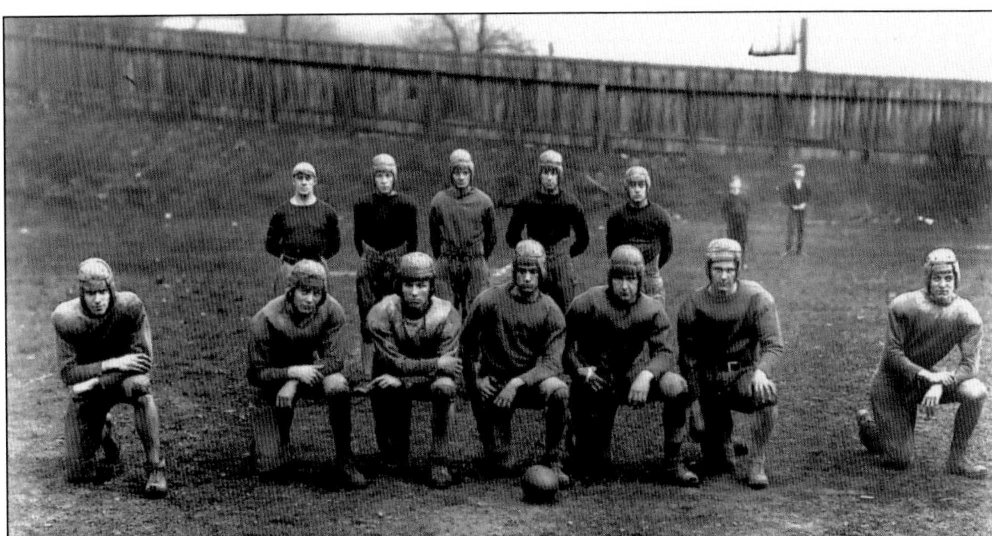

The 1927 Titusville High School football team is seen here. On the far left in the first row is Raymond Tesser, who in 1933 played on the very first Pittsburgh Steelers National Football League team. Tesser had the best of both western Pennsylvania worlds. He worked in a steel mill after his football career ended. (Courtesy of the Titusville High School Alumni Association.)

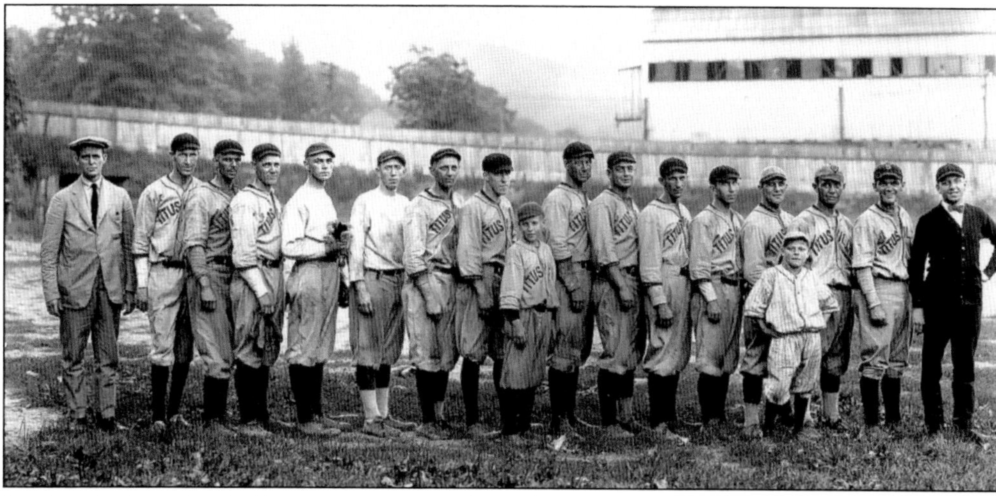

Semiprofessional baseball was once popular throughout western Pennsylvania. This photograph is of the 1923 Titusville Independents. From left to right are Robert McKie, Charles "Red" Giffen, George "Snig" Wig, Bill Lynn, Clint Brown, "Apple" Holland, John "Beans" Beck, Tom Murphy, Ed Lynch (the batboy), Gene McNamara, Ed Alderman, "Skee" Fulton, Leo Hartary, Art Brady, George Schriver, Mike Philbin, and William Smith. Clint Brown was later a relief pitcher for the Chicago White Sox and Cleveland Indians. William Smith later entered the priesthood and was pastor of the St. Titus Roman Catholic Church in Titusville during 1960s and 1970s. The mascot in the front right is unidentified. The Titusville Forge plant can be seen in the background. (Courtesy of the Titusville High School Alumni Association.)

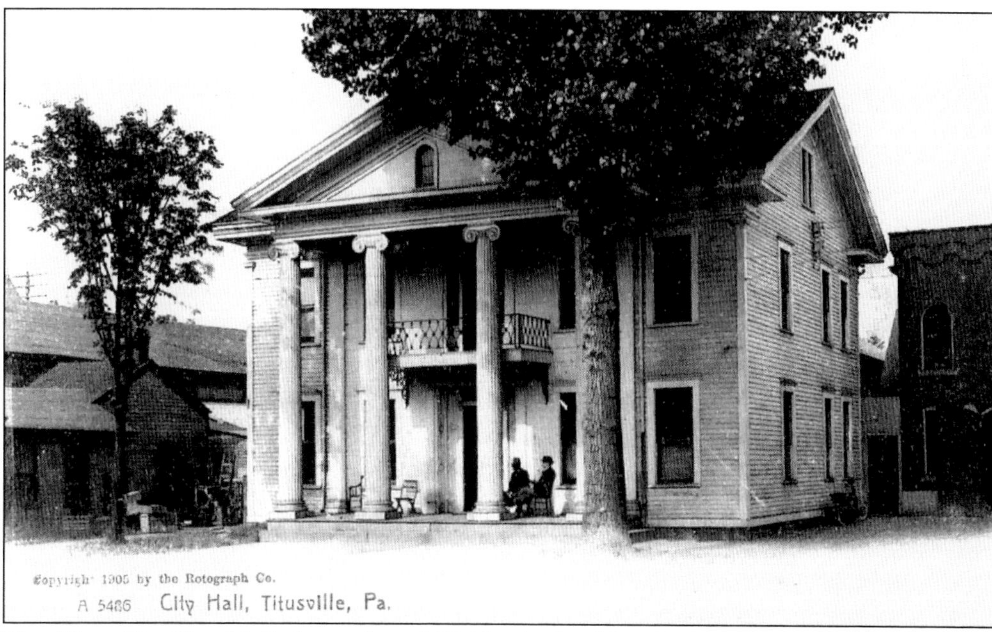

The Titusville City Hall, located at 107 North Franklin Street, was originally the 1862 residence of lumberman Nelson Kingsland. It later became a hotel, the Bush House. Titusville's municipal government has occupied the venerable landmark since 1872. On the right in this c. 1905 photograph is the old firehouse. (Courtesy of Kathryn Newson.)

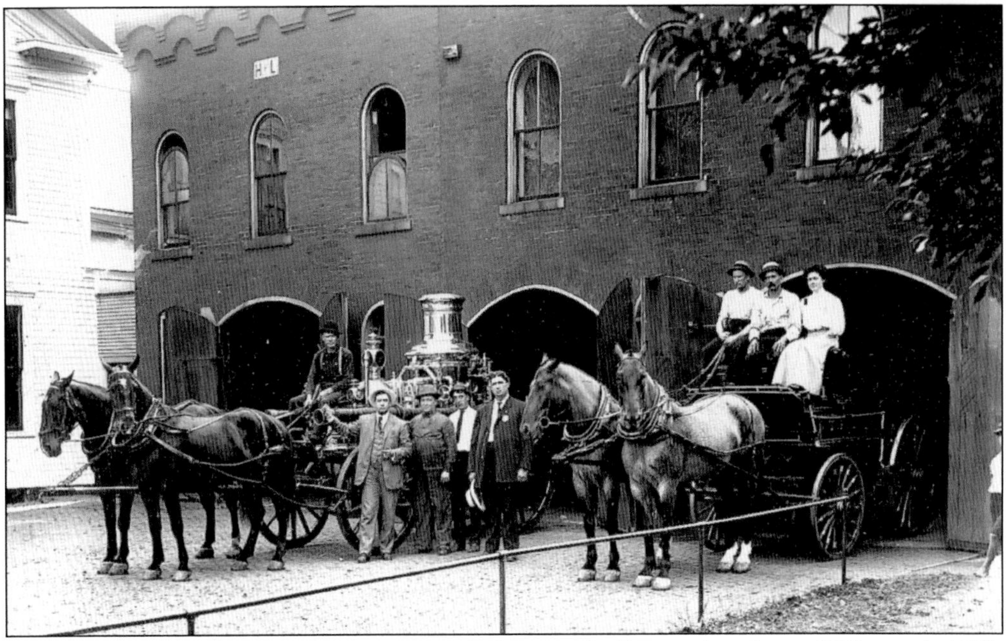

Titusville's No. 1 fire station was part of the city hall complex from 1872 until 1957. This nostalgic early-20th-century view shows the *Colonel Drake*, a fire engine, now displayed at the Drake Well Museum. On the right is the ladder wagon. The people in photograph are unidentified.

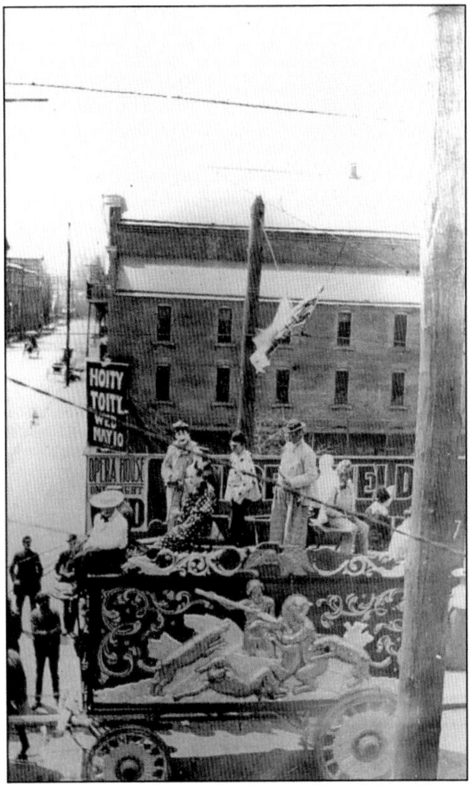

Elaborate circus parades were once common throughout America. This early-20th-century view shows Titusville when the circus was in town. An elaborately carved wagon carrying several clowns can be seen at the corner of West Spring and South Washington Streets. In the background are the Titusville Iron Works foundry and Titusville Opera House. (Courtesy of the Drake Well Museum.)

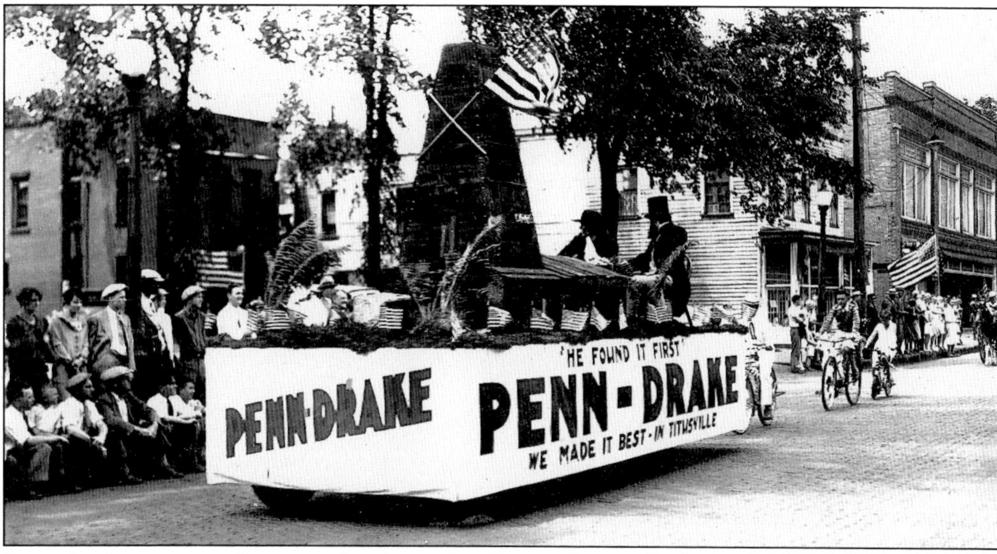

Penn-Drake motor oil was refined by the Pennsylvania Refining Company at Titusville and Karns City. This 1931 photograph of a Fourth of July parade on North Franklin Street shows the Penn-Drake float, which recreated the 1859 Drake Well. In the left background is Titusville's police headquarters, which was on that site for 120 years. Behind the float is Harry Coburn's bakery.

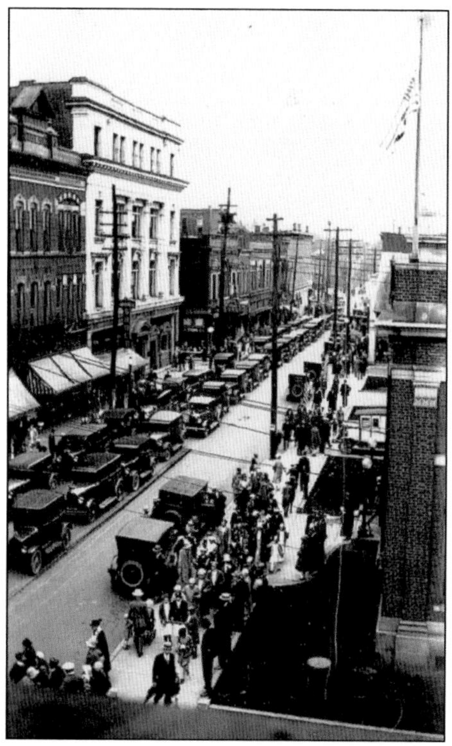

A 1919–1920 view of West Spring Street shows a Memorial Day parade crowd. Buildings on the opposite side of the street included the Exchange Block, Commercial Bank, Reuting Block, and Cohn and Oakleaf department store. The Spring Street traffic flow was two way at this time.

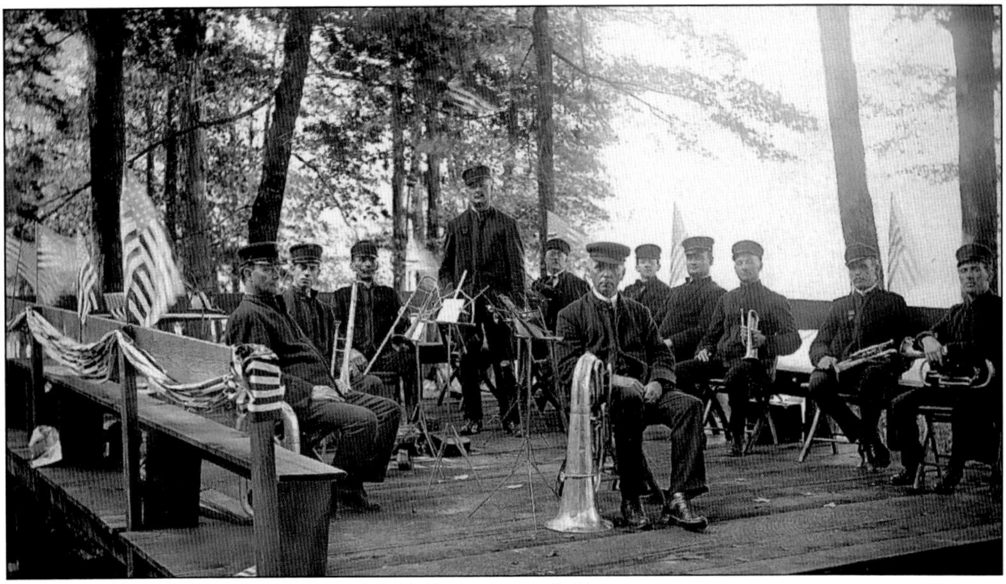

John "Professor" Coleman (1845–1924), a son of German immigrants, was one of many Union army veterans who arrived in Titusville. Coleman, who played the cornet and violin, organized a band and orchestra that performed at area functions until World War I. This *c.* 1907 photograph shows Coleman's band during a Fourth of July concert at Fieldmore Springs Park. John Coleman is standing in the center. Other musicians included J. W. Brown, Bert Benedict, Fred Coleman, Harry Kerr, George McNaughton, and Edward Bartholomew.

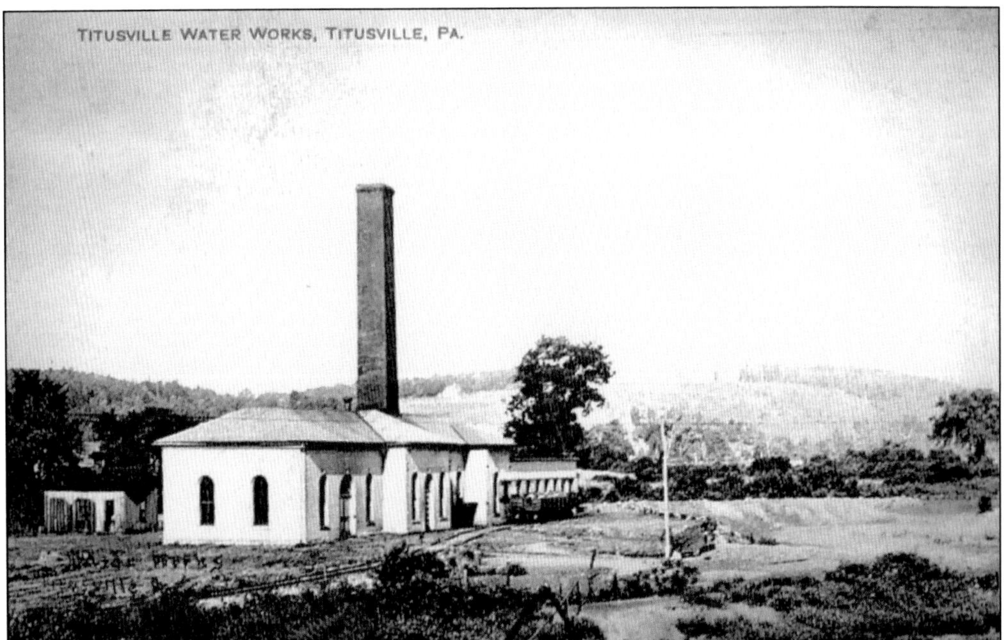

Titusville's water system has been in use since 1874. The waterworks, located in the west end, still operates from this station today. Part of the structure was demolished during the 1960s. (Courtesy of Kathryn Newson.)

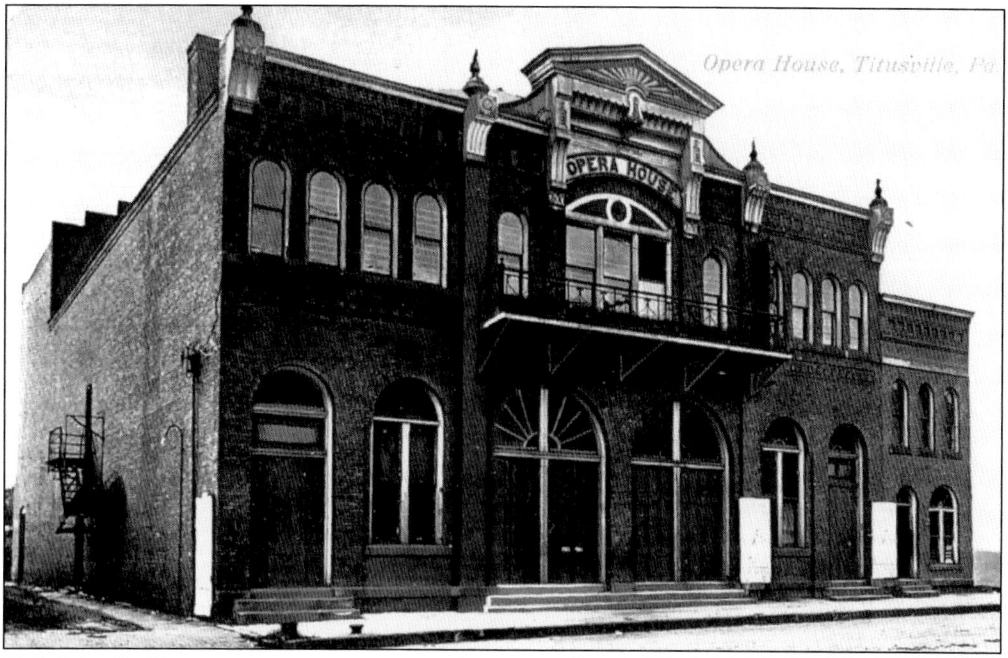

Col. John J. Carter constructed an opera house on South Washington Street in 1887. The Titusville Opera House was used for stage presentations and, later, films for over 40 years. Demolition occurred in 1930–1931. (Courtesy of Kathryn Newson.)

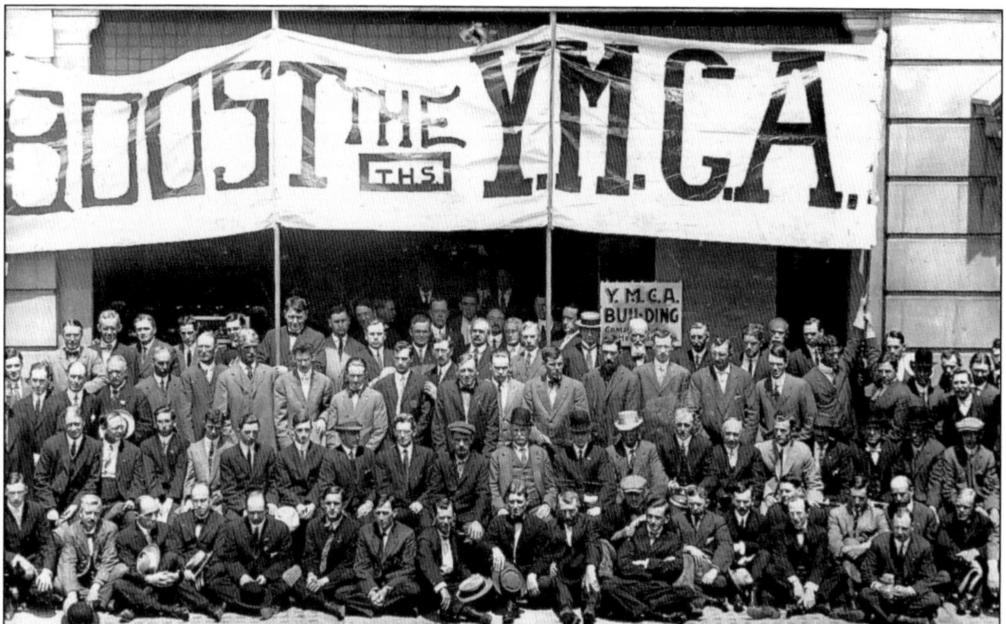

A campaign to raise $75,000 for a new YMCA building was launched by Titusville community leaders on May 20, 1912. Campaign headquarters was located in the Commercial Bank building. The seven-day drive was ended on the fifth day, as $90,000 had been subscribed. (Courtesy of Kathryn Newson.)

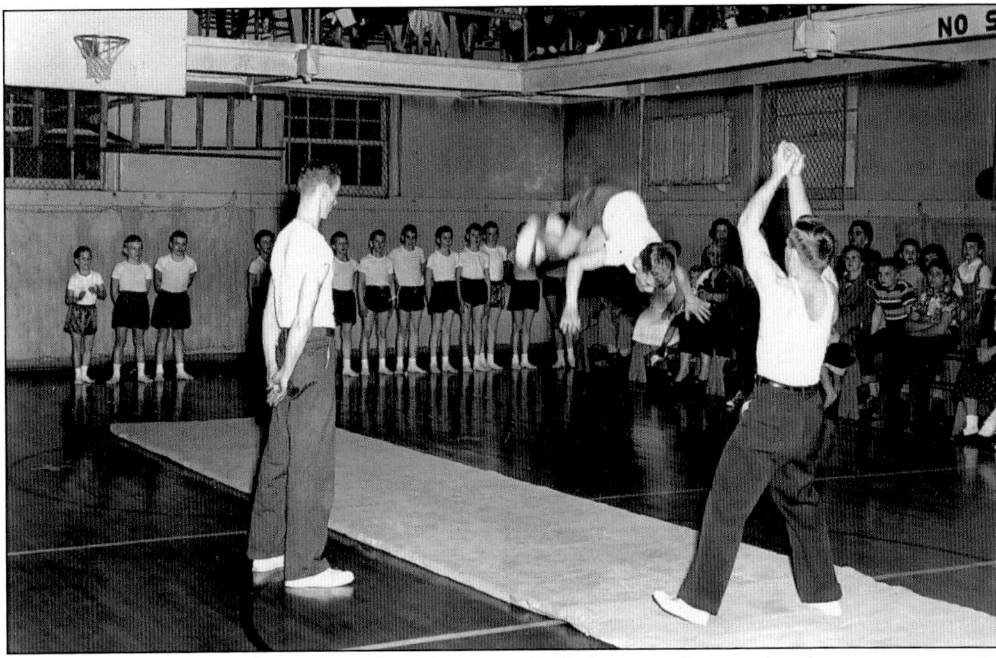

The Titusville YMCA, located at West Spring and Washington Streets, has been a community cornerstone since its facilities opened in 1914. Shown here is a 1958 gymnastics show featuring the YMCA tumbling team. (Courtesy of the Titusville YMCA.)

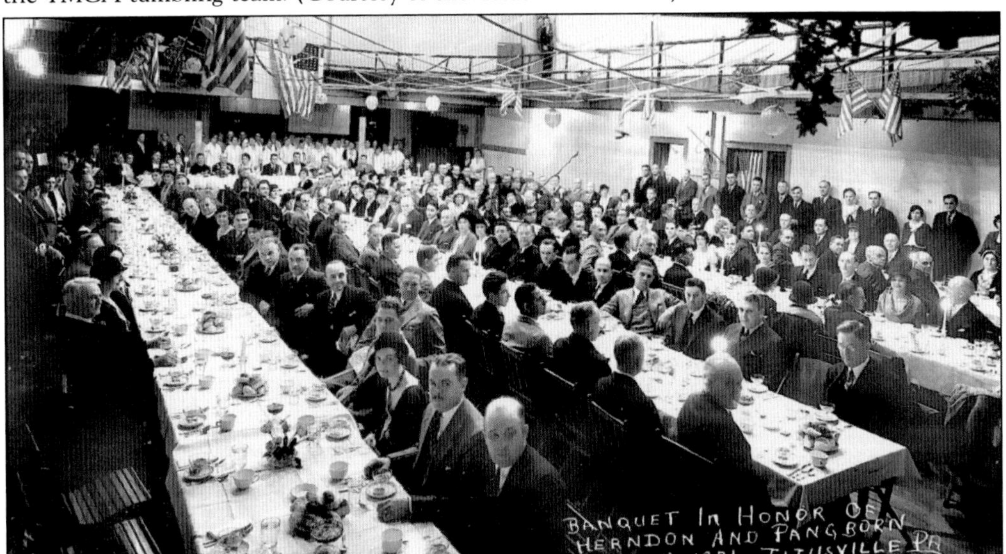

Hugh Herndon (1904–1952) was born in Titusville. He was the grandson of oil producer and industrialist Col. John J. Carter. Herndon achieved fame when he made the world's first nonstop transpacific airplane flight with Clyde Pangborn (1892–1958) from Tokyo, Japan, to Wenatchee, Washington, on October 5, 1931. Both Herndon and Pangborn visited Titusville on October 28, 1931. A banquet was held for the aviators in the YMCA gymnasium. People were enthusiastic about this event, despite the Great Depression. Herndon was married to the former Mary Ellen Farley, daughter of James Farley, postmaster general under Pres. Franklin D. Roosevelt. (Courtesy of the Titusville Herald.)